Engendering Genre
The Works of Margaret Atwood

Engendering Genre
The Works of Margaret Atwood

INCLUDING AN INTERVIEW WITH MARGARET ATWOOD

REINGARD M. NISCHIK

UNIVERSITY OF OTTAWA PRESS

The University of Ottawa Press acknowledges with gratitude the support extended to its publishing list by Heritage Canada through its Book Publishing Industry Development Program, by the Canada Council for the Arts, by the Canadian Federation for the Humanities and Social Sciences through its Aid to Scholarly Publications Program, by the Social Sciences and Humanities Research Council, and by the University of Ottawa.

We also gratefully acknowledge the Association of Canadian Studies in German-Speaking Countries, the University of Constance's Centre of Excellence, "Cultural Foundations of Integration," and the Equal Opportunities Council of the University of Constance whose financial support has contributed to the publication of this book.

www.press.uottawa.ca

uOttawa

Library and Archives Canada Cataloguing in Publication

Nischik, Reingard M

Engendering genre : the works of Margaret Atwood /
Reingard M. Nischik.

Includes bibliographical references and index.
ISBN 978-0-7766-0724-5

1. Atwood, Margaret, 1939- --Criticism and interpretation.
2. Sex role in literature. 3. Atwood, Margaret, 1939- --Interviews.
4. Authors, Canadian (English)--20th century--Interviews.
I. Title.

PS8501.T86Z764 2009   C818'.5409   C2009-907043-X

In Memoriam Hildegard Nischik (1919–2009)

Dearest Mother

What kind of world shall you describe for your readers? The one you can see around you, or the better one you can imagine? If only the latter, you'll be unrealistic; if only the former, despairing. But it is by the better world we can imagine that we judge the world we have. If we cease to judge this world, we may find ourselves, very quickly, in one which is infinitely worse.

Margaret Atwood, Second Words, 333

It *is* more difficult for a woman writer in this society than for a male writer. But not because of any innate mysterious hormonal or spiritual differences: it is more difficult because it has been made more difficult, and the stereotypes still lurk in the wings, ready to spring fully formed from the heads of critics, both male and female, and attach themselves to any unwary character or author that wanders by.

Margaret Atwood, Second Words, 226

You have to understand what the form is doing, how it works, before you say, "Now we're going to make it different ... , we're going to turn it upside down, we're going to move it so it includes something which isn't supposed to be there, we're going to surprise the reader."

Margaret Atwood, interview with Geoff Hancock, 193

If writing novels—and reading them—have any redeeming social value, it's probably that they force you to imagine what it's like to be somebody else.

Which, increasingly, is something we all need to know.

Margaret Atwood, Second Words, 430

Table of Contents

Preface

I still remember when I taught my first course ever on Margaret Atwood, back in 1982. I was thrilled with this new author from Canada, whose literary styles, whose language and themes, and whose personality I found intriguing. Here was literature that I felt strongly attracted to and wanted to bring closer to my students, who at the time were just a few years younger than I. Atwood was my favourite writer in those days, and she has remained so for the decades since then, having certainly kept up my scholarly interest as well as my great pleasure in teaching her works. I have always thought that my seminars on Atwood have been among my liveliest, most successful ones. Many students whom I taught Atwood to, off and on (thirteen times over three decades), were often similarly fascinated by her writing, and they have remained faithful Atwood readers.

Atwood's writing has thus accompanied me throughout my years of teaching and research, and it has spurred three previous, though quite different, books of mine on Atwood: my postdoctoral thesis with a strong theoretical orientation (on mind style analysis, bridging narratology and stylistics, with Atwood's fiction used as textual example; Tübingen: Narr, 1991); an anthology, including accompanying analyses, of her short stories for teaching (Stuttgart: Reclam, 1994); and my scholarly edition *Margaret Atwood: Works and Impact* (Rochester, NY: Camden House, 2000/Toronto: Anansi, 2002), which surveys Atwood's vast oeuvre as well as her reception and influence as writer and critic.

Why, then, another book on Margaret Atwood? Again I am reminded of my early seminars on this author. One of the many reasons Atwood's works have attracted me has always been her shrewd and level-headed gender consciousness. In my earlier classes in the 1980s, my students did not have such an awareness. Curiously many of them, especially the female students (in a rather sexist German society at the time), could not relate to Atwood's statements on gender, could not see the justification for her criticism, or at least her questioning, of traditional gender roles and mentalities. If at all, it was the male students at the time who, at least in the classroom, followed Atwood in her implicit analyses and often agreed with them. It has been one of the many joys of teaching over the decades to observe how Atwood's cutting-edge statements on gender have come to be appreciated by my female students too, so much so, in fact, that nowadays often they more than I raise issues of gender in the classroom.

Surely Atwood's writing has contributed its share to our heightened sense of gender issues, of gender equality and discrimination, and of gender roles. Surveying and analyzing her works over the decades, from her early through her middle to her more recent creative periods, this book traces Atwood's frequent involvement with gender, significant changes in her representation of gender, as well as her innovative linking of gender and genre. In its developing treatment of gender issues over five decades in an impressively high number of (sub)genres—practically all of them dealt with in this book—Atwood's oeuvre is a remarkable cultural document of our times.

Several people were very helpful in the preparation of this volume: Julia Breitbach, Georgiana Banita, and Florian Freitag went through the manuscript and made excellent suggestions for change, as did Emily Petermann and Christina Duck Kannenberg. Anja Ging and Julia Sutter were helpful research assistants and acted as troubleshooters. Annette Regina Lang delved into forms of address when I was updating chapter 4. Christine Schneider conscientiously produced the files and again proved a wizard at deciphering my handwriting. Björn Brumann and Benjamin Kannenberg were helpful with scanning images. Florian Freitag reliably produced the index and, together with Julia Breitbach, helped with proofreading.

I am very grateful to Sherrill Grace from the University of British Columbia in Vancouver for reading the manuscript and for giving good pieces of advice. I also thank John Shoesmith of the Thomas Fisher Rare Book Library at the University of Toronto for being very helpful at short notice with the Margaret Atwood Papers. I particularly thank Margaret Atwood for giving permission to reproduce as many as nine of her comics in this book, which makes it a small collection of close to one-third of her produced comics. I also thank her for finding time between book tours to grant me the interview in Toronto and for providing useful information only she could know. My meetings with Margaret Atwood over the years have been not only "educative" but also and always great fun.

Financially, the project was supported by grants from the Association of Canadian Studies in German-Speaking Countries, from the University of Constance's Centre of Excellence, "Cultural Foundations of Integration," and from the Equal Opportunities Council of the University of Constance in Germany.

Chapters 2 and 3 are revised, updated, and extended treatments of issues I explored earlier in my articles in *Margaret Atwood's Textual Assassinations: Recent Poetry and Fiction*, ed. Sharon Rose Wilson (Columbus: Ohio State University Press, 2003), and in *The Cambridge Companion to Margaret Atwood*, ed. Coral Ann Howells (Cambridge: Cambridge University Press, 2006). Chapter 4 is a revised, updated, and substantially extended version of an earlier article published in *Orbis Litterarum* (1994).

This book is dedicated to my beloved mother, who did not live to see its publication. She indirectly taught me about gender by living her own life strictly according to traditional gender roles and at the same time putting her daughter in a position to be able to choose. I am enriched and extremely grateful for having had such a wonderful mother.

Introduction

One important aspect of Margaret Atwood's extraordinary creativity and productivity over the past five decades—her first book, the poetry collection *Double Persephone*, appeared in 1961—has been the wide range of genres in which she has been productive. To date, Atwood has as many as twelve poetry collections to her credit (not counting four selections of previously published poems; see chapter 1), as many as twelve novels (1969–; see chapter 4), four short-story collections (1977–; the latest one, *Moral Disorder*, being her first short-story cycle; see chapter 3), three collections of prose poetry and short fictions (1989–; see chapter 2), as many as seven books of literary and cultural criticism (1972–; see chapter 6), six books of children's fiction (1978–), some thirty cartoons and comic strips (uncollected; see chapter 7), and a few screenplays based on her own works (1970–; see chapter 5).

In addition, Atwood has acted as editor/anthologist of books of Canadian verse, of collections of Canadian as well as American short stories, and of more unusual books such as *The CanLit Foodbook: From Pen to Palate—A Collection of Tasty Literary Fare* (1987).[1] She has also engaged in visual artwork of various kinds (see the interview with Atwood at the end of this volume), with several of her visual works included in her books or reproduced on some of her book covers. She has also written a few libretti for operas, including one on E. Pauline Johnson. Finally, July 2007 saw her professional debut as a dramatist, when her own drama adaptation of *The Penelopiad* premiered—stage drama had been a gap in the impressive range of generic formats that Atwood had tackled over the years. Perhaps in her creative writing she is not so much interested in an exclusive focus on dialogue, on what characters directly say, and perhaps she prefers to keep greater control over the finished product than is possible when the dramatic text becomes theatre (see also chapter 5 on her experiences in regard to adaptations of her works for TV and cinema).

Atwood's achievements in all the literary genres she has chosen to approach are high—one would be hard put to argue that she excels more in one literary genre than in the others. As if to prove this, Atwood received Canada's most prestigious literary prize, the Governor General's Literary Award, for her second collection of poetry, *The Circle Game* (1966), and then again for her novel *The Handmaid's Tale* (1985). Internationally she is one of only three novelists to be shortlisted for the Man Booker Prize four (in her case) or more times, and she won the award for *The Blind Assassin* (2000). Along with Alice Munro and Mavis Gallant, Atwood is one of the three most frequently anthologized Canadian writers of short fiction. She is also among the most influential critics of Canadian literature and culture—not a small achievement for someone who regards herself first and foremost as a creative writer. Last but not least, she has been shortlisted for the Nobel Prize for Literature and has long been a hot candidate for it.

Atwood's overwhelming publication record, her status as Canada's leading writer and as one of the best and best-known contemporary writers worldwide, her political consciousness and critical awareness, coupled with her media-savvy and media-friendly personality, have resulted in numerous public appearances often connected to her own writing or to writing in general. As for the print media, there are first of all the many interviews conducted with Atwood over the decades (two collections of interviews exist so far, both edited by Earl Ingersoll). With her vast knowledge and sharp wit, her humour and engaging presence of mind, Atwood must be one of the most frequently interviewed writers on an international scale. Then, too, she engages with any political, social, and cultural affairs that she feels called upon to speak or write, or even "draw," about: on the occasion of readings (see chapter 8 on her *Book Tour Comics*), speeches (e.g., her invitation to give the renowned Clarendon Lectures at Oxford University, the Empson Lectures at Cambridge University, and the Massey Lectures at five different locations in Canada), and articles written for newspapers and journals. Be it the Conservative Harper government's anticultural policies in Canada, the persecution of writers on political grounds in some parts of the world, ecological problems, or systematic discrimination against women, Atwood speaks out. She is not only a *poeta doctus* but also the epitome of a writer who regards her vocation as an essential part of the social conscience.

Interweaving the generic threads of her vast oeuvre even further, several of her works have been transposed into other artistic formats (with greater or lesser success). Some of her novels have been adapted for the big screen (*Surfacing, The Handmaid's Tale, The Robber Bride*; see chapter 5); six of her short stories have been adapted for television (*The Atwood Stories*); *The Edible Woman* and *Good Bones* have appeared on stage; there is an opera based on *The Handmaid's Tale*; some of her poetry has been set to music and adapted for television (see chapter 5). As Susan Walker (2001) has stated, "Margaret Atwood is no mere writer. She's an industry. The spinoffs from the products of her imagination and intellect could fill a theme park."

An essential thematic strand in Atwood's oeuvre dealt with here concerns her preoccupation with issues of gender. This study demonstrates first of all that Atwood's writing, in all the genres she has tackled, indeed has been gender conscious right from the beginning—that is, even at a time when the second wave of the Women's Movement had not yet fully gotten under way[2]—through to her most recent works. Atwood has moved on the cutting edge concerning the representation of women and men, the relationship between the sexes, and gender hierarchies. Although we can discern a falling-off of explicit concern with gender in a few of her later works, such as the novel *Oryx and Crake* and the poetry collection *The Door*, her interest in gender issues has been noticeable all through her works: "gender troubles" may have changed somewhat in the course of the past five decades, yet they do remain an issue (see chapter 4). Atwood's involvement with gender in all genres shows interesting variations and developments over the decades (see, e.g., chapters 3, 4, 6, and 7). We can generalize that it affects several important aspects of her writing: most notably, next to general thematic impact, the fields of characterization, character constellation, discourse structures, dialogue, linguistic variants, symbols and imagery, and, last but not least, genre.

To show the broad impact of Atwood's gender awareness and gender involvement, I will be concerned with all of these literary aspects in various chapters. I will pay specific attention to the interaction of genre and gender in Atwood's oeuvre. Coral Ann Howells characterizes Atwood's position on genre as "represent[ing] a balance between respect for generic traditions and an insistent challenge to traditional limits," a position that Linda Hutcheon generally describes as "that postmodern paradox of complicity and critique" (in Howells 2000/02, 139). Howells rightly speaks of Atwood's "continuous experimentation across genre boundaries, and the political and ideological significance of such revisions" (139), and she points out that genre theory nowadays by no means regards genres as fixed categories but "as rhetorical strategies or social institutions which are responsive to particular historical and ideological imperatives" (140). I argue that for Atwood such imperative influences on generic formats go back, to quite some extent, to issues connected with gender.[3] As Barbara Lewalski has pointed out in more general terms, "Recognition that generic codes change over time has engaged modern genre critics with issues of history, politics, gender, and audience expectation as well as with complex literary historical issues of mixed genre and generic transformations" (cited in de Bruyn 2000, 83). In keeping with Hutcheon, we might thus argue that genre and gender in Atwood's oeuvre intertwine in a combination of complicity and critique. Sharon Wilson (2003b), in a different context, speaks of Atwood's "textual assassinations." In the present context, Atwood's focus on gender issues tends to result in revising the traditional design and demarcation lines of (sub)genres, concerning both content/theme (see, e.g., chapters 1 and 7) and form (see, e.g., chapter 2).

Atwood's complications and transformations of (sub)genres might also be seen in the light of Chris Baldick's following definition of "genre":

> French term for a type, species, or class of composition. A literary
> genre is a recognizable and established category of written work
> employing such common conventions as will prevent readers

or audiences from mistaking it for another kind. Much of the confusion surrounding the term arises from the fact that it is used simultaneously for the most basic modes of literary art (lyric, narrative, dramatic), for the broadest categories of composition (poetry, prose fiction), and for more specialized sub-categories, which are defined according to several different criteria including formal structure (sonnet, picaresque novel), length (novella, epigram), intention (satire), effect (comedy), origin (folktale), and subject-matter (pastoral, science fiction). While some genres, such as the pastoral elegy or the melodrama, have numerous conventions governing subject, style, and form, others—like the novel—have no agreed rules, although they may include several more limited subgenres. (2001, 104–05)

To complicate matters even further, I will follow Atwood's versatility and breadth of involvement with different genres and media by also dealing in detail with, strictly speaking, non-literary genres Atwood has turned to, such as cartoon art, essay writing, and film.

As to the other two basic concepts informing this study, gender and engendering, they are more or less indebted to Gayle Rubin's (1975) original differentiation between "sex" and "gender." While "sex" is regarded as an anatomical-biological category, "gender" is a social category, refering to a social process, subject to change, that *constructs* what a given society chooses to regard as "femininity" and "masculinity" and that is, according to Judith Butler (1990), a result of performative acts, those, in other words, that constitute gender.

With the concept "engendering genre," I refer to the role gender plays in constituting genre, Atwood's play with intersections of gender and genre, as well as, vice versa, the role genre plays in constituting gender. In a less rigorous manner, "engendering genre" may simply refer to a foregrounding of gender in a specific generic format (practised by Atwood).

This book is structured, first of all, according to genre. Chapter 1 deals with Atwood's poetry, chapter 2 with her prose poems and short fictions, chapter 3 with her short stories, chapter 4 with her novels, chapter 5 with adaptations of her works, specifically the film made of her novel *The Handmaid's Tale*, chapter 6 with Atwood's literary and cultural criticism, and chapter 7 with her cartoons and comics, before chapter 8 looks at her career by means of an interview conducted with Atwood in Toronto in November 2006.

Chapter 1 deals with a specific subgenre (love poetry) of the genre dealt with (poetry) by focusing on a particularly seminal text by Atwood, *Power Politics* (1971), which may be called a threshold text in the development of love poetry. All other analytical chapters of the book (chapters 2–7) aim at a comprehensive analysis of the genre in question by focusing on gender issues in these genres as practised by Atwood.[4] It is significant, of course, that such a comprehensive approach is possible, demonstrating the omnipresence of gender in her oeuvre.

The aspects of interaction between genre and gender in Atwood's works that I will elaborate on are varied. They range from a demonstration of how gender issues thread through a particular genre from the beginning to the recent stages of her career, and how they develop (particularly in chapters 3 and 6), via the more specific question of how particular gender-sensitive linguistic variants develop in a certain genre—again from early to recent texts (chapter 4)—to, most challengingly, how Atwood's blending of genre conventions with a focus on gender results in, indeed "engenders," seminal texts that partly change, shake and extend, conventional generic boundaries (chapters 1, 2, 5, 6, and 7). That the erudite Atwood is certainly familiar with generic conventions before she tackles them also becomes clear in a statement of hers in an interview: "You have to understand what the form is doing, how it works, before you say, 'Now we're going to make it different ... , we're going to turn it upside down, we're going to move it so it includes something which isn't supposed to be there, we're going to surprise the reader" (in Ingersoll 1990, 193). Atwood's conviction is that the writer's task is to evaluate and, if need be, to contest conventions of any kind—be they social systems of hierarchical orders or literary conventions of genre. Her subversion and transgression of generic boundaries, as well as deeply ingrained gender images and prejudices, work together in a sometimes unsettling but often humorous and always liberating manner.

An incisive case in point is Atwood's seminal poetry cycle *Power Politics*, dealt with in chapter 1. This chapter shows in detail how Atwood, in her critique of love as an "earthly religion," disassembles all the ideals and conventions of love poetry. In an antiromantic, uncompromising, highly analytical stance, she superimposes the critical code of gender politics over the idealistic code of romantic love. Atwood points out parallels between power structures in macropolitical spheres—such as global "imperialist" power politics—and micropolitical spheres—such as human love relationships—which in this poetry collection constitute a miniature war scenario of attack and defence, though not without consolation and hope. In *Power Politics*, not only the female character but also the male character—conceived as gender representatives as well as individuals—are depicted as victims of ruling conventions, such as the romantic code of love. One of Atwood's representative principles is inversion: thus, the male figure is sometimes reduced to his body, whereas the female figure is associated with the mind. Atwood's sharp diagnosis of the sexes is presented with a bluntness that is highly unusual, if not unique, in the long history of love poetry, as is her emphasis on the female potential for aggression. The female lyrical I rejects preconceived patterns of romantic behaviour, thereby denying her partner the idealized approach he longs for, including making him into a hero. Thus, his question "Do you love me" is countered by the lyrical I with one of the oddest (and shrewdest) "professions of love" in literature. By embedding love in the context of political thought and activity, in power structures, Atwood creates a new semantics of love and redesigns the subgenre of love poetry—adapting it to the twentieth century, which saw a gradual displacement of an idealistic romantic code of love by a more realistic cooperative and egalitarian code of love. Chapter 1 shows how Atwood, locating herself firmly within the tradition of love poetry, inscribes this threshold situation into the texts of her poetry cycle, thereby also partly explaining why the book provoked such polarized and even polemical reactions at the time of its publication in the early 1970s and demonstrating its courageous, clear-headed ingeniousness, with a literary and sociological impact.

Chapter 2 turns to Atwood's prose poems and short fictions. The received small/large dichotomy ("bigger is better," "significant is big")—often also connected to gender issues—is relativized and partly inverted by Atwood in turning to these genres in the first place (she introduced the genre of the prose poem into Canadian literature) as well as in the remarkable ways in which she uses them for her thematic purposes. Often highly intertextual, these short texts create networks of meaning and significance despite their limited scope, with Atwood's poetics of inversion being a crucial structural principle that engenders a multifaceted interplay between explicit and implicit meaning, a prismatic multiplication of sense. Since this technique of intertextual inversion is used in a very restrictive space, it almost inevitably results in strongly delineated, suggestive, and highly intensified representations, which partly explain the satirical and parodic tendencies in many of these texts. The chapter demonstrates that received views of gender, discriminating against and fixing women, in particular, into prescribed roles, act as the greatest incentive for Atwood to rewrite pretexts, drawn from both world literature and popular culture. As for her revisionist treatment of world literature, she engages, for instance, in an intensive intertextual dialogue with Charles Baudelaire, whose prose poems of the later nineteenth century became the template for the genre as a whole. Whereas Baudelaire's texts are clearly written from a male perspective, denying female agency and subjectivity, Atwood—who switches the perspective to a female one—uncovers the misogynist tendencies in Baudelaire's prose poems and assesses gender roles and relations anew. Her technique of inversion—as shown in chapter 1—goes beyond a mere mirroring and, supported by intertextual double coding, has a fundamentally (gender-) political aim, which can be seen particularly well in her later collection *Good Bones* (1992). Here Atwood resorts to increasingly radical—but at the same time self-consciously ironic and humorous—inverted counter-representations, thereby also drastically remixing and extending the thematic range of these generic formats. "Making a Man," for instance, facetiously mimics the style of women's magazines: taking the anti-essentialist constructedness of gender images at face value, Atwood inverts the traditional commodification of women and applies it to the hilarious "recipe" of "making a man"—which in turn makes the reader laugh about and question biased constructions of gender images. Although her engendered poetics of inversion apply to other genres of her oeuvre as well, it becomes especially effective in her prose poetry and short fictions.

Chapter 3 goes on to consider Atwood's short-story oeuvre, following the development in the representation of gender relationships from her earliest through to her latest works in this genre. Her first short-story collection, *Dancing Girls* (1977), was influenced by Ronald D. Laing's psychiatric study *The Divided Self: An Existential Study in Sanity and Madness* (first published in 1960), and her early characters, affected by "ontological insecurity" (to use Laing's term), are usually portrayed in unfulfilling, dysfunctional, or disintegrating relationships. Often a character's poor self-image, or some other personality defect, results in dependence on rather than love for his or her partner. The gloomy view of the relationships between woman and man, the characters' inability to unite intellect and emotion, and the resulting preoccupation with schizoid or even schizophrenic mental states in Atwood's early short-story collection are supplanted in her second collection, *Bluebeard's Egg* (1983), by a move away from individual psychological problems toward sociopsychological themes. Individuals are increasingly rendered as members of specific groups (see, e.g., her "family stories"). Nevertheless, in this second collection, too, relationships in their terminal stages and partnerships in crisis remain one of Atwood's favourite themes. The third collection, *Wilderness Tips* (1991), in turn moves away from family-oriented stories and often presents characters at their workplaces—among them, most notably, talented women who have to face male resentment and envy on the cumbersome way up the career ladder. This collection also introduces gender problems for the first time in a same-sex context that goes beyond the mother-daughter and father-son relationships with which Atwood had hitherto dealt. Emotional and intellectual friendships between women occasionally turn out to be the deepest and most formative relationships in their lives. Relationships between women and men, in contrast, are marked by conventional gender patterns or rituals and tend to hamper the women's individual development. In her latest short-story collection, *Moral Disorder* (2006), published when Atwood was in her mid-sixties, gender no longer seems to play such a significant role. However, there are two important stories set in the 1950s and 1960s in which Atwood, in a retrospective setup, explores the formation of gender in earlier stages of life, thereby demonstrating the social constructedness of gender, the performance status of femininities and masculinities. In this recent collection of short stories, a largely non-essentialist view of gender relations seems to be achieved eventually. Altogether, delineating her treatment of gender in her short stories and short fictions over some four decades, I argue that it has largely developed according to the various stages of "victim positions" Atwood described as early as in *Survival: A Thematic Guide to Canadian Literature* (1972).

Chapter 4 looks at gender in Atwood's vast novelistic oeuvre by focusing on the development of forms of address and reference particularly in connection with female characters in these novels. Again a diminishing of gender relevance is noticeable in her latest novel that deals roughly with the present and beyond, the dystopia *Oryx and Crake* (2003), yet not in her later works that return to the past. Thus, in her novels, too, with the exception of *Oryx and Crake*, gender plays a crucial role. The chapter demonstrates Atwood's observant sensibility regarding the opportunities involved in forms of address. She systematically chooses specific options in the characters' communication with the other sex that suggest the attitude of the speakers toward their interlocutors and particularly show the relevance of a systematic use of sexist forms of address and reference for the creation and/or perpetuation of stereotyping and prejudice in connection with women. The chapter traces the highly telling development of forms of address in Atwood's novels from the late 1960s through the late 1980s to the early 1990s and beyond. Atwood has moved from subtle as well as drastic illustrations of sexist attitudes—largely unperceived and undiscussed by the characters—in the early novels toward an explicit awareness of the communicative relevance of forms of address in Elaine Risley's comments in *Cat's Eye* (1988). In *The Robber Bride* (1993), in which most of the communication takes place between female characters, forms of address are predominantly neutral and symmetrical in terms of gender representation. In her later novels from *Alias Grace* (1996) onward, her choice of settings in the past results again in a largely traditional system of reference that reflects the historical period represented, with men regarded as superior to and also ready to trivialize or even denigrate women. In her recent novel *The Penelopiad* (2005), Atwood playfully blends traditional with more symmetrical forms of address as her twenty-first-century perspective intentionally leaks into the representation of antiquity in this hilarious rewriting of the Odysseus-Penelope myth.

Chapter 5 extends chapter 4 by looking more comprehensively at the significance of gender in one of Atwood's novels, *The Handmaid's*

Tale, and then, in particular, at what happens to this aspect in the film adaptation by German director Volker Schlöndorff. The analysis of this best-known adaptation of her works is embedded in a first-time multimedial survey of (film, TV, radio, drama, opera) adaptations of works by Atwood. It becomes clear that her works have altogether not fared particularly well with adaptations, of which Schlöndorff's is a case in point. After sketching the truly adventurous production history of the film, I analyze the degree to which Schlöndorff Hollywoodized the film in his desire to create an "American" film for an "American" audience. In doing so, he partly twisted or obscured the more sophisticated statements of Atwood's novel. In his severe reorientation of the plot (one critic called the film "The Filmmaker's Tale"), Schlöndorff streamlined the complexity of the book into an easily consumable "mainstream" film. He also "mainstreamed" the representation of gender by inflecting Atwood's statements on gender in a male-oriented direction. This becomes clear in analyses of crucial scenes of the film, such as the Scrabble scene or the ending. The film adaptation altogether "remasculinizes" the traditionally masculine dystopian genre, which Atwood precisely complements in her novel by rendering the events from a female and largely internally focalized perspective.

Chapter 6 reaches beyond Atwood's texts that are "literary" in a strict sense and offers an overview of gender issues across her considerable literary and cultural criticism. Her critical prose extends from reviews of literary texts and introductions to her own works and those by other authors, via statements on politics such as US-Canadian relations and human rights, to lecture series on the myth of the North in Canadian literature and culture as well as on writing and the position of the writer. In the present context, her special contribution lies in her emphasis on the role of women in both society and literature and on the significance of being a woman writer. In her early creative period between 1972 and 1982, Atwood produced several essays in this vein that may be considered classic statements on the issue. She comments on the individual female writer's potential stances toward the Women's Movement, astutely pointing out many traps laid out in this context. She uncovers sadly gender-prejudiced reviewing practices concerning books by women writers and the persistence of a deep-rooted essentialist view of women that also concerns the writer's craft, as literature itself has long been part of this essentializing view of women and men. Atwood argues that women, both in real life and in literature, must be regarded as individuals, just as men are, rather than as predominantly typical representatives of their gender. She demands that women should be granted their imperfections as well, just as men are, without being immediately slurred and generally damned: "perhaps it is time to take the capital W off Woman," she suggests in *Second Words: Selected Critical Prose* (1982, 227). In her literary and cultural criticism, too, Atwood thus gives us a female view of women and literature—based on her wealth of first-hand experience in the literary world and her breadth of knowledge of world literature—that counters the male master discourse. As with her fiction, she offers the rare case of a critic reaching both scholars and the general reading public by practising "criticism as creative art" (Pache 2000/02, 133).

In a first-time extensive survey as well as detailed treatment of Atwood's achievements as a cartoonist, chapter 7 demonstrates to what extent Atwood also engenders her comic art. After a concise contextualizing treatment of the development of comic art in the United States and Canada, and of the status of female cartoonists and heroines in the comics industry, the chapter goes on to articulate Atwood's stance toward comics and her development as a "cartoonist." The ensuing detailed analysis of her *Kanadian Kultchur Komix*, published between 1975 and 1980 in *This Magazine*, focuses on a selection of those seventeen of some twenty-four comics in the series in which her creation "Survivalwoman" features as (anti)heroine a pictorial self-stylization of Atwood. Through the correlation of *Survival* and Survivalwoman, this figure comes to epitomize (the state of) Canada in Atwood's typical— and typically Canadian—self-ironic, sarcastic, allegedly self-deprecatory view. Through the doubling of "Canadian" and "female"—next to, for instance, America's "Superman," here sarcastically called "Superham"— the status of Survivalwoman appears to be particularly precarious. Power structures are seen in gendered terms, and oppression and the restriction of individual rights are presented as particularly pronounced in the case of women. In this comics series, Atwood refers to political and cultural events and agendas in, or of relevance to, Canada at the time, such as the War Measures Act of 1970, the International Women's Year of 1975, the Canadian federal election of 1979, and, of course, Quebec nationalism and Canada's precarious relationship with the United States. Since Canada at the time was occupied with a cultural decolonization of its postcolonial status and mentality, Atwood's decision to make her Canadian comics hero female establishes a telling parallelism between power politics and gender politics. Survivalwoman/Canada is rendered as the supposedly smaller, weaker sex, aiming at "soft" (cultural) power, against a physically overpowering Superham/United States relying on traditional means of wielding power, such as physical/military supremacy.

Apart from the *Kanadian Kultchur Komix* series, Atwood's other types of comics, the early autobiographical comics, self-ironically stylize a literary star in the making (indeed definitely a female writer, considering the problems she faces), whereas her later *Book Tour Comics* supplant "the fighting failure" Survivalwoman with a female star author who has made it professionally but nevertheless still has to fight against a context of cultural ignorance and various hurdles of the writing profession—not all but some connected to gender. Thus, in contrast to their male colleagues, women in this profession (as the comics pinpoint) are often subjected to a physical code, which in the final analysis also functions as a signal as to who dictates the evaluative criteria—for the physical appearance of a writer, of course, has nothing to do with (the quality of) her writing. In her comics, too, Atwood cleverly refutes, reverses, or at least disturbs such gendered power codes.

The book closes with an interview I conducted with Atwood in Toronto in November 2006 (chapter 8), thereby letting this outspoken writer have "the last word." This is first of all meant as a symbolic gesture at the beginning of the twenty-first century, with retroactive reference to John W. MacDonald's 1982 review of Atwood's essay collection *Second Words:* "Women, according to the conventional wisdom, are not expected to have 'the last word' (except in last wills and testaments). Equally frowned upon is it for women to initiate 'the first word'—it is regarded as inappropriately forward (except in writing 'forewords' to books of poetry). Second words, however, are presumably acceptable entry points for women into male-dominated discourse." The interview, titled "From Survivalwoman to Literary Icon," however, also deals with a remarkable creative career spanning some five decades. We talked at length about Atwood's little-known development into a "cartoonist," her creative techniques and visual arts in general, her early writing for the student-run magazine *Acta Victoriana* of Victoria College at the University of Toronto, the joys (and woes) of gardening, modern technology and the writer's craft, the cultural climate in Canada at the time Atwood started to publish, her support of publishing houses and writers in general and in which areas a writer should withhold support, and, last but not least, her status and the consequences of being a celebrity writer in Canada in contrast to the United States. I made a point of not asking her any questions about gender issues (except, indirectly, in connection with her choice of a male pseudonym for the *Kanadian Kultchur Komix*) because I was interested in getting to know about aspects of her creativity and activities not traceable from her texts.

As I finish proofreading this introduction and thereby this book manuscript (with Atwood's productivity having kept me on the run), a new book by Atwood was published in fall 2008, *Payback: Debt and the Shadow Side of Wealth*, the text of her Massey Lectures, and another one in fall 2009, *The Year of the Flood*, her latest novel. The cultural concepts of debt and paying it back may also be associated, of course, with the writer-reader relationship, and it cuts both ways. Readers, for sure, and especially female readers, are indebted to Atwood not least for her early (and, though now to a lesser degree, continuing) outspoken and level-headed statements in the interest of women (and, in the final analysis, of men)—at a time when it was unpopular to make such statements and when words such as *feminism* were often used as weapons rather than as descriptive terms for pointing out the obvious: namely, that women should be granted the same chances and respect men are granted. Thus, in her 1976 essay "On Being a 'Woman Writer,'" collected in *Second Words*, Atwood cogently remarks that "The woman writer, then, exists in a society that, though it may turn certain individual writers into revered cult objects, has little respect for writing as a profession, and not much respect for women either. If there were more of both, articles like this would be obsolete. I hope they become so" (1982, 204). More than thirty years after this statement, in "postfeminist" times at the beginning of the twenty-first century, gender is of ongoing relevance, if in new contexts, degrees, and forms. In its developing treatment of gender issues over five decades in diverse genres, Margaret Atwood's oeuvre is a significant cultural document of our times.

NOTES

1. For a comprehensive list of Atwood's works structured according to genre up to the year 2000, see the bibliography in Nischik 2000/02, 319–21.
2. See Atwood's introduction to her first novel, *The Edible Woman*, and chapters 4 and 6.
3. As Frans de Bruyn has argued in general terms, "Female writers have responded in various ways to the male-oriented genres they have inherited, from the self-doubt that perceives the obverse of literary 'paternity' to be 'female literary sterility' and the self-denying acceptance of the lesser sphere of minor genres (journals, diaries, children's books), to a subversion or deconstruction of patriarchal generic norms and a questioning of the male-dominated generic tradition" (2000, 83).
4. This could also have been done in connection with Atwood's poetry in chapter 1, of course, but my focus is different there.

1

Power Politics
Or, The End of Romantic Love Poetry?

The good life is one inspired by love and guided by knowledge.

BERTRAND RUSSELL, *What I Believe*, 10

Margaret Atwood's career as a creative writer began during her student days in Toronto and at Harvard University, and her first major published works were volumes of poetry. *The Circle Game* (1966), her second poetry collection, won her the Governor General's Literary Award, Canada's foremost literary prize, heralding the start of a meteoric literary career both in Canada and abroad. Next to her productivity in a range of other genres, Atwood has produced a poetry oeuvre that is as impressive in quality and quantity as it is varied: to date, she has published sixteen volumes of poetry, including, most recently, *Morning in the Burned House* (1995), *Eating Fire: Selected Poetry 1965–1995* (1998), and *The Door* (2007).

Although Atwood started out as a poet and although poetry constitutes such an impressive part of her oeuvre, her work in this genre has not attracted the same attention among a larger audience as did her short prose and particularly her novels, which have been translated into roughly thirty languages. Thus, it is worth noting that, in spite of Atwood's popularity in, for instance, the German-speaking countries (see Ferguson 2007), only two of her poetry collections have been translated into German: *Morning in the Burned House* (*Ein Morgen im verbrannten Haus*, 1996) and *True Stories* (1981) (*Wahre Geschichten*, 1984). This chapter aims to redress the balance somewhat by exploring the significance of Atwood's seminal poetry collection *Power Politics* (1971). It is an excellent starting point for this study, since *Power Politics* is a groundbreaking book and cultural document, and it is characterized by a typical Atwoodian blending of genre and gender revisions.

SIGNIFICANCE AND SOCIOCULTURAL CONTEXT OF *POWER POLITICS*

Since its publication by the Toronto House of Anansi Press in 1971, *Power Politics* has been received in strikingly contradictory terms. There has been little extensive or exclusive criticism;[1] most of this criticism tends to be limited to brief references within broader surveys of Atwood's poetry or her oeuvre as a whole.[2] On the other hand, when I asked a number of prominent North American authors for statements on the importance of Margaret Atwood (for inclusion in a collection edited on the occasion of her sixtieth birthday, *Margaret Atwood: Works and Impact* [Nischik 2000/02]), *Power Politics* was repeatedly cited as a groundbreaking text that transformed the perception of issues of gender and genre. As Canadian poet Phyllis Webb put it, "*Power Politics* changed the definition of the love poem, the long poem, and, I believe, the course of Canadian poetry. It cuts like a laser beam. It goes beyond sexual politics into the dark heart of a tottering global village" (in Nischik 2000/02, 305).

One point should be stressed from the start: *Power Politics* is a collection of love poems, not antilove poems. There is a love relationship at stake in *Power Politics* after all, which sometimes seems to have been forgotten by critics when focusing on the bitingly recriminating lines in the book. Indeed, in this poetry cycle, Atwood radically refuses to view love and gender relations through rose-tinted glasses. She poignantly reveals that the power structures inherent in broader sociopolitical and cultural contexts are also present in the most intimate of human relationships and that received codes of love are founded on power issues. Consequently, *Power Politics*—critically and parodically, with Atwood's typical biting humour—sets out to expose the harsher realities behind idealized notions of romantic love. As Anne Michaels puts it, "*Atwood dares to imagine realpolitik at the heart of love's mystery*" (in Nischik 2000/02, 305).

As so often in Atwood's works, gender is a crucial theme in *Power Politics*, yet it is by no means the only essential one: *Power Politics* goes beyond a critique of gender relations, developing a wide-ranging piece of cultural criticism along the way, as Phyllis Webb's statement above suggests.

The collection was often glibly and unfairly dismissed as a poetic version of Women's Lib, however, and therefore denied serious treatment by many critics. Rosemary Sullivan, in her biography of Atwood, points out that the American edition of *Power Politics* (published by Harper and Row) came out in 1973, two years after the Canadian edition, and she contrasts the volume's differing reception in the two countries, which she sees as a result of the dissimilar stages of development of the Women's Movement in Canada and the United States: "The American reviews of *Power Politics* seemed less personal; mostly they looked directly at the poetry. Dick Allen, in *Poetry*, described *Power Politics* as 'an honest, searching book which touches deeply'" (1998, 254).[3] It is significant in this context that Atwood herself rejects the notion that the Women's Movement influenced the conception of *Power Politics* or of her debut novel, *The Edible Woman* (1969)—these works had, after all, been written in the 1960s, at a time when Women's Lib had not yet risen to prominence in North America. Atwood's statement in a foreword written in 1979 for the Virago edition of *The Edible Woman* (at the time already a cult text for the Women's Movement) is hence equally applicable to *Power Politics*:

> *The Edible Woman* appeared finally in 1969, four years after it was written and just in time to coincide with the rise of feminism in North America. Some immediately assumed that it was a product of the movement. I myself see the book as protofeminist rather than feminist: there was no women's movement in sight when I was composing the book in 1965, and I'm not gifted with clairvoyance, though like many at the time I'd read Betty Friedan and Simone de Beauvoir behind locked doors. (8)[4]

In both *The Edible Woman* and *Power Politics*, Atwood tackled the problems of gender relations from a new, indeed "protofeminist," perspective, analyzing gender-based structures of domination and repression from a female point of view and providing an elaborate reaction to such imbalance. In her early works, then, Atwood sensed the zeitgeist of a highly important cultural moment in the 1960s. In fact, these texts can be regarded—in their more (*Power Politics*) or less (*The Edible Woman*) radical reconceptualization of gender relations—as seminal texts of literary gender studies. The following statement by Helmut Frielinghaus, Atwood's editor at her first German publishing house (Claassen), makes clear the cultural explosiveness of her themes at the time:

> Those who remember the early sixties, or know how much they at first resembled the fifties, will have an idea of how much Margaret Atwood risked in striking out on her own with her first novel. What she had written was something new; it was extremely intelligent and witty, but that did not distract from the fact that it was also aggressive and challenging. (in Nischik 2000/02, 296)

Without intending to play down Atwood's remarkable achievement in her early works, I think that it is necessary to put into perspective that "striking out on her own" on which Atwood and her German editor place so much emphasis. Poetry linked to the Women's Movement had already been published in North America in the early 1960s, collections such as H.D. (Hilda Doolittle), *Helen in Egypt* (New York: New Directions, 1961); Anne Sexton, *To Bedlam and Part Way Back* and *All My Pretty Ones* (Boston: Houghton Mifflin, 1960, 1962); Adrienne Rich, *Snapshots of a Daughter-in-Law* (New York: Norton, 1963); and Sylvia Plath, *Ariel* (New York: Harper and Row, 1965). Alicia Ostriker (1984) includes *Power Politics* among the second wave of the *American* feminist movement. Sullivan states that "the new feminism was an American phenomenon" while also demonstrating that Atwood was indeed aware of some of the relevant texts by 1969 (1998, 242), "But Margaret Atwood and Margaret Laurence had had their consciousness raised long before official feminism" (243). In 1970, an *annus mirabilis* in this respect, a number of long-overdue works of cultural criticism were published that clearly fell within the scope of the feminist movement, such as Robin Morgan's *Sisterhood Is Powerful: An Anthology of Writings from the Women's Liberation Movement* (according to Sullivan, 242, Laurence had sent Atwood a copy of this book), Leslie Tanner's *Voices from Women's Liberation*, Shulamith Firestone's *The Dialectic of Sex: The Case for Feminist Revolution*, Vivian Gornick and Barbara Moran's *Woman in Sexist Society: Studies in Power and Powerlessness*, and, of particular interest for those interested in literature, Kate Millet's classic work *Sexual Politics*.[5]

In the following quotation, Atwood herself highlights the cultural upheavals of the 1960s and 1970s—a period when gender represen-tations and relations at last became a matter for political debate—and discusses the reception of *The Edible Woman* and *Power Politics* at the time of publication. Her survey of the reception of her early work is so significant that it is worth citing in full. The polarized reactions as Atwood presents them indicate the extent to which she challenged cultural barriers:

> Incredible as it may seem, the publisher misplaced the manuscript [of *The Edible Woman*] for two years; but because of this delay it was assumed by some that the novel was a product of what is commonly termed the Women's Movement. It wasn't, and neither is *Power Politics*. I see both books as amplifications of themes that have been present in my work since I first started writing and publishing. To say this is not to disparage anyone's politics. It is merely to indicate that parallel lines do not usually start from the same point, and that being adopted is not, finally, the same as being born.
>
> If the Women's Movement had little to do with the composition of *Power Politics*, however, it had a lot to do with its reception. In general, response divided rather neatly along sex lines, women greeting the book with recognition, men with fear; ten years ago women would probably have ignored and men dismissed it. Women, both critics and ordinary readers, spoke of the book as though it was about them, about the way it was; for them it was realistic. Men tended to use adjectives like "cruel" and "jagged" and to see it either as a display of perversity on my part or as an attack, a conspiracy, a war or an inhuman vivisection of Love, nasty and unfair as cutting up a puppy. (cited in McCombs 1988a, 52)

I will now approach this seminal book first of all by commenting on the resonant cover of the original publication, in which Atwood had a hand and which visually prepares readers for some of the essential statements of *Power Politics*.

THE COVER ILLUSTRATION FOR *POWER POLITICS*

The cover illustration for *Power Politics* matches the uncompromising and radical manner in which Atwood reconceives love and gender relations in that volume. She often contributes to the design of her book covers, or even designs them herself, as with the collage on the cover of *Good Bones* (1992)[6] (in this case, the cover illustrates Atwood's revisionist version of the children's story "The Little Red Hen," modified in *Good Bones* to "The Little Red Hen Tells All"; see chapter 2). Although the cover illustration for *Power Politics* was

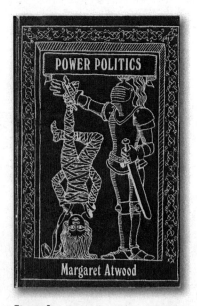
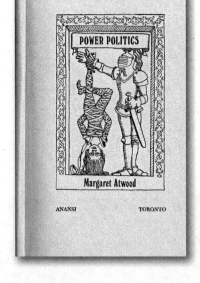

Figure 1.

executed by William Kimber, the idea came from Atwood herself, and she authorized the final version.[7] This illustration is so relevant to the subsequent poems as to merit a closer look.

The illustration is disturbing and irritating. It shows two figures tied to one another, preventing each other from pulling loose and restricting each other's mobility. The figure on the right is clad from head to toe in armour; the hands are covered by thick gauntlets, and even the visor is lowered, hiding the face. The figure stands rigid and restricted, reduced as it is to its protective armour and aggressive sword. The martial outfit, the general shape of the body, and the contrast to the second, female figure suggest to the viewer that the first figure is male, although there is no definite proof of this assumption. This figure, hiding from the outside world, and tightly gripping its weapon, the sword in its sheath, is completely obscured by its offensive and defensive equipment. It seems to symbolize physical strength, with its statuesque pose and strong arm. But this impression is reduced to absurdity, for the very pose that encapsulates his power—with the woman dangling from the male figure's arm—must also cause him severe physical discomfort; in fact, the pose is hardly sustainable for a longer time. So the question is who of the two is suffering more? The woman hangs head down, her hair falling onto the ground; she is defenceless and dependent on the male figure. Her body is almost entirely bandaged, suggesting horrendous wounds or even mummification, yet she is in no way repulsive. Whereas the man's face is covered with a visor obstructing his view, she looks directly at the viewer with eyes wide open, seemingly ignoring the armour-clad knight and challenging the viewer with her gaze. Her posture—with crossed legs and arms held behind her back—is that of the hanged man on the twelfth card of the *Major Arcana* of the Tarot card game. This pose, and the woman's facial expression, suggest a certain openness if not power in spite of her uncomfortable position. In Tarot, the twelfth card "represents the turning point of psychological development when one must confront unconscious forces."[8] It stands, among other things, for patience and renunciation, out of which come the opportunity, indeed the obligation, to achieve a new perspective on life through profound understanding.[9] This is similar to the basic situation in *Power Politics*. It is perhaps not coincidental that the colour of the cover, rust, is a darker variant of the colour that symbolizes love—red.

ANALYSES OF THE POEMS

Like many of Atwood's collections, *Power Politics* can be described as a poetry cycle: the individual poems are effective in their own right, but the power of the volume is fully realized only when it is taken as a whole, the individual texts being integrated through techniques such as motivic repetition, variation, and intensification.[10] Susan Friedman, in a more general context, points out that when Atwood composed *Power Politics* the cyclical structure constituted a challenge to a gendered tradition: "The short, passionate lyric has conventionally been thought appropriate for women poets if they insist on writing, while the longer, more philosophical epic belongs to the real (male) poet" (cited in Ostriker 1982, 78). This integrative effect is enhanced by the fact that most of the poems have no title. The book is divided into three sections, each of which is introduced by an untitled, quasi-programmatic quatrain. Part I contains fourteen poems, of which six have titles; Part II consists of sixteen poems, of which only four are titled; and Part III has fifteen poems, only two of which have titles. *Power Politics*, the fifth of Atwood's twelve volumes of poetry, has many characteristics in common with the others, which have come to be seen as the hallmarks of her poetry: free rhythms, without rhyme or fixed meter, and an idiosyncratic voice—authoritative, confident, distanced (further heightened during poetry readings by Atwood's seemingly unemotional reading style). This deadpan gesture has even engendered a new adjective: *Atwoodian*.

> **At·wood·i·an** (at'wood'ē-an) *adj. Literary*. 1. Of or relating to Margaret Atwood's unique manner of expression, as charac-terized by her virtuoso wit and unmistakable style. [First coined by Clark Blaise in the *Chicago Tribune*.] 2. Wickedly observant. 3. Deliciously entertaining. 4. Darkly humorous. 5. Superbly controlled. 6. Brilliantly imagined. 7. Compassionate and empathetic. 8. Outrageously true. *SYNONYMS: wry, sly, hilarious, amusing, sophis-ticated, delightful, satisfying, sardonic, exuberant, droll, exhilarating.*[11]

This proposed definition fits in well with Atwood's poetry and prose and is therefore applicable to *Power Politics* (with the possible exception of point 7).

Power Politics opens with the following quatrain, which has achieved considerable notoriety and which sets the tone for the whole collection:

> You fit into me
> like a hook into an eye
> a fish hook
> an open eye (1)[12]

Here an image of psychological and physical brutality is superimposed—through the double meaning of "eye"—on the seemingly straightforward structure and simple vocabulary of the epigram, and metaphor suddenly becomes metonymy. As is often the case in Atwood's work, the starting point for this transformation is the perception of everyday reality, which is transported to a more complex level of consciousness by being examined from an unusual, alienating perspective, thus forcing the reader to question the value and justification of conventional categories of perception. This effect is often achieved through the use of subversive or inverse modes of representation (see chapter 2) that expose the norms of perception and language and question them critically from a female perspective. In this way, traditional, "received" stories are complemented or revised by being juxtaposed with "a repertoire / of untold stories, / a fresh beginning" (see chapter 3).[13]

Although identification of the "I" as female and of the "you" as male takes place only in subsequent texts of the volume,[14] the association is already suggested by the quatrain's imagery. The simile of the hook fitting into the eye at first suggests a complementary, logical combination, in which two contrasting parts join to form a unit: the active element is the "you," the passive or receptive element the "me." Even this image, however, not only conveys the harmony of a perfect match but also suggests a scenario of possessive penetration. The superimposition of the second part of the epigram almost entirely erases the largely positive connotations of the first part, specifying the meaning of "hook" and "eye" as fish hook and human (or animal) eye and relating them to each other in a completely different, brutal manner. The image of a steel hook in an open eye painfully evokes wounding and destruction.[15] The hook seems to have hunted down and captured its object of desire, thereby destroying the fragile, unprotected eye/I, that is, the woman herself. The superimposition of this image is sexually and emotionally motivated. The idealized and romanticized view of the natural harmony of gender relations, so often encountered in traditional love poetry, is juxtaposed in this linguistically playful but semantically ruthless quatrain with an aggressive and damaging element of gender relations.[16] Right from the volume's onset, then, a painful, uncomfortable picture of gender relations is unleashed, the man being represented as aggressor and the woman as victim. It is hardly surprising that, particularly in the 1970s, this volume should have provoked such polarized and polemical reactions from readers.

Following in the line of this rather unconventional overture, Atwood in the subsequent poems throws all the conventions and ideals of love poetry by the wayside, as I will show with a few examples. In "He Reappears," the alleged ability of lovers to communicate without words leads to a communicative dead-end and ends with the female speaker's desperate, unanswered question: "Can't we / be friends I said; / you didn't answer" (2). In the next poem, untitled, love is compared to a bad movie with its standardized plot and characters. It feeds off hackneyed aphorisms taken from popular culture's hoard of quotations, which stand in the way of authentic self-expression. Yet the lyrical I cannot but be attracted to this miserable substitute for a loving relationship; love's clichés stick with her just like "melted celluloid" clings to her body:

> You take my hand and
> I'm suddenly in a bad movie,
> it goes on and on and
> why am I fascinated
>
> We waltz in slow motion
> through an air stale with aphorisms (3)[17]

In "She Considers Evading Him," the female speaker escapes from this "bad movie," with its preprogrammed codes of behaviour, into a death fantasy:

> collapse across your
> bed clutching my heart

and pull the nostalgic sheet up over
my farewell smile

which would be inconvenient
but final. (4)

The poem, however, also underlines what the book cover already suggested—namely, the "you," the male character, is depicted by Atwood as a victim as well (a fact often ignored by earlier reviewers). The male character also suffers in the relationship, not least because of the "antiromantic" approach of the female speaker, whose analytical thinking and individualistic reaction to the "you" reject preconceived patterns of romantic behaviour, thus denying her partner the idealized approach for which he longs.

Another untitled poem comments,

You say, Do you
love me, do you love me

I answer you:
I stretch your arms out
one to either side,
your head slumps forward. (6)

This is certainly one of the oddest "professions of love" in literature. Indeed, it almost comes across as a denial of love since the "I" does not choose to provide a direct answer to her lover's repeated question. Instead, the "answer" is involuntarily provided by the—questionably "nodding"—questioner himself, demonstrating along the way how self-referential the question is. The lyrical I's refusal to answer even takes on macabre connotations if we interpret the posture of the "you," as guided by the lyrical I, as an image of crucifixion. Instead of the hoped-for confirmation that he is loved, the "you" is presented with the suggestion that he has already been executed.[18] Complicating the web of potential meanings even further, we might note that the archetype of the crucified man is Jesus, the very symbol of love, who rose from the dead. Similarly

strange and ambiguous is the following "declaration of love" in a
subsequent untitled poem (see below for further comments on this
passage):

> I love you by
> sections and when you work.
>
> Do you want to be illiterate?
> This is the way it is, get used to it. (9)

In "Their Attitudes Differ," the lyrical I analyzes relationships, and
herself, with diamond-sharp perception, again a far cry from the issues
and style of conventional love poetry:

> I approach this love
> like a biologist
> pulling on my rubber
> gloves & white labcoat
>
> You flee from it
> like an escaped political
> prisoner, and no wonder
>
> You held out your hand
> I took your fingerprints
>
> You asked for love
> I gave you only descriptions
>
> Please die I said
> so I can write about it (10)

Atwood parodies here, perhaps, the inclination of women to analyze
relationships, to frequently make a topic of relationships or their
partners in their conversations and discussions.

Finally, in "They Travel by Air," a typically Atwoodian gender
inversion takes place:

> A different room, this month
> a worse one, where your
> body with head
> attached and my head with
> body attached coincide briefly
>
> I want questions and you want
> only answers ...
>
> we collide sightlessly and
> fall, the pieces of us
> mixed as disaster (11)

Here the male figure is reduced to its body and the female associated with the mind—a mind that questions and rejects the preprogrammed answers that its partner wants to impose on it.

As can be seen in "My Beautiful Wooden Leader," Atwood's characteristic humour shines through even in the darkest of situations, in this case at the expense of the male figure. Of all the poems in the collection, this one most closely relates to Kimber's cover illustration analyzed above. The poem parodies the traditional tendency to idealize the male lover as a hero, showing how he is dependent on others in his desire to come across as a triumphant, dominant champion:

> we follow you
> scattering floral tributes
> under your hooves.
>
> Magnificent on your wooden horse (7)

or, "General, you enlist / my body in your heroic / struggle to become real" (7). The poem's imagery of fringed clothing and horses suggests the virile, hero-generating environment of the western, all the more so since the man's arm points westward, and the poem ends with a characteristic western-style sunset. Yet this pompous gesture, already presented ironically in the same pose on the cover illustration, is depicted as miserably ineffective posturing:

> Magnificent on your wooden horse
> you point with your fringed hand;
> the sun sets, and the people all
> ride off in the other direction. (7)

Due to the lyrical persona's refusal to view him unquestioningly as a hero, the male figure appears as a "wooden leader" with only "wooden medals." His ostensibly heroic triumphs turn out to be mere faked posturing ("fixing it each time so you almost win"), and the allegedly brave, independent man seems in fact to be helpless and consumed by self-pity: "you long to be bandaged / before you have been cut" (7; also compare the man's protective coat of armour on the cover illustration). In the face of such posturing, love ossifies to defensive stasis:

> My love for you is the love
> of one statue for another: tensed
>
> and static. (7)

In Part II of the cycle, the situation becomes even worse. The quatrain introducing this section indicates that the relationship will now be examined against a social and political background. In doing so, Atwood indirectly comments on the conventional social separation of the public and the private spheres, the former being associated with male autonomy, the latter with female dependence (see Benjamin 1988, 178). As George Bowering puns, "The book [*Power Politics*] is a sequence of lyrics on the state of affairs which tend to become affairs of state" (1981, 43). The term "imperialist" suggests unequal power relations and global power politics directed against humanity and the environment:

> Imperialist, keep off
> the trees I said.
>
> No use: you walk backwards,
> admiring your own footprints. (15)

Here, too, the gender conflict is still implied: the "I" is in the right but lacks the power to enforce it—her words, warnings, and exhortations cannot prevent the imperialist from taking the path he wants, a path not of progress but, in its self-reflexiveness and disdain for nature, of regression.[19]

Parts II and III in particular contain scathingly depressing diagnoses of the contemporary human condition, depicting an almost Beckettian endgame situation in an analysis whose scope ranges far beyond the theme of gender relations:

> These days my fingers bleed
> even before I bite them (17)

> and there isn't anything
> I want to do about the fact
> that you are unhappy & sick

> you aren't sick & unhappy
> only alive & stuck with it. (16)

> the entrails of dead cards
> are against me (41)[20]

> There is no way I can lose you
> when you are lost already. (54)

Power Politics suggests several possible causes for this state of stasis and decay: physical and psychological power relations (on personal and national levels); the threat posed by dangerous political situations; violence directed against humanity and the environment;[21] and the increasing influence of technology on life, which comes to dominate immaterial relationships, too (see "annunciation" in the following passage):

> I walk the cell, open the window,
> shut the window, the little
> motors click

> and whir, I turn on all the
> taps and switches (19)

> you become slowly more public,
> in a year there will be nothing left
> of you but a megaphone
> ...
> having long forgotten the difference
> between an annunciation and a parking ticket (30)

> I judge you as the trees do
> by dying (32–33)

In such a sociopolitical context, Atwood sees love, too, as being infected by power politics and imperialistic behaviour. Love in *Power Politics* is cleverly exposed as a political theme, constituting a miniature war scenario of attack and defence:[22]

> We are hard on each other
> and call it honesty,
> choosing our jagged truths
> with care and aiming them across
> the neutral table.
> ...

> A truth should exist,
> it should not be used
> like this. If I love you

> is that a fact or a weapon? (24, 25)

> Next time we commit
> love, we ought to
> choose in advance what to kill. (35)

To sum up, Atwood in *Power Politics* presents the reader with a challenging, uncompromising diagnosis of the contemporary human condition, penetratingly analyzing even the most intimate of relationships. As the title of the collection suggests, she sees political, social, and private power structures at the root of evil. Basically two theoretical conceptions of power are implied in *Power Politics*, entering into dialogue with one another. Max Weber's autocratic view of power (seen rather from the perspective of the wielder of power) defines it as a process of domination. In this context, power means imposing one's will on that of others. Hannah Arendt's democratic view of power (seen rather from the perspective of those who empower), on the other hand, sees power as a process of (political) formation and persuasion, based on empowerment for a limited time. A given power can also be revoked by the empowerer, and power can only be wielded in collaboration with others (see Florence Kennedy's idea of the "circularity of oppression" in Morgan 1970, 438).[23]

In her treatment of power politics, Atwood undermines the conventional thought patterns that are so often the cause of facile binary oppositions: winner and loser, dominance and subordination, aggressor and victim. Although in *Power Politics* she asks questions rather than provides answers, she does suggest one possible way out of the impasse: the concept of the "third eye" (see her "Instructions for the Third Eye" in *Murder in the Dark*, 61–62).[24] *Power Politics* emphasizes that it is only by breaking down fixed, binary power structures that mutual dependence can be overcome (such mutual dependence is visualized in the cover illustration) and an open, trusting relationship be built. In this, *Power Politics* suggests one of the basic assumptions of gender studies, as Nancy Chodorow, for instance, puts it:

> It is crucial for us feminists to recognize that the ideologies of difference, which define us as women and as men, as well as inequality itself, are produced, socially, psychologically, and culturally, by people living in and creating their social, psychological, and cultural worlds. Women participate in the creation of these worlds and ideologies, even if our ultimate power and access to cultural hegemony are less than those of men. To speak of difference as a final, irreducible concept and to focus on gender differences as central is to reify them and to deny the reality of those *processes* which create the meaning and significance of gender.

> To see men and women as qualitatively different kinds of people,
> rather than seeing gender as processual, reflexive, and constructed,
> is to reify and deny *relations* of gender, to see gender differences as
> permanent rather than as created and situated. (1980, 16)

POWER POLITICS AS A SEMINAL TEXT OF LOVE POETRY

I would finally like to focus on, and put into context, the question of
why *Power Politics* can be considered one of the seminal, groundbreaking
texts of literary gender studies and to what extent it gave love poetry a
new direction toward the end of the twentieth century. At the turn of
the 1970s, a period of cultural upheaval during which traditions and
conventions were violently called into question, Atwood produced a
daring, merciless analysis of love, which recognized that the power
structures at work in a sociopolitical context were also present even in
the most private and intimate of spheres. Her diagnosis is delivered with
bluntness and a disregard for conventions that is extraordinary in the
long history of love poetry. This was reason enough for the Women's
Movement of the 1970s to claim Atwood's work for itself, a claim
that Atwood has rejected. It is important to note that her treatment
of woman and of female gender roles is almost as withering as her
sarcastic, humorous deconstruction of male posturing—once again
also with the purpose of dismantling binary structures. In emphasizing,
for instance, the female potential for aggression, Atwood broke new
ground in the genre of love poetry. (She followed up this view of
women in various ways in her later novels *Cat's Eye*, *The Robber Bride*,
and *Alias Grace*.) Atwood repeatedly portrays women as accomplices
to their own victimization. In *Power Politics*, she puts the blame on all
those, whether male or female, who allow themselves to be caught up
in power structures: "You refuse to own / yourself, you permit / others
to do it for you" (30). The poems are highly cerebral, they do not
take sides, they dissect the romantic myth beyond all its clichés and
taboos, and they aim at identifying the algorithms of love for the
emotional benefit of both woman and man. One may indeed argue that
Power Politics constituted the most complex, innovative, and radical

work dealing with romantic love in Western poetry up to its time of publication.[25]

Did the publication of *Power Politics*, then, herald the end of romantic love poetry or even the end of romantic love? It would, of course, be a crass exaggeration to suggest that the volume could have had such far-reaching aims, to say nothing of consequences. Atwood in *Power Politics* locates herself, however, firmly within the tradition of love poetry, and the poems can be interpreted as an attempt to reform and renew that tradition.[26] Her often parodic intertextual dialogue with traditional love poetry is in evidence throughout the volume. For example, the following lines, cynical as they may at first appear, are in fact a metapoetic reference to the "alarming mortality rate of lovers, in song and film, as well as in books" (McCombs 1973, 58): "Please die I said / so I can write about it" (10). Indeed, love and death, the two great themes of literature,[27] especially when combined in *Liebestod*, have been a favourite motif of great love stories from Shakespeare's *Romeo and Juliet* to Michael Ondaatje's/Anthony Minghella's *The English Patient*. These literary as well as popular tales of love and death contribute massively to the romanticization of love, for the simple reason that death implies the end of a love relationship, at least in this life—whereas Atwood insists on facing up to a love that lives and breathes, with all its challenges posed by the everyday. In statements such as "Please die I said / so I can write about it," Atwood parodies the ideal of love in death so frequently found in literature.[28]

The previously quoted passage,

> I love you by
> sections and when you work.
>
> Do you want to be illiterate?
> This is the way it is, get used to it. (9),

with its suggestions of ignorance and illiteracy on the part of the loved one, seems to be an inverse reference to the love poetry of earlier centuries, when the idealized, worshipped object of love was a woman, who as such was often denied access to education and literacy. Atwood's equivocal statement concerning the lover, "I love you by / sections and when you work," is, seen from this perspective, ambiguously ironic. It also calls into question the absoluteness of romantic love and contains an ironic reference to the tradition of Petrarchan love poetry (highly popular from the Middle Ages to the emergence of romantic love poetry in the eighteenth and nineteenth centuries). In this tradition, the unattainable object of love is usually worshipped from a distance and presented via a description of her individual physical characteristics (leading A. H. Schutz to speak of a "synthetic woman").[29] With Atwood, however, the woman is now the author, while the man as the object of love is represented by her and thereby exposed to her judgment. Like Sylvia Plath and Anne Sexton before her, but reaching even further,[30] Atwood inverts the traditional premises of love poetry, which Judith McCombs, with considerable clarity, has summarized as follows: "In the past the tradition has been heavy on male = author = lover = I, female = object = beloved = her: a genre which might be called The Love Story of Sir Hero and his unequal, the Ignoble Savaged Miss" (1973, 54).

Power Politics also settles the score with the motifs of heroification (usually of the man) and idealization (usually of the woman's physical beauty) so prevalent in traditional love poetry, and it does so with regard to both sexes. Since the poems hardly seem to depict a specific relationship (although Atwood wrote these poems at a time of crisis with her then husband James Polk),[31] but are concerned rather with examining the effects of social and sociopsychological influences on gender relations from a gender studies perspective, the "I" and the "you" in the poems appear to be generic rather than specific. Atwood doubly confuses traditional gender roles by occasionally presenting the man as victim (of his self-image and of the image of him provided by the lyrical "I") and the woman as verbal aggressor (when fighting back the man's attacks). *Power Politics*, then, presents a new, challenging perspective within the framework of a time-honoured literary genre, acting, so to speak, as "a hook in the reader's eye"[32] by questioning conventional, polarizing views, attitudes, and forms of behaviour.

After the early, heated reactions to the book in the 1970s, the reception calmed down, and reviewers began to focus on Atwood's considerable intellectual achievement in *Power Politics*, on the volume's avant-garde, seminal significance, and on its comic elements. Three examples may serve to illustrate this point. Bowering noted in 1981 that, "If there is one thing that Margaret Atwood was on top of in the early Seventies, it was the sense of love as a political struggle. .... In *Power Politics* Atwood gave voice and leadership to post-Sixties attitudes here concerning relationships between the sexes and between the English-speaking peoples of North America" (43).[33] The same year Canadian poets Douglas Barbour and Stephen Scobie published *An Anthology of Comic Canadian Poetry* under the main title of *The Maple Laugh Forever*. In their statement for *Margaret Atwood: Works and Impact* in 2000, they reminisce,

> We had one section titled "Brevity Is the Soul of Wit." Fully aware that we would get some flack for doing so, we opened the section with the epigrammatic opening quatrain to *Power Politics*. Margaret Atwood didn't question our choice, although many reviewers did. We stand by our sense then that it is a superb example of black humor. Well, we laughed, anyway. (in Nischik 2000/02, 306)

It is debatable whether that quatrain contains any form of humour other than wordplay or whether the poem can fulfill Barbour and Scobie's stated aim in the anthology of making readers laugh (11).[34] Theirs nevertheless represents a further legitimate approach to this text: via black humour as an alienating, subversive agent that casts new light on the seemingly familiar.

German scholar Lothar Hönnighausen goes even further in this direction in his survey article on Atwood's poetry. He comments on *Power Politics*,

> Readers who recognize that poetry is not a direct expression of personal feelings, and who take it for granted that women reflect upon love relations as critically as men, will have no difficulties with these witty poems. ... If we approach these poems as inheriting the zeitgeist of change and inversion, of William S. Burroughs, Allen Ginsberg, Robert Rauschenberg and Claes Oldenburg, of Beat, Pop Art, the civil rights movement, and women's lib, we will not be shocked by the "cruelty" of Atwood's [opening] epigraph ... but will rather intuit and enjoy its black humor. (2000/02, 105–06)

This intellectual domestication of *Power Politics* goes too far by defusing the explosive power of an unruly text.[35] The relatively relaxed reception of the book thirty years after its publication is, however, an indication of the decisive change that this text marked. What then seemed shocking now seems—after the student movement, the various waves of the Women's Movement, the establishment of gender studies (and of men's studies)—an integral and largely uncontroversial part of culture. Although the book is still highly relevant, it no longer has quite the same power to shock, at least not in intellectual circles.

Atwood in *Power Politics* calls the concept of idealized romantic love into question. This concept is more closely related to literary texts than is usually recognized—not only because most studies of romantic love have been undertaken by scholars of literature but also because sociologists, who have begun postulating a "sociology of love," trace the creation of romantic love back to English literature of the eighteenth century (Samuel Richardson), to *Sturm und Drang* literature in Germany, and particularly to German Romanticism at the end of the eighteenth century: Novalis, Schlegel, Fichte, Brentano, Varnhagen, Günderode.[36] Particularly interesting for the present purposes are the paradoxes inherent in the code of romantic love and, from today's perspective, the far-reaching absence of cultural patterns that correspond to this code (Lenz 1998, 71).[37] According to German sociologist Karl Lenz, the code of ideal romantic love has seven components: the unity of sexual passion and emotional attraction; the unity of love and marriage; the integration of parenthood into the ideal of romantic love; the exclusivity and lastingness (indeed permanence) of the emotion; the limitlessly expandable individuality (Niklas Luhmann) of the lovers; the absoluteness of the relationship and the concomitant degradation of other aspects of life; and, finally, reciprocity: only requited love is romantic love.

In the last quarter of the twentieth century, the ideal of romantic love was, if not suspended, then at least called into question and challenged by the concept of "egalitarian love" (German philosopher Peter Sloterdijk [2000, 146] speaks of "de-mythologized passion" and "love on an equal footing"). From the 1960s onward, cultural critics working within the Women's Movement and others demonstrated how asymmetrical gender relations, and therefore gender-related power structures, had been superimposed on the code of romantic love, generally to the disadvantage of women. This was the first step toward the demystification of romantic love and of its integration into the discourse of gender politics. To clearly illustrate two of the anti-egalitarian asymmetrical pitfalls of the code of romantic love, I quote a statement by the German Romantic Fichte relating to the first characteristic of romantic love mentioned above, the unity of sexual passion and emotional attraction: "The uncorrupted woman possesses no sexual instinct; none manifests itself in her. Rather is she filled with love, and this love is the natural instinct of a woman to satisfy a man. It is, however, an instinct that desperately needs to be satisfied, but its satisfaction lies not in the sensual satisfaction of the woman but of the man" (in Lenz 1998, 78). To put it bluntly, the unity of sexual passion and emotional attraction applies only to the male partner. A second pitfall: the chastity of women—and only of women—had been idealized as a prerequisite for love and marriage. In this case, too, asymmetrical power structures are superimposed on the so-called ideal of romantic love. As late as the mid-1800s, a scientific work with the revealing title "The Natural History of the People as Basis for German Social Politics" states that "Sexual immorality is one of the few crimes that a woman can commit against the state."[38] Asymmetrical gender structures like these were able to persist for a considerable period, hidden as they were behind the ideological mask of the one and true love—everlasting, passionate, individual, absolute, and requited.

In *Power Politics*, Margaret Atwood tears back this ideological mask and targets every single characteristic of romantic love. In doing so, she repeatedly depicts her male opposite, the "you," as a romantic anachronism. Both sexual passion and emotional attraction become embroiled in power games—who will gain the upper hand?—and cannot be unified. Love and sexuality are disassociated; their romantic union is dissolved. Sexuality in *Power Politics* is located outside love—"it does not move like love" (46)—and is portrayed as a fundamentally self-referential, if not selfish, act. On this level, too, idealization of the partner, which the romantic code prescribes, crumbles. There is no mention in *Power Politics* of marriage or parenthood, and the last poem in the collection, "He Is Last Seen" (56), describes the separation of the lovers. As far as the fourth item of the romantic code sketched above is concerned, *Power Politics* views a relationship not as necessarily unique and everlasting but rather as transitory. Each partner's desire for self-determination leads to a situation in which, "in a conflict situation, individuality takes precedence over perpetuating the relationship" (Lenz 1998, 81). *Power Politics*, however, also demonstrates the paradox inherent in this desire for individuality. The code of romantic love promises to unite, indeed to merge, two individuals spiritually, emotionally, and physically. In Atwood's poetry cycle, however, the code repeatedly breaks down in the face of the antagonism between two partners who are mainly concerned with their own defensive strategies. As German sociologist Georg Simmel has put it, "Love is pure tragedy: only individuality can bring it to life, yet it is destroyed by the impossibility of overcoming individuality" (cited in Lenz 1998, 81). The desire for an absolute relationship is consistently undermined in *Power Politics*, and ignoring other aspects of life outside the relationship was hardly feasible for thoughtful contemporaries in the 1970s, faced as they were with political, military, technological, and environmental threats. As Atwood said in 1971, "*Power Politics* depicts the power that is our environment" (cited in Grace 1980, 53). And, finally, as to the seventh item of the code of romantic love, it remains unclear whether love is reciprocal here, an uncertainty that forms a leitmotif of a collection that, as we have seen, is suffused with power games.

CONCLUSION

At a time when love had more than ever attained the status of an "earthly religion"[39] (see the hippie movement, the student movement, and the sexual revolution), Atwood's *Power Politics* takes up the ideal of romantic love and shows that its implications for power and gender politics are out of date and inadequate. Atwood points out parallels between power structures in macro- and micropolitical spheres. By embedding love in the context of political thought and activity, she creates a new semantics of love. In *Power Politics*, she is fighting not against dualities but against polarities, binary gender relations that leave even the most intimate love affairs exposed to political power structures. The code of idealized romantic love is crossed by the code of political (gender) equality, making the reality of love part of political activity. With her conception of the omnirelevance of gender equality, Atwood placed herself, at the beginning of the 1970s, on the threshold between a romantic and a cooperative, egalitarian conception of love. Equality and symmetry are fundamental objectives of cooperative love (elements of this concept are absence of dominance, the self-expression of *both* individuals, the reconciliation of rationality and emotion, the separation of love and marriage, and, last but not least, gender equality). Power relations are rejected in favour of egalitarian forms of communication and strategies of negotiation, exchange, and persuasion.[40] Relationships can be critically analyzed without calling them completely into question. The threshold situation that characterizes *Power Politics* as a whole is constantly inscribed into the text by Atwood, who repeatedly superimposes the critical code of gender politics over the code of romantic love:

> I love you by
> sections and when you work. (9)

> You are the sun
> in reverse, all energy
> flows into you and is
> abolished (47)

Or, in an ambivalent transformation,

> In the room we will find nothing
> In the room we will find each other (51)

I suggested at the beginning of this chapter that *Power Politics*, in spite of its often disillusioning if not depressing atmosphere, is a work of love poetry and not of antilove poetry.[41] Atwood questions traditional values and behavioural patterns in both private and public spheres; she exposes, exhorts, and warns. In the final analysis, however, there is still a love affair, albeit an unsatisfactory one, at the heart of *Power Politics*. In Atwood's rewriting of the concept of love and the genre of love poetry, love still answers to an unquenchable longing of the individual for recognition by the other. Love poetry is still being written, also and particularly in *Power Politics*, to address a "you" across all dividing lines and against all odds and to engage in a lifelong dialogue of togetherness. In this way, love (and with it love poetry) may be able to renew itself from the silent bareness that is left after battle—"In the room we will find nothing/In the room we will find each other" (51)—even if, for the two lovers in *Power Politics*, there seems to be no happy end eventually. Indeed, the volume thus also includes hopeful, conciliatory passages suggesting that overcoming conventional power politics in public and private life, macro- and micropolitical life, is essential for the survival of humanity, of women and men. The combination of public and private comes across most clearly in the warning tone of the final poem of Part II, "They Are Hostile Nations" (37–38). This combined view of macro- and micropolitics, of the code of romantic love and gender-related codes of behaviour and power structures, the implied knowledge of generic traditions of love poetry, as well as a daring, mercilessly uncovering, and imaginative use of language are the essential factors in how Margaret Atwood revisions love and redesigns love poetry in her seminal poetry cycle *Power Politics*.

NOTES

1. See McCombs 1973; Irvine 1979; Bowering 1981; Cooley 1994; and Somacarrera 2000, 2006.
2. See Onley 1974; Grace 1980, 53–63; Blakely 1983; Mallinson 1985, 44–46; McCombs 1988a, 5–6, 35–36, 50–52; and Hönnighausen 2000/02, 105–07.
3. For a brief overview of *Power Politics*, its historical context, and its often disturbingly unperceptive reception, see Sullivan 1998, 196–98, 237–59.
4. See also her fascinating later comments on the 1960s and 1970s in Atwood 1990, esp. 18–21, which underline her statement above.
5. I take this information from Ostriker 1984, an interesting article, whose analysis and conclusions, however, I disagree with in a number of cases. More convincing is Ostriker 1982. In the foreword to Eisenstein and Jardine 1980, the "rebirth of the women's movement" (i.e., the second wave) is located in the "late 1960s" (xv).

6. Atwood has also executed, or contributed to, illustrations (drawings, paintings, collages) for the covers of *Double Persephone, The Journals of Susanna Moodie, Two-Headed Poems, Interlunar,* and *Morning in the Burned House.* See in this context her statement "When I was five, I did write a book of poetry. First I did the cover and the title; then I assembled the pages and inserted them in the book, and then I wrote the poems. So you could say that I'm a bookmaker first. And that's a reasonable thing to call a writer, somebody who makes books" (interview with Margaret Kaminski, in Ingersoll 1990, 30).

7. See McCombs commenting on "the cover of *Power Politics* (conceived by Atwood and executed by William Kimber)" in Davidson and Davidson 1981, 47. The basis for this statement is a letter Atwood wrote to McCombs in 1973. For Kimber and the development and importance of the Canadian publisher House of Anansi, which published *Power Politics,* see chapter 3 in Fetherling 1994, 103–63. For Atwood's cover design for *Power Politics,* an untitled watercolor (1970) that was the basis for Kimber's cover design, see Plate 8 in Wilson 1993a.

8. For the history and importance of Tarot, see, e.g., Olsen 1995, here 313.

9. Significantly, Atwood emphasizes in a letter to me that "the Hanged Man is a lucky sign in the tarot." See also the use of this motif at the end of T. S. Eliot's poem "The Waste Land": "I do not find / The Hanged Man" (ll. 54–55). For further links between *Power Politics* and "The Waste Land," see Mallinson 1984, 74–75, notes 54 and 55.

10. In connection with the short-story cycle, Forrest L. Ingram speaks of "the dynamic pattern of recurrent development" (1971, 200).

11. From a publisher's advertisement by Nan A. Talese and Doubleday for Atwood's *The Robber Bride* in the *New York Times Book Review.* See also Aritha van Herk's more complex, highly elaborated, literary composition on *Atwood (noun, verb, adjective, and adverb atypical),* which van Herk wrote for Nischik 2000/02 (310).

12. All quotations from this work are taken from the edition included in the Bibliography. Sullivan's biography of Atwood states that this epigram was written in Edmonton, Alberta, in February 1970, apparently on the back of an information leaflet of the University of Alberta's Department of English, where Atwood was teaching at the time (1998, 247–48).

13. The quotation is taken from Atwood's poem "A Paper Bag," from *Two-Headed Poems* (1978), reprinted in *Eating Fire: Selected Poetry, 1965–1995* (1998, 198–99, here 199).

14. "He Reappears" (2); "She Considers Evading Him," "switch back in time to the woman image left" (4).

15. See George Woodcock: "For the eye sees, and is hurt, and so perception and feeling merge into each other" (1975, 313).

16. The epigram thus also criticizes the assumptions and imagery often encountered in masculinist literature à la Henry Miller, where the sexual act is presented as a power game in which women are humiliated. Passages illustrating this, for instance from Miller's *Sexus* (1945), are much more shocking than Atwood's supposedly "cruel" epigram. The following represents a relatively harmless scene from *Sexus* in which the female character is presented as hanging from the man's "hook," wriggling like a fish: "In a moment I had her in the tub, stockings and all. ... She was just like a bitch in heat, biting me all over, panting, gasping, wriggling like a worm on the hook. As we were drying ourselves she bent over and began nibbling at my prick. ... She kneeled at my feet gobbling it. After a while I made her stand up, bend over; then I let her have it from the rear. She had a small juicy cunt, which fitted me like a glove" (cited in Morgan 1970, 311). Whereas Miller's sexist perspective suggests a "natural harmony" in sexual relations (however cruel), in which the roles are grossly imbalanced, Atwood destroys this supposed harmony by emphasizing the destructive potential of such relations (particularly for women). Further analysis of such sexist passages can be found in Millett 1970.

17. For a more extensive analysis of this poem, see the first section of chapter 5.

18. This interpretation is suggested by Bowering 1981, 43.

19. See also McCombs 1973, 60.

20. This is a possible reference to Tarot.

21. The book was written in the middle of the Cold War (e.g., the Cuban Missile Crisis) at a time when political assassinations were frequent (consider Robert Kennedy and Martin Luther King) as well as during the rise of the ecological movement.

22. See also Dux (1992, 439): "Just as any form of power can only be countered by the reaction of those who feel exposed to it, so can equal rights for women only be achieved by organizing their reaction. No further justification is necessary; the fact that power is being wielded is reason enough to react against it" (my translation; subsequent translations from German into English are always mine unless stated otherwise).

23. Pilar Somacarrera differentiates three conceptions of power in Atwood's works, two of which go back to quotations by Atwood herself: "the capacity of powerful agents to realize their will over the will of powerless people. ... 'the desire for power over the physical universe through experiment and the intellect.' ... '[T]he hardest form of power to acquire ... is power over

oneself'" (2006, 55). For the political potential of poetry in general, see Montefiore 1994, 7.

24. In a similar context, Rachel Blau du Plessis talks of "both/and vision" (Eisenstein and Jardine 1980, 132 passim). Sullivan paraphrases a relevant comment Atwood made in an interview as follows: "Women would be better off thinking of themselves in a context beyond the universe of two, creatively engaging with the world. In the end we must all take responsibility for ourselves since the only destiny we hold in our own hands is our own. And only we hold our own destiny" (1998, 255). See also Atwood's reply to an interviewer's question, "What do you think an ideal relationship between a man and a woman would be?": "A happy one" (in Ingersoll 1990, 142).

25. Dorothy Livesay's love poems of the late 1960s may be said to point toward *Power Politics*. Although not as explicitly as Atwood, Livesay in *The Unquiet Bed* (1967) also tackles the issue of romantic love as a power game or as a struggle for dominance, and Livesay's *Plainsongs* (1969) occasionally anticipates the approach to love that can be found later in Atwood's *Power Politics* (e.g., the lover who hurts and is hurt in turn or the superimposition of intimacy and separateness in love). I am indebted for this contextualizing comparison to Carmen Otilia Teodorescu, who completed her PhD dissertation, "Re-Writing Love: North American Love Poetry of the Twentieth Century," at the University of Constance in 2009 and who investigated thoroughly the love poetry of thirty-five American and Canadian poets, thereby writing an illuminating history of North American love poetry of the twentieth century.

26. Other North American books of poetry that effected drastic changes in love poetry and the reconceptualization of romantic love before *Power Politics* are, for instance, from the United States, Amy Lowell, *What's O'Clock* (1925); Edna St. Vincent Millay, *The Harp-Weaver and Other Poems* (1923); H.D., *Helen in Egypt* (1961); and Adrienne Rich, *The Diamond Cutters* (1955), *Snapshots of a Daughter-in-Law* (1963), *Necessities of Life* (1966), and *Leaflets* (1969); from Canada, Phyllis Webb, *Naked Poems* (1965); and Dorothy Livesay, *The Unquiet Bed* (1967). It can be argued, however, that Atwood's *Power Politics* is the most uncompromising revisionist contribution in this line of love poetry.

27. See also Leslie Fiedler's classic *Love and Death in the American Novel* (1960).

28. See also Mitchell 1984, 316n37.

29. In Hoffmeister 1973, 25; see also Forster 1969, esp. 10, 13, 14.

30. McCombs points out that Plath's and Sexton's poems still reflect the polarizing system of representation, where *he* equals active aggressor,

and *she* equals passive victim; Atwood transcends, to some extent, this limitation in *Power Politics*. For the poetic tradition and its conventional gender representation, see Montefiore's (1994) extensive comments, esp. chapters 1 and 2.

31. For the danger of the "intentional fallacy," which seems to occur especially in reference to texts by female authors, see Montefiore 1994, 5–8. Atwood describes the volume's combination of private and public spheres as "halfway between letter and newspaper" (cited in Grace 1980, 53). Atwood and Polk separated in 1972 and were divorced in 1977. (Since 1976, Atwood has been living with Canadian writer Graeme Gibson.) In a discussion of Margaret Drabble's interview with Atwood for *Chatelaine* ("their generation was the first among women writers to be able to write whatever they wanted"), Sullivan makes clear how strongly the cultural upheavals of the 1960s and 1970s affected personal circumstances: "The women of their generation were breaking down old paradigms at a time when new ones hadn't yet been invented and there were costs ... [such as] a husband who ... 'then felt that something had been sprung on him that he hadn't bargained for—namely the success of the woman'" (1998, 258, 259; the quotation within the quotation is from Atwood).

32. This fitting description comes from Grace 1981, 61.

33. See also McCombs 1973, 54; and Sullivan 1998, 252–55.

34. I also disagree with Barbour and Scobie's opinion, in terms of both *Power Politics* and Atwood's other poetry, that Atwood is a "feminist romantic poet" (1981, 11): Atwood is a gender-aware, (post)modern poet, but it would be wrong to limit her to this aspect of her work, which is heavily cognitive in its orientation. Linda Wagner also calls *Power Politics* a "comic scenario," although she qualifies this statement in the course of her subsequent argumentation (in Davidson and Davidson 1981, 89–91). See also the exchange on this between Atwood and Linda Sandler in an interview (in Ingersoll 1990, 51).

35. Hönnighausen's overall conclusion is that "What seems most original in *Power Politics* is a new breathtaking irony and brutality in the rendition of love, where previous generations of poets had felt obliged to offer slush" (107).

36. See Günter Burkart and Karl Lenz in Hahn and Burkart 1998, 66, 22.

37. In our context, it is not so important that the remarkable cultural success story of romantic love from the nineteenth century onward did not progress beyond the level of discourse until the twentieth century, after which it came to influence the norms of relationships and therefore affected social behaviour in a concrete way (see Lenz 1998, 70).

38. Wilhelm Heinrich Riehl, *Die Naturgeschichte des Volkes als Grundlage einer deutschen Sozialpolitik* (1855), cited in Hahn and Burkart 1998, 72.
39. Thus German sociologist Ulrich Beck, speaking, however, about the 1990s (in Beck and Beck-Gernsheim 1990, chapter 6).
40. Cancian 1987 differentiates between "traditional marriage" (dependence), "independence," and "interdependence" as the three main conceptions of love. She is in favour of the third type, which she calls "love with self-development," linking it to the cooperative conception of love (3, 4, 8–10 passim).
41. See also McCombs: "[The book] reveals, with craft and wisdom, many verdicts but no Verdict" (1973, 54).

2

Murder in the Dark
Atwood's Inverse Poetics of Intertextual Minuteness in Her Short Fictions and Prose Poems

The distortion of a text is not unlike a murder.

SIGMUND FREUD (cited in Irvine 1988, 265)

The lake, vast and dimensionless,
doubles everything, the stars,
the boulders, itself, even the darkness
that you can walk so long in
it becomes light.

MARGARET ATWOOD, "Interlunar," 103

INTRODUCTION

The dichotomy between *small* and *large* is a motif that recurs frequently in the works of Margaret Atwood. This is particularly evident in her various cartoons (see chapter 7), but she also makes repeated use of the small/large dichotomy in her literary texts, inverting norms to significant effect. In *The Robber Bride* (1993), for instance, the importance of physical size is reduced, thus implicitly increasing the value of smallness: "Tall people's heads are too far from the ground, their center of gravity is too high. One shock and they topple" (39). In "Weight," from Atwood's short-story collection *Wilderness Tips* (1991), the reader is told that "Molly was pushy. Or you could call it determined. She had to be, she was so short. ... She'd made it on brains"

(182). Here non-physical qualities can be seen to compensate, or more than compensate, for a small physique. A similar point is made in the following fictional interview from *Cat's Eye* (1988), which surely touches on Atwood's diverse experiences in the media circus of literature:[1]

> "I thought you would be different," says Andrea as we settle.
> "Different how?" I ask.
> "Bigger," she says.
> I smile at her. "I am bigger." (92)

This quotation indeed suggests that Atwood's preoccupation with the small/large dichotomy may also have an autobiographical basis.[2] Yet her own small stature is only a superficial explanation for the strategy of inversion present in her works. Rather, it is part of a general tendency in Atwood's oeuvre to expose conventions (e.g., "bigger is better" or "significant is big")—that is, the social, psychological, linguistic, and mythical structures that underpin everyday perceptions and judgments—and to question their values and functions.[3]

Since the 1980s, Atwood has employed new textual formats for her challenging explorations and rewritings, short texts that are hard to classify and have few genuine forerunners in Canadian literature. Texts in these hybrid genres appeared in the collections *Murder in the Dark: Short Fictions and Prose Poems*, *Good Bones*, and *The Tent* (published in 1983, 1992, and 2006 respectively[4]), featuring pieces that operate within the generic parameters of the short story, yet it would be inaccurate to describe them simply as short short-story (or prose poetry) collections. Among the various "genres" they contain are mini essays, "essay-fictions," short dialogues, dramatic monologues, and reflections, to name but a few. Atwood's commentators have yet to discover an appropriate collective critical term, if there is one, for these highly diverse short texts (one critic simply called them "gems"). Arguably because of the category-defying originality of their forms and modes of representation—combined with a possible confusion of smallness/ shortness with minor significance (see William French's summing up in his 1983 review of *Murder in the Dark*: "not quite a major work but hardly minor as its length might indicate")—these pieces were neglected by critics for a long time.[5]

It has now been recognized, however, that, especially with *Murder in the Dark* and *Good Bones*, Atwood imported a largely unfamiliar genre into English Canadian literature: the Baudelairean prose poem.[6] In addition, the short texts in these two collections constitute a radical, "postmodern" contribution to the development of generic hybridization.[7] A closer evaluation of many of the texts reveals Atwood's literary art at work in the smallest of spaces. In an intertextual manner,[8] they create networks of meaning and significance despite their limited scope, frequently going hand in hand with what I would like to call Atwood's poetics of inversion: her technique of undermining conventional thought patterns, attitudes, values, or textual norms by turning them on their heads. The result is a multifaceted interplay between explicit and implicit meaning or, to put it another way, a prismatic multiplication of sense. Since this technique is used in a very restricted space, it almost inevitably results in strongly delineated, suggestive, and highly intensified representations, thus providing a possible explanation for the satirical and parodic tendencies discernible in many of the texts.[9]

Figure 2.

One of Atwood's drawings (see figure 2), included in the American edition of *Good Bones and Simple Murders* (a compilation of selected texts from *Murder in the Dark* and *Good Bones*),[10] perfectly illustrates this type of inverse portrayal. This drawing appears within the text of the prose poem "Good Bones."[11]

One may interpret this drawing in many ways depending on perspective and focus of perception. One might, for instance, see an undulating, moonlit[12] lake or river landscape at twilight. On the other hand, there appear to be two sets of two female profiles looking at one another, different from each other (light/dark) yet still very similar. Or, looking at it the other way around, two female profiles emerge but turn away from each other while still constituting two complementary halves of the same figure. One might also discern a side view of two dissimilar women (one larger, one smaller), who are nevertheless harmoniously looking in the same direction, or silhouettes of female physical forms (to put it plainly, stylized female genitals and breasts). Finally, one can even find a stylized bone in this image—a "good bone" indeed!

MURDER IN THE DARK

Atwood's inverse poetics of intertextual minuteness can be seen at work particularly clearly and pithily in a number of texts in *Good Bones*, yet it nevertheless constitutes an underlying principle in the conception of the earlier collection *Murder in the Dark*, too. *Murder in the Dark* opens with a series of eight vignettes (grouped together as Part I), which are linked by their presentation of epiphanic events from the childhood of the lyrical I. The first text, "Autobiography" (9), introduces not only this context but also Atwood's technique of inversion. As Christl Verduyn rightly says of this text, which is no more than half a page long, "As in subsequent texts, the form of 'Autobiography' is in itself unsettling; this must be the world's shortest, not to say oddest, autobiography!" (1986, 125).

Atwood's uses of the first-person singular and the past tense are redolent of the genre of autobiography. What is being evoked, however, is a fragmentary, epiphanic situation that undermines the sequence of events encountered in traditional autobiographies: a mental painting—

the almost static description of a landscape as seen and felt—is used to demonstrate the power of artistic perception and representation to alter and, indeed, *create* reality. This highly condensed "Autobiography" refers to no human beings other than the "I" (and to the products of human civilization: "dam, covered bridge, houses, white church, sawed-off trunks of huge trees," etc.). Important here is the "I's" perception of the almost lifeless landscape as well as the reconstruction and mental working-over of this perception on another, artistic level of reality: "Once, on the rock island, there was the half-eaten carcass of a deer, which smelled like iron, like rust rubbed into your hands so that it mixes with sweat. This smell is the point at which the landscape dissolves, ceases to be a landscape and becomes something else." The change of perspective sweeps aside the inherently static nature of landscape description, just as on a linguistic level Atwood's mental painting is lent an added dynamism by the use of verbs of motion. The latter convey the process of perceiving and the transforming power of artistic perception and representation: "the lake disappeared into the sky," "trunks of huge trees coming up through the water," "a path running back into the forest," "the landscape dissolves ... and becomes something else." The traditionally diachronic sequence of events in autobiographies is thus replaced by a synchronically situated metamorphosis, developed within the artistic conscience through its powers of transformation (see the two similes introduced by "like"). Significantly it is precisely this ability to transform (the perception of) reality that marks the basic hinge for many artists' (auto)biographies (compare the concept of the "third eye" in the final text of this collection, "Instructions for the Third Eye," in many ways an extension of "Autobiography"). Atwood's provocatively titled "Autobiography" takes as its theme the individual point of view ("there was a white sand cliff, although you couldn't see it from where I was standing," "the entrance to another path which cannot be seen from where I was standing but was there anyway") and implies that even autobiographical texts are quasi-fictional constructs—though this does not make them less important or "true." This skeletal, highly condensed inversion of the genre of autobiography at the beginning of *Murder in the Dark* is a metapoetical commentary not only on the genre but also on the collection of "Short Fictions and Prose Poems" that it introduces.

Any author writing in the genre of the prose poem is heavily indebted to the work of Charles Baudelaire, all the more so in the case of an English Canadian writer working in a literary tradition to which the genre is unfamiliar (see Merivale 1996).[13] Concrete proof of Atwood's reception of Baudelaire's poems and prose poems can be found in the highly ironic ending of "Let Us Now Praise Stupid Women"[14] in *Good Bones*: "*Hypocrite lecteuse! Ma semblable! Ma soeur!* / Let us now praise stupid women, / who have given us Literature" (37). The French quotation modifies Baudelaire's famous closing gambit in "Au lecteur," the introductory poem to *Les fleurs du mal* (1963, 8) ("—Hypocrite lecteur,—mon semblable,—mon frère!"), and, not without a certain linguistic irreverence ("lecteuse" instead of the correct form "lectrice"), places the emphasis firmly on the female sex. This reversal ironically highlights a tradition of misogynist representations of women (see Clack 1999, 1–9), a tradition in which Baudelaire plays a central role. Atwood's revisionist attitude to this tradition, her exposing and rewriting of such misogynist portrayals, has been pointed out by Merivale in relation to *Murder in the Dark*:

> Atwood's prose poems of the sex wars invert or subvert the misogyny, bordering on highbrow pornography, of Baudelaire's prose poems, while maintaining, but recontextualizing, in her lyrical transvestitism, the irony of the Baudelairean ... voice. In that whole misogynist repertory, whose most powerfully intelligent exponent is Charles Baudelaire, woman, reified and dangerously idealized, is seen as perfect only insofar as she reflects the man to himself. ... These are neat inversions of the misogynist patterns in Baudelaire's poems of Woman reified by the Poet; in Atwood the Poet watches the man reify her. (1996, 105, 102)

I would like to develop Merivale's excellent analysis in two ways. First, with reference to two texts from *Murder in the Dark*, I will examine more closely Atwood's revisionist approach to gender, particularly her reaction to the portrayal of gender in intertexts by Baudelaire. Second, looking at four texts from *Good Bones* that are also devoted to the representation of gender, I will differentiate between Atwood's subversions and inversions, with *subversion* here taken to be the more inclusive concept.[15]

Merivale's observation that the poet watches man reifying woman holds particularly true for Atwood's prose poems "Worship" and "Iconography," from Part IV of *Murder in the Dark*. Such texts can be seen as radically critical rewritings of Baudelaire's texts, for instance his poems "Le serpent qui danse" and "Le chat," both from *Les fleurs du mal*, or his prose poems "Un hémisphère dans une chevelure" and "Un cheval de race" from *Le spleen de Paris*. In Baudelaire's texts, woman, as perceived by the lyrical I, is reduced to her physical existence and is reified by ostensibly flattering comparisons to animals and objects:

> A te voir marcher en cadence,
> Belle d'abandon,
> On dirait un serpent qui danse
> Au bout d'un bâton. ("Le serpent qui danse," 50)
> [When you walk in rhythm, lovely
> With abandonment,
> You seem to be swayed by a wand,
> A dancing serpent.] ("The Dancing Serpent," 37)

> Usée peut-être, mais non fatiguée, et toujours héroïque, elle fait penser à ces chevaux de grande race que l'oeil du véritable amateur reconnaît, même attelés à un carrosse de louage ou à un lourd chariot. ("Un cheval de race," 370)
> [Deteriorated perhaps, but not wearied, and still heroic, she reminds you of those horses of pure breed recognized by a true connoisseur's eye, even when hitched to a hired coach or a heavy wagon.] ("A Thoroughbred," 99)

In "Worship" (51), Atwood subtly highlights and lays bare, through a strongly ambivalent use of language, the sexuality hinted at in texts by Baudelaire such as "Le serpent qui danse." She furthermore subjects Baudelaire's attitude to sexual gender roles to a radical critique from a female point of view. Indeed, the beginning of "Worship" ("You have these sores in your mouth that will not heal. It's from eating too much sugar, you tell yourself") seems to act as a retort to the following lines from "Le serpent qui danse":

Comme un flot grossi par la fonte
Des glaciers grondants,
Quand l'eau de ta bouche remonte
Au bord de tes dents (50, 52)
[When, like a stream by thawing of
Glaciers made replete,
The water of your mouth rises
Up to your teeth] (37)

"Worship" is based on two fundamental themes—religious veneration and physical unification—that are related to each other within the text and mingle in a stretto-like combination. Thus, the admiring, not to say worshipping, attitude of the man toward the woman is compared to religious adoration, and its deficiencies and compensatory function are subjected to a complex and pointed analysis: "Thanksgiving. That's why he brings you roses, on occasion, and chocolates when he can't think of anything else. ... Prayer is wanting. ... You aren't really a god but despite that you are silent. When you're being worshipped there isn't much to say." The worshipping attitude is ruthlessly exposed, by means of vaginal (uteral?) imagery, as man's self-reflection, even selfishness, while reifying woman: "Jesus, Jesus, he says, but he's not praying to Jesus, he's praying to you, not to your body or your face but to that space you hold at the centre, which is the shape of the universe. Empty. He wants response, an answer from that dark sphere and its red stars, which he can touch but not see."[16]

Reified woman, sexuality, and religious veneration are inextricably intertwined at the close of "Worship," where words such as "use/d" and "service/d" take on a kaleidoscopic range of meanings, and a phrase such as "like a chalice, burnished," evokes a manifold sense, with woman an instrument in the ceremony of sexual love (see, e.g., "to burnish": "to polish by friction with something hard and smooth"): "that's you up there, shining, burning, like a candle, like a chalice, burnished; with use and service. After you've been serviced, after you've been used, you'll be put away again until needed." The term "service," correlating with the religious conceit of the text in its possible reference to religious service, may have yet another, even more radical, meaning here. "Service" also refers to the insemination of animals; this would imply that human sexual love, in spite of its pretensions, may be based on a primitive need to dominate and control. The couching of this idea in religious ritual and imagery renders the representation of woman as an object of sexual love, rather than an active participant in it, all the more shocking. The suppressed implications of Baudelaire's gender portrayals are thus brought to the fore by Atwood in a subtle act of deliberate subversion. Whereas the text by Baudelaire is written exclusively from a male perspective, denying female subjectivity and agency, she also takes account of and assesses the female role in gender relations; her use of the second person ("you") illustrates a universalizing, perhaps even didactic, tendency.

This rearrangement of perspectives both within Atwood's prose poems and in the intertextual dialogue with texts by Baudelaire, which nevertheless leaves room for the male point of view as an ironic accompaniment, becomes a full-fledged inverse portrayal in Atwood's "Liking Men" from *Murder in the Dark* (53–54; see also "Simmering" in the same collection). In the case of "Liking Men," Merivale's observation that "in Atwood the Poet watches the man reifying her [woman]" is no longer valid. Here a reversal of roles takes place, with woman portrayed as reifying man, and an undercurrent of irony is present from the outset: "It's time to like men again. Where shall we begin?" (53). With Baudelairean symmetry,[17] the text is divided evenly into two halves by the crucial phrase "You don't want to go on but you can't stop yourself" (53). After various parts of the male body have been rejected as too problematic, the seemingly harmless feet are ironically reified and singled out, pars pro toto, as objects for "liking men." But a positive approach ("You think of kissing those feet, ... you like to give pleasure" [53]) proves almost impossible to maintain: the associations called up by footwear, benign at first ("Rubber boots, for wading out to the barn in the rain in order to save the baby calf. ... Knowing what to do, doing it well. Sexy" [53]), lead inexorably—from "dance shoes," "golf shoes," and "rubber boots," via "riding boots," "cowboy boots," and "jackboots"—to scenes of war and rape in which man is the aggressor. Going beyond Baudelaire, the "I" in "Liking Men" still attempts to differentiate between man as a category, which includes warmongers and rapists, and men as individuals: "Just because all rapists are men it doesn't follow that all men are rapists, ... you try desperately to retain the image of the man you love and also like" (54). This attempt takes the "I" back to the birth of the man and from there back to the social conditions that have influenced his upbringing and life story: "Maybe that's what you have to go back to, in order to trace him here, the journey he took, step by step" (54).

"Liking Men," then, points both intra- and intertextually to the constructedness and thereby mutability of gender roles and images. Atwood's technique of inversion—as we have already seen in the apparently reflected double moonscape in her drawing—goes beyond mere mirroring and, in its intertextual double-coding, reaches beyond Baudelaire's self-reflective portrayal of women; as Margery Evans says of Baudelaire, "in *Le Spleen de Paris* ... the descriptions of women are, quite self-consciously, a series of fictions which may help to give the poet a sense of his own existence ('à sentir que je suis et ce que je suis') but which in no way purport to be an objective rendering of a common, shared reality" (1993, 56–57). In contrast, Atwood's inverse portrayal of women and gender relations has a fundamentally political aim, as can be seen even more clearly in her later collection *Good Bones* (see, e.g., "Making a Man," with its humorous attack on the reification of women as commodities of popular culture). In fact, Atwood's acute awareness of gender differences may be seen as an integral part of her humanitarianism, her being a champion for human rights in both her literary and her non-literary public roles (as, e.g., a member of Amnesty International).

GOOD BONES

In introducing the genre of the prose poem to the English Canadian literary scene, Atwood enters into an intertextual dialogue with Baudelaire in a number of ways: in her choice of genre, of theme (notably the representation of gender), and of specific intertextual references. In this last respect, "A Beggar" from Part II ("Raw Materials") of *Murder in the Dark* can be interpreted as a rewriting of Baudelaire's "Assomons les pauvres" from *Le spleen de Paris*, and "Bad News," the opening text of *Good Bones*, recalls Baudelaire's "Au lecteur" from *Les fleurs du mal* (see also the aforementioned direct reference to

Baudelaire in "Let Us Now Praise Stupid Women" from *Good Bones*).
It is nevertheless Baudelaire's self-reflective, discriminatory gender
representations (see, e.g., "L'homme et la mer," "Le chat," "Le serpent
qui danse," or "Un cheval de race") that act as the greatest spurs to
Atwood and that, as she progresses from *Murder in the Dark* to *Good
Bones*, lead her to increasingly bold counter-representations (see, e.g.,
"Men at Sea" from *Good Bones* as a rewriting of "L'homme et la mer").
The development of Atwood's more and more radical technique of
inversion—based also on her frequent injection of playful and comic,
facetious elements—becomes clear in a comparison of, for example,
"Worship" and "Liking Men" (from *Murder in the Dark*) with "Making
a Man" (from *Good Bones*) or "Iconography" (*Murder in the Dark*) with
"Gertrude Talks Back" (*Good Bones*).

Atwood's prose poem "Men at Sea"[18] is an intertextual inversion
of Baudelaire's poem "L'homme et la mer" from *Les fleurs du mal*
(1963, 21–22). In Baudelaire's text, the relationship between man(kind)
and the sea is raised to a mythological level, with the sea portrayed as
a mirror of the soul and the subconscious, "its eternal billows surging
without end" (21). Just as the wild depths of the sea remain unfath-
omable, so too the soul of self-obsessed man is darkly brooding: "You
plunge with joy into this image of your own ... , no one has mapped
your chasm's hidden floor" (22). In Baudelaire's poem, the immeasur-
ability of the "inner sanctum" is metaphorically intentionalized: "no
one knows your inmost riches, for / Your jealousy hides secrets none can
repeat" (21). The poem also suggests a typically Baudelairean treatment
of gender relations, provoked by the double meaning in French of
l'homme (meaning both "man" and "mankind") and by the homonyms
la mer/"sea" and *la mère*/"mother." The female, then, is presented as a
passive and expressionless, yet mysteriously fascinating, object in which
man is reflected and onto which he projects his desires. In the closing
part of the poem, the meaning of *l'homme* is indeed narrowed down to
the sense of "man" ("oh, relentless brothers!" [22]), and the relationship
between man and the sea becomes, in a stylized way, the ultimate
expression of danger and adventure: "You two have fought without pity
or remorse, both / From sheer love of the slaughter and of death" (22).

In the prose poem "Men at Sea," Atwood deconstructs the self-centred
heroic machismo of the Baudelairean intertext, and her revision ruthlessly

exposes the gender stereotyping that is merely hinted at in the pretext. Her inverse poetics and (gender) politics are crystallized in the minimalist yet radical modification of the poem's title, "Men at Sea," in its closing line. Through the cleverly simple addition of a comma—"Men, at sea"— the title takes on completely new connotations: heroic, virile seafarers are reduced to a state of insecurity and helplessness. This insecurity is a result of the female perspective from which "Men at Sea" is written and that promotes woman (who is completely neutralized in "L'homme et la mer") to the same level as Baudelaire's (brooding, self-centred, introverted) male heroes. In doing so, Atwood employs clichés just as Baudelaire does—yet intentionally and ironically.

Atwood's text, then, begins with a subject that Baudelaire ignored: the line "You can come to the end of talking, about women, talking" suggests, ambivalently, that women talk about all sorts of things with varying degrees of definiteness but especially "about what they feel" (71). Male profundity, in contrast, is initially supplanted in Atwood's text by an energetic male desire for action for its own sake. Nevertheless, neither man's need for emotional compensation ("to drain the inner swamp") nor the unpredictability of gender relations ("and above all no women. Women are replaced by water, by wind, by the ocean, shifting and treacherous; a man has to know what to do") is lost from sight. In this hyperbolically caricatured world of adventure, where men assert themselves through their physicality ("a narrowing of the eyes, sizing the bastard up before the pounce, the knife to the gut ... , all teeth grit, all muscles bulge together"), there is no place for women, not even in their supposedly favourite pastime—talking: "out here it's what he said to him, or didn't say" (72).

The ending, with its more realistic restaurant setting, alludes to the start of the text. The one-sidedness of the male narration, its concentration on action and rejection of emotion, is countered by: "She says: But what did you feel?" The reaction to the question at first mirrors Baudelaire ("Your jealousy hides secrets none can repeat" [22] versus "never give yourself away" [73]). Atwood's inverse intertextual counter-representation, however, not only highlights the weaknesses of the myth of virility, with its suppression of emotion, but also shows it to be completely false: "They're all around her ... , one per woman per table. Men, at sea" (73).

The principle of counter-representation via inverse intertextuality, with an emphasis on gender themes, can also be seen at work in "Gertrude Talks Back" in *Good Bones* (15–18), in which Atwood applies this technique irreverently and hilariously to one of the greatest works of world literature, Shakespeare's *Hamlet*. More than any other of Shakespeare's plays, this drama concentrates on the figure of its protagonist: Hamlet *fils* is present in thirteen of the twenty scenes and speaks more than half the text, in dialogues as well as in numerous monologues and asides. The figure of Hamlet provides the perspective through which we view the action as well as the focus of our sympathies. This takes place at the expense of the drama's female characters: Ophelia, Hamlet's platonic lover, and even more so Gertrude, his mother. Critics agree that Gertrude's direct involvement in the play, in terms of spoken lines and presence on stage, is not representative of her importance in the context of the play as a whole. Gertrude rarely speaks, and when she does she says little, even in the famous "closet scene" with Hamlet (III.4.). She hardly acts, but rather reacts (even the "closet scene" was arranged by Polonius and Claudius, not her), and frames her speech usually in the form of questions and requests or to support another character (particularly Claudius, her second husband, or Hamlet). Her speeches are usually confined to a single line, her longest speech encompassing only nine lines.

In the revisionist short dramatic monologue "Gertrude Talks Back," Atwood rewrites Shakespeare's plot, making Gertrude the title figure and giving her freedom of speech—to such an extent that she now embarks on a monologue, subjecting her supposed dialogue partner Hamlet to passive silence (we can only infer his reactions from what Gertrude says in her monologue). Apart from this drastic reversal of allocated speech, Atwood also takes up various other aspects of the Shakespearean pretext and parodically inverts them in the smallest of spaces. Whereas Gertrude in the original text is submissive, addressing her royal husband (appropriately for the period) as "my lord," in Atwood's revised version she speaks with considerable self-confidence about her two husbands, Hamlet *père* and Claudius. She brands the fact that Hamlet should have been named after his father as selfish ("It was your father's idea"; "I wanted to call you George" [15]). Hamlet's long, resentful lecturing of Gertrude in the original, in which Hamlet compares Claudius unfavourably to his father,[19] is countered by Gertrude's version of the story and the two men. In doing so, Atwood revises the representation of Gertrude, and that of Ophelia, as passive sexual adjuncts to the male figures—representations that complied with the sexual morality of the time. In the original, Ophelia is expected to preserve her chastity until marriage, as, for instance, her brother Laertes admonishes her to do; Gertrude is classified by her son as an older woman who has no right to express her sexuality:

> Then weigh what loss your honour may sustain
> If with too credent ear you list his [Hamlet's] songs,
> Or lose your heart, or your chaste treasure open
> To his unmastered importunity.
> Fear it, Ophelia, fear it, my dear sister,
> And keep you in the rear of your affection,
> Out of the shot and danger of desire.
> (Laertes to Ophelia, I.3.29–35)

> You cannot call it love, for at your age
> The heyday in the blood is tame, it's humble,
> And waits upon the judgement ...
> Rebellious hell,
> If thou canst mutine in a matron's bones,
> To flaming youth let virtue be as wax
> And melt in her own fire
> (Hamlet to Gertrude, III.4.67–69, 81–84)

Hamlet's use of sexual innuendo when speaking to Ophelia—which Hamlet uses simultaneously to attract and reject her (thus pushing her further toward madness and suicide)—similarly demonstrates male control and definition of female gender roles in the original intertext.

Atwood's modernized Gertrude strongly rejects such gender inconsistencies, openly acknowledging that Hamlet *père* was a failure in bed who could not fulfill her sexual desires. She rejects the restriction of female sexuality to youthful women—in fact, the older Gertrude seems much more sexually at ease than her son: "I must say you're an awful prig sometimes. Just like your Dad. *The Flesh*, he'd say. You'd think it was dog dirt. You can excuse that in a young person, they are always so intolerant, but in someone his age it was getting, well, very hard to live with, and that's the understatement of the year" (17). The manner in which Atwood's Gertrude dismisses Hamlet *père* on account of such sexual deficiencies, while upgrading the "energetic" Claudius for equally sexual reasons, not only serves as justification for her remarriage (an act that is not so clearly motivated in Shakespeare's *Hamlet*) but also makes a case for female sexuality, which had been reduced to passivity, and places it in the centre of the action. Atwood gives this inversion a final twist when Gertrude at the end of the text openly acknowledges, in the ultimate daring inversion, "It [the murder of Hamlet *père*] wasn't Claudius, darling. It was me" (18).[20] Atwood's Gertrude openly proclaims her guilt, whereas Shakespeare's character relies on strategies of displacement, repressing her emotions. Atwood's Gertrude contradicts, defends, and justifies herself, whereas the original Gertrude, even when under fire from Hamlet's patriarchally declaimed accusations in the "closet scene," remains silent. Atwood's Gertrude has a zest for living and robust self-confidence. She is concerned mainly (but not only, if we consider her remarks about the difficulties caused for Hamlet by his name) with her own needs, and she accepts responsibility for her own actions. Yet Atwood's character, whose conception has many similarities to the female protagonists in her novels *The Robber Bride* (1993) and *Alias Grace* (1996), is not the "better" Gertrude. She is, rather, the freer, more self-determined Gertrude, whose self-image no longer depends on how she sees herself mirrored by men[21] ("Darling, please stop fidgeting with my mirror. That'll be the third one you've broken" [15]).[22] To that extent, her "talking back" almost four hundred years after the original text is an appropriate and necessary riposte to Hamlet's "frailty, thy name is woman!" (I.2.146).[23]

Atwood's gender-oriented intertextual dialogue covers a wide range, from an engagement with world literature (in the form of Baudelairean and Shakespearean intertexts) to her equally telling encounter with popular literature. Whereas "Men at Sea" is mainly concerned with the (self-)conception and representation of men, "The Little Red Hen Tells All" in *Good Bones* (11–14), just like "Gertrude Talks Back," is an outstanding example of Atwood's gender revisionism regarding the representation of women. It again demonstrates her ability to juxtapose an original and a revisionist version in the smallest of spaces, creating a new complexity that opens up significant new meanings. In the case of "The Little Red Hen," we again have before us an "official," conventional story and an "unofficial" version. Here the differences between the two versions are openly explored and, so to speak, made public. The parable-like tale is also an example of Atwood's recurring revisionist use of received stories from popular culture, that is, folkloric texts such as fairy tales and myths. Atwood rewrites these stories, especially the gender portrayals perpetuated by such influential tales. The outcome is a typically Atwoodian mixture of themes and motifs from popular literature, imaginatively juxtaposed with their intellectual significance in an often humorous way. The resulting combination of approachable textual structures, witty impact, and impressive intellectual strength is an important reason for Atwood's appeal to a broad readership.

"The Little Red Hen Tells All" is based on a widely known children's tale in the English-speaking world. Atwood reproduces the basic structures of this fable but adds imaginative amplifications and ambivalent wordplay (e.g., "A grain of wheat saved is a grain of wheat earned" [12]) as well as precisely integrated comments on the plot, which expose with apparent casualness the popular tale's intellectual implications—for instance, the capitalist ideology supporting pro-duction and maximization of profits: "Sobriety and elbow-grease. Do it yourself. Then invest your capital. Then collect" (11).

Atwood's most important reinterpretation in this story, however, concerns gender difference. By highlighting the gender of the female "narrator," Atwood brings to light the ideological impact of the tale, in both its original and its new versions. The gender roles in the original folk tale (which is often passed on orally from mothers to their children) are, on closer inspection, somewhat strangely conceived. The egocentric, hoarding, greedy behaviour of the female "narrator," the hen ("*I'll eat it myself, so kiss off*" [13]), does not comply with the typical female image of nourishment and generosity; it rather resembles the typical behaviour of a "rooster." Atwood further parodies the original story by reconciling this selfish demeanour with traditionally associated "feminine" qualities. The conflict is thus transferred from the external to the internal: because of her gender-specific socialization, the hard-working hen acts contrary to her own interests and needs in a way that is very much in favour of the common good but verges on self-denial. The capitalist ideology of the folk tale is modified in Atwood's retelling through a foregrounding of gender difference. Atwood makes clear the pitfalls of gender differentiation, to which "hens"/women fall victim far more often than "roosters"/men. The story also makes clear that women's self-image, propagated by gender-specific socialization and social context, is one of the main causes of this phenomenon. All in all, next to its biting critique of gender roles, "The Little Red Hen" is also a humorous story, even "horrible fun."[24]

In "Making a Man" in *Good Bones* (53–58), Atwood turns from folk stories to popular journalism and, with palpable delectation, inverts the commodification of women so often encountered in this popular genre. Mimicking the style of women's magazines, she gives the reader tips on how to "make a man." The text takes the form of a recipe, which presents various creative possibilities for baking, sewing, or even inflating figures of men, smugly parodying the stylistic conventions of cook and other how-to books. "Making a Man" opens as follows:

> This month we'll take a break from the crocheted string bikinis and Leftovers Réchauffées to give our readers some tips on how to create, in their very own kitchens and rumpus rooms, an item that is both practical and decorative. It's nice to have one of these around the house, either out on the lawn looking busy, or propped in a chair, prone or erect. Choose the coverings to match the drapes!
>
> When worn out, they can be re-covered and used as doorstops.
> (53)

Different ways of man-making are then presented, for instance the "Traditional Method," which parodies the biblical creation myth: "Take some dust of the ground. Form. Breathe into the nostrils the breath of life. Simple, but effective! (Please note that although men are made of dust, women are made of ribs. Remember that at your next Texas-style barbecue!)" (53–54). Another suggested method of production is the "Clothes Method," an episode laced with linguistic play and a critique of traditional gender roles: "Clothes make the man! How often have you heard it said! Well, we couldn't agree more! However, clothes may make the man, but women—by and large—make the clothes, so it follows that the responsibility for the finished model lies with the home seamstress" (55). The "Marzipan Method" of making a man refers directly to the small/large dichotomy ("We've often thought men would be easier to control if they were smaller. Well, here's a tiny rascal you can hold in the palm of your hand!" [56]), and the "Folk Art Method" continues this reductive reification of man: "You've seen these cuties in other folks' front yards, with little windmills attached to their heads. They hammer with their little hammers, saw with their little saws, or just whirl their arms around a lot when there's a stiff breeze" (57). Such Atwoodian representations of man—stylized like the portrayals in her comics (see chapter 7)—take the anti-essentialist constructedness of gender images at face value and show her playfully intertextual poetics of inversion at work in the smallest of spaces.

CONCLUSION

With her contributions to the genre of the prose poem and other forms of short prose, Atwood documents the fact that, as Umberto Eco puts it in his afterword to *The Name of the Rose*, "the post modern discourse ... demands, in order to be understood, not the negation of the already said, but its ironic rethinking. ... The past, since it cannot be destroyed, ... must be revisited; but with irony" (cited in Spriet 1989, 29). Or, as Linda Hutcheon has summarized the postmodern condition,

> What we currently call postmodernism has entailed a re-valuing of difference in culture: difference in terms of gender, race, ethnicity, class, sexual preference. The "excentric" or off-centre is valued over the centre. The postmodern distrust of centres and the hierarchies they imply can be seen in many ways. ... Part of this is simply an inversion of pre-existing hierarchies, since all binaries indeed conceal hierarchies, as Jacques Derrida has taught us. Poststructuralist thought like his has also suggested that all meaning is created by differences and is sustained by reference to other meaning. ... The postmodern ... tries to rethink binary

oppositions completely in terms of the multiple, the plural, and the heterogeneous: "and/also" thinking replaces "either/or." (1991, 51–52)

Atwood's subversive "textual assassinations" (see the book title of Wilson 2003b), her "murders in the dark" (see the epigraph to this chapter), seek to question the basis, justification, and consequences of traditional judgments and prejudices, particularly concerning issues of gender. They call into question the singular, one-sided point of view— without, however, seeking to negate it. Atwood's subversive poetics of inversion defamiliarize, irritate, disturb, and amuse, opening up explanatory chasms as soon as they close them. The author as murderer of conventional "daylight" stories—to take up the playful symbolism of the title story "Murder in the Dark"—teaches us the meaning of fear in order to point out new and often uncomfortable views (see the end of "Iconography" in *Murder in the Dark*: "Watch yourself. That's what the mirrors are for, this story is a mirror story which rhymes with horror story, almost but not quite. We fall back into these rhythms as if into safe hands" [52]). In Atwood's prose poems, this is rendered in a language closer to poetry than to prose. As Margaret Atwood herself puts it in an interview on the differences between prose, prose poetry, and poetry, "The difference between a prose poem and a short story for me is that the prose poem is still concerned with that rhythmical syllabic structure. You're as meticulous about the syllables in a prose poem as you are in a poem" (in Hammond 1979, 79).

NOTES

1. For further details, see Becker 2000/02.
2. Pertinent references can also be found repeatedly in Atwood's non-fictional texts; for instance, from *Survival* (1972), "where there is a David in Canadian literature there is usually a Goliath, ... the evil giant (or giantess)" (58), or in numerous interviews (e.g., in Ingersoll 1990).
3. For details, see Lakoff and Johnson 1980, e.g., 22 and 50.
4. The idea, hinted at by some Atwood critics, that such a prose-lyric hybrid could eventually replace her purely poetical work has been disproved by

the more recent publication of her collections of poems *Morning in the Burned House* (1995) and *The Door* (2007).

5. As late as 1996, Patricia Merivale could still refer to *Murder in the Dark* as "Atwood's most critically neglected text" yet "one of her most difficult, challenging, and rewarding" texts (99). More than two decades after the first publication of the earlier collection, relevant literary studies of *Murder in the Dark* and *Good Bones* are still comparatively rare: see Verduyn 1986; Irvine 1988; Spriet 1989; Merivale 1995, 1996; Delville 1997; and Wilson 2003a.

6. See Merivale (1995, 268): "Subversion of prose genres through compact parody and canny intertextuality ... has been a recipe for one branch of the oxymoronic genre of the prose poem since the time of Baudelaire. ... It is this kind of prose poem that interests Atwood, rather than the lyrically surreal and melodious prose poems of the 1890s ... , or the more abstractly meditative and philosophical kind represented by, say, John Ashbury ... , or those found in the works of many Canadian poets influenced more by the 'redskins' (Pound-Williams-Olson-Black Mountain) than by the 'palefaces' (Baudelaire and Eliot ...). Atwood has, for the moment, the Baudelairean mode almost to herself in Canadian poetry, as she quite brilliantly demonstrates in *Murder in the Dark*. *Good Bones* consolidates her generic monopoly in such prose poems, while extending her range."

7. For generic hybridization in general, and specifically in Atwood's novels, see Howells 2000/02.

8. Referring to Baudelaire's prose poetry in particular, critics have pointed out the highly intertextual nature of the prose poem. See Merivale 1996, esp. 100: "a multiplicity of generic allusions, to different kinds of prose narratives, seems characteristic of the prose poem."

9. For a general overview of parody in Atwood's works, see chapter 5 in Kuester 1992.

10. This book was published by Doubleday, the publishing house of Atwood's American publisher Nan A. Talese, in 1994; the only text in this book not included in the earlier collections is the murder mystery parody "Simple Murders."

11. On "Good Bones," see Merivale 1995, 266–69.

12. The portrayal of the moon (here as crescent) suggests a wealth of additional allusions (see Daemmrich and Daemmrich 1987; and Frenzel 1992, under the heading "moon"/"Mond"): the moon is a symbol of the divine and a source of inspiration; the moon is a ruler over the element water, controlling the tides and being the source of life; its reflection in the water at night doubles its brightness; the Moon God was regarded as being

female or androgynous; the moon is connected to fertility, creation, and imagination and to emotions or passions, especially love. Concerning the crescent moon, a conventional representation is a female figure on the crescent as a source of life; the crescent moon is traditionally associated with good weather or luck; Archibald MacLeish puts it poetologically: "A poem ought to be like a crescent moon" (cited in Frenzel 1992, 539).

13. Although Aloysius Bertrand's *Gaspard de la nuit* (1842) is generally considered to be the first sequence of prose poems, its influence was minor compared with that of Baudelaire's *Le spleen de Paris: Petits poèmes en prose* (1862) (see Evans 1993), which became the template for the genre as a whole.

14. The title probably also alludes to James Agee and Walker Evans's *Let Us Now Praise Famous Men* (1941), the classical example of American documentary fiction and photography in the 1930s.

15. Although *The Tent*, which I do not discuss here, is similar to *Good Bones* with respect to genre and generic hybridity, gender in this later work is not a particularly foregrounded issue in this collection of short fictions and "musings," which deals with issues such as the tortuous creative process or mortality.

16. See Baudelaire: "Un ciel liquide qui parsème / D'étoiles mon coeur!" ("Le serpent qui danse," 52) ["A liquid sky that sows its stars / Within my heart!"] ("The Dancing Serpent," 37).

17. See Evans 1993; and Merivale 1996, 102.

18. From *Good Bones* (71–73), previously published in "New Poems" in *Selected Poems 2: Poems Selected and New 1976–1986* (1986).

19. "See what a grace was seated on this brow—/ Hyperion's curls, the front of Jove himself" (III.4.54–55), whereas he refers to Claudius as "the bloat king" (III.4.182).

20. For further intertextual interference between *Hamlet* and "Gertrude Talks Back," see, e.g., "Leave wringing of your hands, peace, sit you down, / And let me wring your heart" (III.4.33–34) versus "I am *not* wringing my hands. I'm drying my nails" (15); "Nay, but to live / In the rank sweat of an enseamed bed / Stewed in corruption, honeying and making love / Over the nasty sty ... " (III.4.90–93) versus "The rank sweat of *what*? My bed is certainly not *enseamed*, whatever that might be! A nasty sty, indeed! Not that it's any of your business, but I change those sheets twice a week, which is more than you do, judging from that student slum pigpen in Wittenberg" (16).

21. See Hamlet to Gertrude in III.4.17–20: "[*Seizes her arm.*] Come, come, and sit you down, you shall not budge, / You go not till I set you up a

glass / Where you may see the inmost part of you." It is significant that this produces Gertrude's only strong reaction in the entire play, which can also be read metaphorically: "What wilt thou do? Thou wilt not murder me?" (III.4.21).

22. For the conception of love in Atwood's works, see chapter 1.

23. For further brief examples of Atwoodian "talking back," see, e.g., her poems "Orpheus (1)" and "Eurydice" in *Eating Fire: Selected Poetry, 1965–1995* (1998), in which Atwood "edits" the classical myth of Orpheus and Eurydice.

24. Atwood, speaking about her dystopian novel *The Handmaid's Tale*, in an interview with Katherine Govier, *Quill and Quire* (September 1985): 66–67.

3

"Untold Stories, Fresh Beginnings"
Atwood's Short Stories

A repertoire / of untold stories, / a fresh beginning
                    MARGARET ATWOOD, "The Paper Bag," 1991

Considering earlier criticism of Margaret Atwood's short fiction, one becomes aware of a seeming critical paradox: Atwood is a major figure on the contemporary literary scene, and she is the figurehead of Canadian literature. The short story, in turn, has been hailed as "the most active ambassador of Canadian literature abroad" (Bonheim 1980–81, 659), a statement that could be applied with similar justification to Atwood. Her short stories, however, have long been passed over in survey works on her writing, have been treated as mere preparatory exercises, or simply have been seen as less important than her novels and poetry collections.[2] There is indeed always the danger that one branch of a multitalented author's work will languish in relative critical neglect—a particularly relevant danger in the case of a prolific writer such as Atwood, who is, in addition, a renowned literary critic (see chapter 6) as well as a highly sought-after media personality (see chapter 8). There is also the barrier of an implied generic hierarchy, which, at least in the minds of general readers, still gives precedence by and large to the novel over other forms of literary expression. Seen from this perspective, the critical fate of Atwood's short fiction for some two decades reflects that of the reception of the genre as a whole.

The decade leading to the turn of the century, however, also saw a change in the reception of Atwood's short fictional prose, with several contributions that either exclusively or in combination with other genres finally directed attention to her short stories.[3] Since *Wilderness Tips* (1991), Atwood's third collection of short stories, the kind of attention given to her short stories has been close to that lavished on her novels—see, for instance, the immediate and highly positive reviews of her latest short-story collection *Moral Disorder*.[4]

It is true that Atwood has published less in this genre (so far four short-story collections) compared with her productivity in the novel or even poetry (twelve novels and twelve collections of poetry, not counting four volumes of "selected" poetry), and that there have been—for her standards—relatively long intervals between the publication of her short-story collections: *Dancing Girls* (1977), *Bluebeard's Egg* (1983), *Wilderness Tips* (1991), and *Moral Disorder* (2006). The fifteen years between her acclaimed *Wilderness Tips* and *Moral Disorder* may also be explained by her venturing out into new generic territories of short fiction and prose poetry with *Murder in the Dark* (1983), *Good Bones* (1992), and *The Tent* (2006) (see chapter 2), only to see her return triumphantly to the short-story genre with another generic debut in her oeuvre, the short-story cycle *Moral Disorder*.

From the perspective of teaching, Atwood's short stories have always been a favourite that could perhaps even rival her novels. And, indeed, her short stories alone would suffice to place her in the forefront of twentieth- (and twenty-first-) century writers. Although there are discernible currents and even cross-references linking Atwood's short stories to her poetry and novels,[5] her work in the genre is as free of derivativeness as it is varied. This chapter traces some of this work's main themes, techniques, and lines of development, taking the prominent theme of gender relations in Atwood's short stories as its cue.

DANCING GIRLS

Atwood's exceptional thematic and structural variety is already evident in her debut short-story collection, *Dancing Girls* (1977), the individual stories of which were first published between 1964 and 1977. In looking for a common denominator to link these stories, a statement from Atwood's poetry springs to mind: "This is not a debate / but a duet / with two deaf singers"[6]—for these early stories often portray individuals in unfulfilling, dysfunctional, or disintegrating relationships:

> This is an interval, a truce; it can't last, we both know it, there have been too many differences, of opinion we called it but it was more than that, the things that mean safety for him mean danger for me. We've talked too much or not enough: for what we have to say to each other there's no language, we've tried them all. ... We love each other, that's true whatever it means, but we aren't good at it.[7]
>
> I want to tell him now what no one's ever taught him, how two people who love each other behave, how they avoid damaging each other, but I'm not sure I know.[8]

In *Dancing Girls*, the characters often confuse their dependence on their partners with love. The stories make clear that dependence is usually the result of a character's personality defects or poor self-image—ideal prerequisites for becoming embroiled with an unfulfilling, harmful, and often loveless partner (see, e.g., "The Man from Mars," "Polarities," "Under Glass," "Hair Jewellery," "A Travel Piece," "Training," and "Lives of the Poets"). "Ontological insecurity," as Ronald D. Laing puts it in *The Divided Self* (1965, esp. 39–61), a lack of self-confidence, the feeling of being trapped within the wrong body—such feelings of inadequacy lead many characters in *Dancing Girls* into relationships that only serve to confirm and reconfirm their negative opinions of themselves, whether through their partner's open lack of interest, attitude of dominance, or sexual betrayal. The stories demonstrate how the failure to come to terms with oneself is inextricably linked to an inability to form meaningful relationships: the protagonists are, ultimately, defeated not by their partners but by themselves.

A number of stories in *Dancing Girls* seem to be literary reworkings of *The Divided Self* (first published in 1960), a psychiatric work popular in the 1960s. Laing's study presents a theory of the schizoid or schizophrenic personality, which Atwood took up in her writings of the 1960s and 1970s. *Schizo-id* means "almost split"; (neurotic) schizoid behaviour therefore constitutes a preform of (psychotic) schizophrenia: "The term schizoid refers to an individual the totality of whose experience is split in two main ways: in the first place, there is a rent in his relationship with his world and, in the second, there is a disruption of his relation with himself."[9] Atwood's early short stories examine the grey area between (still "normal") neurosis and (abnormal) psychotic behaviour, repeatedly portraying the incursion of the irrational into everyday life or even the descent into madness.[10] Following the unorthodox, "unpsychiatric" approaches of Laing, Gregory Bateson, and others, Atwood questions the very concepts of "normality" and "abnormality." Her open-ended stories repeatedly imply that it is the social context that is "sick" and that its rigorously anti-emotional conformism prevents the normal development of the "wilderness" of the individual psyche, pushing sensitive individuals (most frequently women) over the brink into what is—for these characters—a more acceptable world of madness.

An excellent example can be found in the short story "Polarities." Morrison, the protagonist, is a classic case of the schizoid personality. Although he initially seems to fit well enough into his social environment, Atwood's use of a combined authorial and figural third-person narrative allows the reader a deeper insight into his mental world. It becomes obvious that there is a conflict between Morrison's behaviour on the one hand and his thoughts and opinions on the other. Morrison often asks his colleague Louise questions that signal some kind of interest in her—a tactic that takes her in for large stretches of the narrative. The narrator's comments, however, expose Morrison's emotionally dysfunctional personality. Morrison confuses Louise with his combination of apparent interest in her on the one hand and distance and coldness on the other: "'What's finished?' he asked. He hadn't been paying attention" (40); "'What aspect?' Morrison asked, not interested" (46). He thus distorts the purpose of questions, using them as a defensive tactic. He wants to prevent any meaningful communication that might force him to commit himself and overcome his emotional distance. Louise, desperate for certainty and dependent on Morrison in her state of mental crisis, thus falls over the edge into the "sanctum" of madness, which she can, after all, control.[11]

Louise's communicative strategies are diametrically opposed to Morrison's. Her statements carry the dialogue forward rather than slow it down. Louise expresses emotions and even fear, and her questions communicate a genuine interest in Morrison and a desire for information. The title of the story is thus an accurate reflection of the characters' relationship: activity and passivity, action and reaction, directness and indirectness, openness and dissimulation, initiative and blockage, interest and indifference—these polar opposites constantly clash in the dialogues and narrative, inevitably leading to tragedy. Morrison is able to open himself up to Louise, and to come to terms with his feelings, only after she has mentally divorced herself from reality and is no longer in a position to place any demands on him. In a crisis himself now, he becomes aware of his own psychological inadequacy: "He saw that it was only the hopeless, mad Louise he wanted, the one devoid of any purpose or defence. A sane one, one who could judge him, he would never be able to handle" (62).

"Polarities," like many of Atwood's early short stories, closes on an open, ambiguous note. The text suggests several possible interpretations of the ending: that Morrison mentally and physically freezes or even freezes to death or that, as is the case with Louise, his mental defences cave in and he falls into psychosis. In both cases, the closing scene should be interpreted metaphorically as an expression of his fantastic visions, for the sequence of perceived objects is unrealistic and goes far beyond what the human eye can see ("the mountains"—"then forest upon forest"—"after that the barren tundra and the blank solid rivers"—"and beyond ... the frozen sea" [65]). The vividness of this climactic scene is evidence of Atwood's poetic talent: in the space of only a few lines, Atwood evokes highly complex mental processes and developments.

Morrison's characterization in this story is based on a homogeneous series of metaphors, which often suggest constraint and limitation (e.g., "He would never survive a winter *buried* like that or *closed* in one of the glass-sided *cardboard-carton* apartment buildings" or, even in sexual contexts, "He imagined his long body *locked* in that athletic, chilly *grip*" [41, 44; emphasis added]). His worldview, his attitudes, influence the language and the choice of metaphors used in connection with them. Morrison projects his neurosis, his feeling of congestion and imprisonment, onto everyday objects and the people surrounding him, especially Louise. Language and content are thus inextricably linked (an aspect of "mind style"; see Nischik 1991b, 1993a).

The fundamental image in Louise's world, on the other hand, is that of division—a split in her personality that Louise tries to overcome by creating a circle.[12] Her visions and imagery depend on the contrast between wholeness and division and on the (re-)creation of wholeness. In this sense, Morrison might be an ideal partner for Louise, who, demonstrating reason in madness, recognizes his mental inadequacy far earlier than he himself does.[13] Her metaphoric world clearly demonstrates her attempt to overcome the divisions and repressions from which he is suffering. "Polarities" seems to accept the view of psychosis as socially determined, as in Laing's "antipsychiatric approach": "*Without exception* ... the behaviour that gets labelled schizophrenic is a *special strategy that a person invents in order to live in an unliveable situation*. ... What we call 'normal' is a product of repression, denial, splitting, projection, introjection and other forms of destructive action on experience" (1965, 114–15, 27). If one thinks of the seemingly "normal" Morrison, this view does not seem too extreme. He and Louise share only one thing among the "Polarities" that characterize this story: their inability to unite intellect and emotion and to overcome the divisions in their personalities.

As is often the case in Atwood's works, "Polarities" presents the problems of individuals against a national backdrop. It is no coincidence that Louise, obsessed with the idea of wholeness, is a bilingual Canadian ("her mother was a French Protestant, ... her father an English Catholic" [60]) now living in Anglo-Canada. Interestingly, during one of Morrison's visits to her sickbed, she falls back into French, thus cutting Morrison off from her completely. It is, moreover, a typically Atwoodian conceit that Morrison, who thinks in terms of dominance and power, should be an American teaching at a Canadian university (probably the University of Alberta in Edmonton).[14] Atwood, an ardent supporter of Canada, has often spoken out against the political, economic, and cultural dominance of her country by the United States (see Goetsch 2000/02 and chapters 6 and 7). The polarity between Canada and the United States can be traced throughout the course of "Polarities," for example in Leota's claim that Americans are stealing Canadians' jobs (the question of Americans being employed at Canadian universities was hotly debated in political circles during the 1960s).[15] Atwood also makes use of the USA/Canada dichotomy in stories such as "Hair Jewellery,"

"Dancing Girls," and "The Resplendent Quetzal" from *Dancing Girls* or in "Death by Landscape" from *Wilderness Tips* (as well as in her novels *Surfacing* and *The Handmaid's Tale* and in her poetry) (see Broege 1981; and McCombs 1988a). Finally, "Polarities" also serves to demonstrate the centrality of the (often Canadian) setting of Atwood's texts, which frequently has great importance for the characters involved (see "Death by Landscape"). In "Polarities," external (e.g., climatic) conditions often parallel the characters' mental states, functioning almost as an "objective correlative": external and internal paralysis go hand in hand.

BLUEBEARD'S EGG

Atwood's second short-story collection, *Bluebeard's Egg* (1983), is no longer concerned with schizoid and schizophrenic mental states (although rudimentary traces of this concern might still be detectable in Joel in "Uglypuss"; the protagonists of "The Salt Garden" and "The Sunrise" have other pathological problems to contend with: e.g., epileptic fits). The stories in *Bluebeard's Egg* were written in the 1970s and early 1980s. Noteworthy in this context is also the development in the reception of R. D. Laing, whose considerable influence in the 1960s declined rapidly from the 1970s onward (see Nischik 1991b, 84–85). Correspondingly there was a move away from individual psychological problems toward sociopsychological themes. Individuals were increasingly seen as part of their social surroundings and operating as members of specific groups. It is remarkable in this context, then, that in *Dancing Girls* characters are often presented in exceptional circumstances, separated from their accustomed social surroundings (e.g., on journeys or abroad), reinforcing the rootlessness of these "tourist" characters.[16] In *Bluebeard's Egg*, on the other hand, characters are usually portrayed at home or within their family circles. The collection contains a number of "family stories," such as "Significant Moments in the Life of My Mother," "Unearthing Suite," and "Loulou; or, The Domestic Life of Language," which exude a warmth completely alien to the desperate characters and the dark tones of the earlier stories.[17] Nevertheless, Atwood in this second collection keeps faith with one of her major themes:

relationships in their terminal stages and partnerships in crisis. In contrast to *Dancing Girls*, however, where stories on these themes are suffused with desperation and hopelessness, the stories of *Bluebeard's Egg* hold out a glimmer of hope—alternative realities that provide a source of comfort for the (usually female) protagonists by rendering the situation more tolerable.

The contrasts outlined above between Atwood's first and second short-story collections could be clearly illustrated by a comparison of "The Resplendent Quetzal" (1977) and "Scarlet Ibis" (1983), a particularly appropriate comparison given the strong thematic similarities between the two stories.

"Scarlet Ibis" presents a marital relationship drained of life and any hint of joy. The spouses, Christine and Don, travel to Trinidad with their youngest daughter, four-year-old Lilian, in the hope of finding new impulses for their dreary existence. The trip ostensibly fails in its purpose: Don and Lilian complain about everything, even about the activities Christine proposes for them. Christine, the focus of the story, is repeatedly rejected by her exhausted, overworked husband, and the two seem to be unable to communicate except for banalities. During the climax of the holiday, a boat trip to a bird reserve, conflicts are not aired but transplanted into imaginary worlds, and Christine's internal monologues replace dialogues between her and her husband. She constantly withdraws from the threat of reality by fleeing into a world of the imagination, as when she imagines her (not very rosy) future with Don. Correspondingly the story contains a high number of modal verbs[18] and adverbs, conditional forms, and *if* and *as if* clauses: "*Maybe* he *would, maybe* he *wouldn't. Maybe* he *would* say he was coming on with a headache. *Maybe* she *would* find herself walking on nothing, because *maybe* there was nothing there" (186; emphasis added). The imaginary alternative world exists parallel to the real world of experience and appears at times to have a greater reality for Christine, as it is mentally more present and holds out more hope.

Her escapist fantasies eventually come to a head during the sighting of the rare tropical birds:

> She felt as if she was looking at a picture, of exotic flowers or
> of red fruit growing on trees, evenly spaced, like the fruit in the

gardens of mediaeval paintings. ... On the other side of the fence was another world, not real but at the same time more real than the one on this side, the men and women in their flimsy clothes and aging bodies. (199)

This fleeting, epiphanic experience of remarkable beauty and freedom for a short time leads to a rapprochement between Don and Christine and briefly awakens in her a feeling of existential security ("Don took hold of Christine's hand, a thing he had not done for some time. ... Christine felt the two hands holding her own, mooring her, one on either side" [199–200]). Retrospectively, however, this experience is trivialized by Christine, reduced to a "form of entertainment, like the Grand Canyon: something that really ought to be seen" (201). Brought back down to earth in this way, even the alternative realities can provide no relief for Christine, serving only to increase her existential insecurity and immobility. By conforming to expectations and ignoring her own emotional needs, she prevents change: "She tried to think of some other distraction, mostly for the sake of Don" (182). Untold stories, *no* fresh beginnings.[19]

WILDERNESS TIPS

The stories in *Wilderness Tips* (1991), Atwood's third short-story collection, were written in the 1980s. In these stories, the "untold stories" in the protagonists' lives come to the surface more often. The characters admit their existential needs more readily, both to themselves and to others, and have a greater ability to transcend catastrophes in their lives, achieving at least the suggestion of a "fresh beginning." The collection moves away from the family-oriented stories of *Bluebeard's Egg*, often presenting characters at the workplace. In "Hairball" and "Uncles," we see talented women who have worked their way up the career ladder in the face of resentment and envy among male colleagues.

In "Hairball," calculating, career-oriented fashion designer Kat is met with the fierce opposition of her money- and power-mad colleagues, which in turn leads her younger lover—in a way her pupil and her "creation"—to dethrone his mentor in a *coup d'état* while she is undergoing major surgery. However, this personal and professional betrayal does not, as it might well have done in *Dancing Girls*, result in the female victim's retreat into bitterness and denial (or an escape into severe illness); rather, it leads to a symbolic act of revenge. This retaliation cannot make good the harm Kat has already suffered, but by accepting her pain, by realizing how unhappy her totally work-oriented life has been, and by meeting an outrageous act with an outrageous response, Kat, in the story's last sentence, is preparing herself psychologically for a fresh beginning: "She has done an outrageous thing, but she doesn't feel guilty. She feels light and peaceful and filled with charity, and temporarily without a name" (56). In *Wilderness Tips*, women at times appear as victims of very subtle gender discrimination. They now refuse, however, to participate in their subjugation and domination, taking a stand instead and transforming previously "untold stories" into (symbolically encoded) spoken texts.

A number of stories in *Wilderness Tips* are innovative in Atwood's short-story oeuvre in that they are narrated retrospectively, demonstrating on the one hand how experiences from the past are reinterpreted in retrospect and on the other how formative they can be. "Death by Landscape" contains an additional new feature within Atwood's short prose (see, however, *Cat's Eye*), placing gender problems for the first time in a same-sex context that goes beyond the mother-daughter and father-son relationships Atwood hitherto examined. In this story, the tentative friendship that for several years links the Canadian schoolgirl Lois with the American girl Lucy turns out in retrospect to carry more emotional power than any of Lois's subsequent relationships, including that with her husband, Rob. The lasting bond that links the girls is strengthened by Lucy's mysterious, unsolved disappearance into the Canadian wilderness during a summer camp excursion. After the death of her husband, the adult Lois reviews her life up to that point, recognizing that it has taken two paths: an "official" life she has lived physically, and an "unofficial" inner life of the mind—a typical division with Atwood's characters. In this story, the "untold story" develops into the conscious, dominant path:

> She can hardly remember getting married, or what Rob looked like.
> Even at the time she never felt she was paying full attention. She

was tired a lot, as if she was living not one life but two: her own, and another, shadowy life that hovered around her and would not let itself be realized—the life of what would have happened if Lucy had not stepped sideways, and disappeared from time. (127–28)

Here (as in "Weight" in the same collection), the gender conflicts found in many early stories are reduced in importance by the fact that, for the female protagonists, their emotional and (in "Weight") intellectual friendships with other women turn out to be the deepest, most personal, and most formative relationships in their lives. Relationships between men and women, on the other hand, are marked too strongly by conventional gender patterns (not to say rituals) of behaviour and seem rather to get in the way of the women's individual development.

It becomes clear in examining the configuration of relationships in *Wilderness Tips* that Atwood has come full circle in comparison with her earliest collection. In the later stories, in contrast to her first ones, Atwood presents profound partnerships between kindred spirits who are so closely linked they do not even need physical closeness yet are far away from the claustrophobic relationships of dependency portrayed in earlier volumes. In *Wilderness Tips*, these profound relationships[20] overcome not only physical distance but also marriage to another character and may even outlive the death of one of the partners in the surviving partner's mind (e.g., in "Isis in Darkness" or "The Age of Lead"). These relationships are, however, rarely enjoyed in a conventional sense—the characters always recognize their importance too late, and they do so only tacitly. Fear or death of one of the partners always represents an insuperable hindrance.

"Death by Landscape" and "Hairball" are good examples of Atwood's firmly Canadian perspective. These and other stories work with the huge expanses of the Canadian landscape, its unexplored wildernesses, which, particularly in "Death by Landscape," turn nature into a "protagonist" with a profound effect on plot.[21] They evoke the Canadian tradition of landscape painting, particularly that of the Group of Seven. They tell of canoe trips and summer camps in "Death by Landscape" (and in "True Trash"). They contrast Canada and the United States or Canada and Britain in "Hairball." They examine a curious piece of Canadian exploration lore (the failed Franklin expedition to the Arctic in the nineteenth century) in "The Age of Lead," combined with the contemporary ecological problems that affect Canada so profoundly, not least due to its geographical proximity to the United States. They tackle the theme of immigration in "Wilderness Tips" and contemporary Canadian political problems in "Hack Wednesday." These and other motifs in *Wilderness Tips* (whose stories are nearly all set in Canada) demonstrate how "Canadian" a writer Atwood is in spite of her cosmopolitanism. As well as dealing with supranational themes, such as gender relations, she also conveys specifically Canadian characteristics to an international audience.

MORAL DISORDER

Moral Disorder (2006), Atwood's latest short-story collection, is her first book of short stories in fifteen years. It is her most homogeneous short-story collection to date, in fact her first short-story cycle. *Moral Disorder* is clearly also her most "autobiographical" book, with Atwood the writer and family person in her mid-sixties taking stock and looking back, sketching the development of her protagonist Nell from childhood to adulthood and older age. In contrast to Alice Munro's short-story cycle *Lives of Girls and Women* (1971), *Moral Disorder* is not predominantly a portrait of the artist as a *young* woman; rather, it stresses the personal development of Nell within her family context over a long range of time (only two of the eleven stories deal with Nell's childhood, one with her youth, eight mainly with an adult Nell). Recurring characters next to the protagonist, who is present in all stories, are Nell's parents, her sister Lillie (eleven years younger), plus Tig, Nell's long-time partner, and his ex-wife Oona. Three stories, following each other in the middle of the collection, deal with Nell and Tig's life on a farm ("Monopoly," "Moral Disorder," and "White Horse") before the couple moves back to the city in the following story, "The Entities," and the final two stories then deal with Nell's father and mother, especially their worrisome old age stamped by severe illness.

The structure of the book is predominantly chronological, within a largely retrospective framework and a sometimes montage-like alternation between narrative past and narrative present ("The Headless Horseman," "The Labrador Fiasco," "The Boys at the Lab"). Yet the introductory story, "The Bad News," presented in the present tense, shows an older Nell and Tig ("after this long together" [2]), thus opening the book with the latest chronological story, probably to signal an important aspect and tone of the collection as a whole. "The Bad News" honours its title by exuding a sense of loss—of vitality, of reckless optimism—and a sense of fear and anxiety. Danger seems to lurk everywhere, also on a larger, political scale, since "the leaders of the leading countries, as they're called, those aren't really leading any more, they're flailing around; you can see it in their eyes, white-rimmed like the eyes of panic-stricken cattle" (3). The hope for the future boils down to the unrealistic wish that "things stay the way they are, I pray" (8). Afraid of old age, illness, and a potential loss of mental capacity, Nell is in a precarious mental state: "This has become my picture of my future self: wandering the house in the darkness, in my white nightdress, howling for what I can't quite remember I've lost. It's unbearable. I wake up in the night and reach out to make sure Tig is still there, still breathing. So far, so good" (5).

In such an "existential" context, it is not surprising that gender, for the first time in Atwood's short-fiction oeuvre, does not play a big role in this collection. In her mid-sixties, Atwood seems to be involved mainly with other issues. On the other hand, it is significant that the only two stories in which gender does figure rather prominently come in the first third of the book, which deals mainly with a young/er Nell in her childhood and youth. These periods are crucial for gender socialization, especially given the stories' setting in the 1950s and 1960s, when gender was a particularly prominent social issue:

> I'd never got over the Grade Two reader, the one featuring a father who went to a job every day and drove a car, a mother who wore an apron and did baking, two children—boy and girl—and a cat and a dog, all living in a white house with frilly window curtains. ... My future would not be complete—no, it would not be *normal*—unless it contained window curtains like these, and everything that went with them. (79–80)

"The Art of Cooking and Serving" and "My Last Duchess" thus belong to the relatively few stories in Atwood's short-story oeuvre—similar to "Betty" (*Dancing Girls*), "Hurricane Hazel" (*Bluebeard's Egg*), and "Uncles" and "Death by Landscape" (*Wilderness Tips*)—that show gender at work in the crucial younger, formative stages of life, and they clearly show gender as transmitted and performed, certainly not as in-born femininities and masculinities.

The second story in the book, which also explains the cover images of the Canadian edition (19), shows a young Nell mainly in a daughter-mother relationship and, presumably in the 1950s, under strong conventional gender influences. Under the title "The Art of Cooking and Serving," Atwood renders a female initiation story: initiation into domestic life and giving birth/mothering on the one hand and eventual distancing from familiar influences and turning to peer group activities on the other. The story suggests conventional gender expectations and restrictions in Nell's upbringing, for instance by the fact that knitting is one of her prime pastimes, not least because her mother is expecting a "late" child (who in later stories appears as Nell's younger sister Lillie). Lillie is an unplanned baby and turns out to be "one of *those*" (22), as the doctor puts it, a nervous and nerve-racking child who hardly ever sleeps and who exhausts her family, especially her mother. Before the baby's sex is known, Nell reflects on the gendered colour system for babies, blue for boys and pink for girls (11–12). She is praised by others for knitting diligently for the baby ("a good little worker" [20]), thus being re-enforced in gendered socialization patterns that train little girls in the direction of motherhood. Whereas Nell, "with single-minded concentration" (14), is fully integrated into the family preparations for the birth of the third child, Nell's brother is hardly mentioned. In any case, his task under the new circumstances is not exactly taxing, compared with the change of life the baby's birth means for Nell: "We would all have to pitch in, said my father, and do extra tasks. It would be my brother's job to mow the lawn, from now until June" (13).

When Nell does not knit the layette for the baby or clean the house, another pastime of hers is to read a cookbook published in 1929–30, ten years before she was born (incidentally just like Atwood herself). Sarah Field Splint's *The Art of Cooking and Serving* gives her orientation in a context of female socialization:

Sarah Field Splint had strict ideas on the proper conduct of life. She had rules, she imposed order. Hot foods must be served *hot*, cold foods *cold*. "It just *has* to be done, however it is accomplished," she said. That was the kind of advice I needed to hear. She was firm on the subject of clean linen and shining silver. (18)

Nell's imagination is particularly kindled by the two chapters entitled "The Servantless House" and "The House with a Servant": "Both of them were windows into another world, and I peered through them eagerly. I knew they were windows, not doors: I couldn't get in. But what entrancing lives were being lived in there!" (18). The book sets her thoughts in motion: "Did I want to transform, or to be transformed? Was I to be the kind homemaker, or the formerly untidy maid? I hardly knew" (19). In her insecure, transgressive state of development, Nell is thankful on the one hand for guidance through role models but on the other cannot decide on one or the other—perhaps because both of them are heavily engendered and she is looking for other options. This indeed proves true at the end of the story, when Nell rebels against her mother and the nurturing role her mother is steering her toward in a gender-essentialist manner: "'Why should I?' [help her mother with the baby] I said. 'She's not *my* baby. I didn't have her. You did.' I'd never said anything this rude to her. Even as the words were coming out of my mouth I knew I'd gone too far, though all I'd done was spoken the truth, or part of it" (23). To act against ingrained gender roles in an open manner may entail pain, in more than one sense: "My mother stood up and whirled around, all in one movement, and slapped me hard across the face" (23). Nevertheless, the end of the story sees young Nell drifting away from the domestic, nurturing role supposedly cut out for her, mentally drifting into a new kind of outside world of peer groups, "to all sorts of ... seductive and tawdry and frightening pleasures I could not yet begin to imagine" (23).

Whereas this distancing between mother and daughter in puberty is a usual developmental step, giving birth to a child is rendered in rather unusual problematic terms in this story, thereby also working against any kind of euphemistic motherhood myth. First, Lillie is a late, unplanned baby. Due to her mother's advanced age, her birth is expected with trepidation: "Until my new baby brother or sister had arrived safely my mother would be in a dangerous condition. Something terrible might happen to her" (12). Second, the baby totally disarranges the family with her constant wailing. Third, her mother changes to her disadvantage, physically and mentally, after giving birth to Lillie. Perhaps no wonder, then, that Nell eventually and explicitly opts against this kind of female familial restriction by rejecting responsibility for her younger sister and placing her into her exhausted mother's range of activities and worries. Again the men in the family seem to have little to do with the baby; they are not shown to support the mother in her caring for the child and do not seem to particularly care.

"The Art of Cooking and Serving" thus renders traditional gender roles in problematic terms, showing these roles to work against the independence and freedom of choice particularly of women. Giving birth to a child and nurturing it are shown to be the concerns of women, who must either accept the prescribed role or, painfully, opt out of it, as Nell does at the end of the story, leaving her overtaxed mother in the lurch:

> My mother ... slapped me hard across the face. She'd never done that before, or anything remotely like it. I didn't say anything. She didn't say anything. We were both shocked by ourselves, and also by each other.
>
> I ought to have felt hurt, and I did. But I also felt set free, as if released from an enchantment. I was no longer compelled to do service. On the outside, I would still be helpful. ... But another, more secret life spread out before me, unrolling like a dark fabric. (23)

That Nell may be a budding writer is suggested by her involvement with words and language even when a child: "I was knitting this layette because my mother was expecting. I avoided the word *pregnant*, as did others: *pregnant* was a blunt, bulgy, pendulous word, it weighed you down to think about it, whereas *expecting* suggested a dog with its ears pricked" (12). Even names are evaluated by young Nell: "It was by a woman called Sarah Field Splint, a name I trusted: *Sarah* was old-fashioned and dependable, *Field* was pastoral and flowery, and

Splint—well, there could be no nonsense and weeping and hysteria and doubts about the right course of action with a woman called Splint by your side" (17).

Yet the main issue in this story is Nell's considering and eventually choosing particular (symbolic) options for her future life. Nell is first presented as a conforming eleven-year-old girl who feels responsible for helping her mother with domestic chores ("When I wasn't knitting, I swept the floor diligently" [15]). In connection with Splint's cookbook, she briefly dreams of a domestic existence for herself, yet she focuses only on potential positive aspects of such an existence: "How I longed for a breakfast tray with a couple of daffodils in a bud vase, as pictured, or a tea table at which to entertain 'a few choice friends' ... or, best of all, breakfast served on a side porch" (18). The older Nell gets, the more she comes to realize the disadvantages of an exclusively domestic life, with "woman" equalling maternity and household and, in the case of her mother, apparently making up a whole existence; this becomes especially virulent with/after the birth of the third, unwanted child: "Despite her superior ability, she was slacking off ... , her face pale and moist, her hair damp and lank, her stomach sticking out in a way that made me feel dizzy. ... She always knew what to do in an emergency, she was methodical and cheerful, she took command. Now it was as if she had abdicated" (14). When Nell has turned fourteen and the situation at home has further deteriorated after the birth of her sister ("From having been too fat, my mother now became too thin. She was gaunt from lack of sleep, her hair dull, her eyes bruised-looking, her shoulders hunched over" [21]), she is still following in her mother's footsteps: "I avoided the boys who approached me: somehow I had to turn away, I had to go home and look after the baby, who was still not sleeping. My mother dragged around the house as if she was ill, or starving" (22). It is through her rebellion against her mother's dismal domestic life and against her mother's expectations for her that Nell steers her own life in a new direction—at the cost of alienation between mother and daughter, but with a feeling of release and relief, and with hope for her future life.

After "The Headless Horseman"—which deals mainly with the problem-laden relationship between the two sisters[22] in the narrative past and present—comes "My Last Duchess." This is the second story in the book that foregrounds gender, though already to a smaller extent than "The Art of Cooking and Serving" does. "My Last Duchess"—also the title of a well-known poem/dramatic monologue from 1842 by Victorian poet Robert Browning—deals with Nell at high school age, in particular her boyfriends, here Bill, as well as the relevance that literature and her English teacher, Miss Bessie, have for her. Nell is good in English and rather fascinated by her English lessons, whereas Bill prefers algebra and approaches literature as one would non-fictional texts. He thinks he does not understand Browning's poem and literature in general, and thus at first he accepts Nell as his tutor so that he can pass his English exam. Finally, however, as they begin to quarrel about the poem, disagreeing about how to evaluate the figures of the Duke and Duchess, it becomes the occasion for them to end their relationship.

The reason for the separation is less trivial than it may seem at first because it involves Nell's newly gained critical awareness of the apparent female gender conformity of the Duchess, which Bill defends. His "She was a nice normal girl" Nell counters with "She was a dumb bunny," which eventually leads to Bill indirectly attacking Nell and degrading her intelligence: "At least she wasn't a brainer and a show-off" (72). Their quarrel thus finally boils down to their different conceptions of what a young woman may be or should do. Nell, after she has first drawn up a list of opposite characteristics of the Duke and Duchess "for the purposes of the final exam" (67), a list that conforms to the received critical view of the Browning poem, eventually comes to see the poem in a somewhat different light, not least because of her discussion with Bill. Nell comes to view the Duke with some sympathy (in contrast to Bill, who outright rejects the Duke's ruthless behaviour) yet without defending him. More importantly, she judges harshly the Duchess's pleasing demeanour of always smiling at seemingly everybody, thus taking an unconventional view of the poem: "The more I thought about the Duchess and about how aggravating she must have been—aggravating, and too obliging, and just plain boring, the very same smile day after day—the more sympathy I felt for the Duke" (66–67). With this oppositional, independent-minded view and because she is more knowledgeable about literature than Bill, Nell unwittingly provokes her boyfriend's denigration of her. Thus, both the Duchess and Nell are criticized and rejected by their partners—both, in the final analysis, for having a mind of their own and for refusing to be dominated and controlled by their male partners. For while ostensibly obliging, the Duchess's constant smiling at everybody, especially men, may also be regarded as her indirect opposition to her husband's arrogant and highly possessive stance toward her.[23]

After their quarrel, Nell cries and briefly ruminates about such strange emotional mechanisms ("It was so sad. Why did such things have to disintegrate like that? Why did longing and desire, and friendliness and goodwill too, have to shatter into pieces? Why did they have to be so thoroughly over?" [73]). But she then turns to read Thomas Hardy's *Tess of the d'Urbervilles* in bed, for "Miss Bessie would be tackling it on Monday" (73). Reading this novel makes Nell compare her own fate with that of the literary character Tess ("Tess had serious problems—much worse than mine" [73]), think about questions of canon ("Who chose the books and poems that would be on the curriculum? What use would they be in our future lives?" [74]), and, finally, think about her English teacher, Miss Bessie ("Me, and Miss Bessie. Miss Bessie, too, must have been up late" [74]).

Miss Bessie, rendered in respectful, positive terms from the beginning ("Miss Bessie was the best English teacher in the school. Possibly she was one of the best in the city" [56]), toward the end of the story emerges as a crucial influence on Nell's life, more important than her quickly changing boyfriends at this time of her adolescent life. This influence is due partly to the teacher's personal characteristics: Miss Bessie is a respected, knowledgeable, critical, and strict but well-meaning teacher, ambitious to lead her pupils to the best achievements they are capable of, and she seems to be good-looking and dresses elegantly. But her significance for Nell is due at least equally to her superior knowledge of English literature. Literary texts, this story argues, are a school for life if an "attentive reader" (55) knows how to decode them sympathetically: "They [the teachers] knew something we needed to know, but it was a complicated thing. ... These women—these teachers—had no direct method of conveying this thing to us, not in a way that would make us listen, because it was too tangled, it was too oblique. It was hidden within the stories" (75).

With such considerations, her English teacher, and the teachings of literature transmitted through her, intermingle in Nell's mind. In a kind of epiphany, Nell sees her teacher as someone who has taught her significant lessons for life, but it is the thoughtful pupil herself who has to draw the conclusions from the books: "These girls [literary figures like the Duchess, Tess, or Ophelia] were all similar. They were too trusting, they found themselves in the hands of the wrong men, ... they let themselves drift. They smiled too much. They were too eager to please. Then they got bumped off, one way or another. Nobody gave them any help" (74). Nell learns not to be too compliant but instead to stand up for one's self and opinions. The Browning poem and, in conjunction, her English teacher, who acts as a catalyst for her freshly gained awareness, displace Bill in the order of importance in Nell's ponderings:

> I ought to have been brooding over Bill—didn't he require more tears? Instead, in the bright place at the back of my head, there was an image of Miss Bessie. She was standing in a patch of sunlight. ... She seemed distant but very clear, like a photograph. Now she was smiling at me with gentle irony, and holding aside a curtain; behind the curtain was the entrance to a dark tunnel. I would have to go into the tunnel whether I wanted to or not—the tunnel was the road of going on, ... but the entrance was where Miss Bessie had to stop. (75)

The motif of holding aside the curtain (placed in front of the dark tunnel in Miss Bessie's case, the painting in the Duke's case) also points to some important parallels between Miss Bessie and the Duke, though the former is definitely the more positive and important figure for Nell. Both Miss Bessie and the Duke are correlated with culture and art, with indirect teachings of significant lessons via art. Their complex "untold stories" seem to be weightier, more important, and more resonant than any clear, directly told messages. The deciphering that art requires of the "attentive reader" makes her part of the story, as Nell's ruminations demonstrate, rather than a mere passive listener or viewer. Nell's teacher, by way of instructing her pupils how to appreciate literature, can give Nell knowledge, criteria, and "pattern[s]" (75) by which to perceive the world, but it is Nell who has to make her own experiences, guided by values in which she believes. In her painful situation of yet another broken relationship with a boyfriend, this is the lesson that

Nell slowly learns. A statement from George Bernard Shaw's *Major Barbara* proves true for Nell too: "You have learnt something. That always feels at first as if you had lost something" (1964, 316). In Nell's own words,

> Very soon I would be a last year's student. I would be gone from Miss Bessie's world, and she would be gone from mine. Both of us would be in the past, both of us over and done with—me from her point of view, her from mine. Sitting in my present-day desk there would be another, younger student. ...
>
> Meanwhile, I myself would be inside the dark tunnel. I'd be going on. I'd be finding things out. I'd be all on my own. (75–76)

With this statement, prospectively referring to a "teacherless" Nell dependent on her own resources, the story ends.

"My Last Duchess" may be read as another initiation story—initiation into literature, into the lessons it may teach for life, into mental independence. The story may also be understood as another contribution by Atwood to unearthing the "female tradition" (see Nischik 2007)—here concerning education (all of Nell's teachers seem to have been female), giving significant impulses for life. Miss Bessie, her devoted English teacher, has had a much larger impact than Bill on Nell, a future writer of literature herself, after all. As Nell sees it, the demanding Miss Bessie supports and trains and gives and then lets go, releasing her understanding pupil to write her own life script, in which her devoted English teacher plays a seminal part, as this story demonstrates.

CONCLUSION

Although the recent stories in *Moral Disorder*, which were first published between 1996 ("The Labrador Fiasco") and 2006, foreground gender issues to a lesser extent than the stories in Atwood's previous collections, two of them do explore, in a retrospective setup, the formation of gender in earlier stages of life, a topic partly introduced in some of her earlier stories (see above) but particularly pronounced in her two later short stories. The social constructedness of gender, the performance status of femininities and masculinities, thus become particularly clear in her recent short fiction.

It can thus be said that Atwood's treatment of gender relations and gender difference forms a constant thread running through her short-story works. It can be argued that, in the course of some four decades,[24] Atwood's treatment of gender issues in her short stories and short fictions (see chapter 2) has developed largely according to the various stages of "victim positions" Atwood differentiated early on in *Survival* (1972, 36–38): "*Position One: To deny the fact that you are a victim*" (e.g., Louise in "Polarities"); "*Position Two: To acknowledge the fact that you are a victim, but to explain this as an act of Fate, ... the dictates of Biology (in the case of women, for instance)*" (e.g., Christine in "Scarlet Ibis"); "*Position Three: To acknowledge the fact that you are a victim but to refuse to accept the assumption that the role is inevitable*" (e.g., Kat in "Hairball" seems to be close to it, but she eventually moves on to position four, a creative non-victim; an example of position three is Julie in "The Bog Man" from *Wilderness Tips*); and finally "*Position Four: To be a creative non-victim*" (e.g., Gertrude in "Gertrude Talks Back"; Nell in "My Last Duchess" comes close to this position due to the story's future-oriented ending). Especially in *Murder in the Dark* and *Good Bones*, Atwood's often inverse views on gender conceptions become even more incisive, perceptive, and demanding, though not without a light-hearted, humorous treatment of a complex issue. Atwood exposes with penetrating insight the often gender-linked conventions and psychological, linguistic, and mythological substructures embedded in daily reality. If, as she sees it, human beings tend to transform threatening and irrational elements of their environment into rationally comprehensible ones, then it is the task of the writer to counter this move toward the conventional.

Seen *in toto*, Atwood's treatment of gender relations in her short stories and short fictions may be read as "Instructions for the Third Eye," to take up the title of the resonant rounding-off text of *Murder in the Dark*. Atwood admonishes us, female and male readers, to transcend the dualistic thought pattern of either/or, which chains us to fixed identity positions and gender roles, and to be open to liberating, non-essentialist views of gender relations. In her recent short-story cycle *Moral Disorder*—although its protagonist in her younger years repeatedly feels subjected to gender clichés—an altogether non-essentialist view of gender relations seems to be achieved eventually, so much so that over larger parts of this collection gender is seldom foregrounded. In her short stories and short fictions, too (see the previous chapter), Margaret Atwood acts once again as a chronicler of our times, exposing and warning, disturbing and comforting, and challenging us to question conventions and face up to unarticulated truths. As Nell reflects at the end of "The Entities" in *Moral Disorder*, "All that anxiety and anger, those dubious good intentions, those tangled lives, that blood. I can tell about or I can bury it. In the end, we'll all become stories" (2006, 188).

NOTES

1. From *Two-Headed Poems* (1978), in *Eating Fire* (1998, 198–99). The main title of this chapter is also taken from this poem.
2. See, e.g., Rigney 1987, 108–13, where "A Travel Piece" (1975) from *Dancing Girls* is interpreted as a thematic preform of the novel *Bodily Harm* (1981); or see Grace and Weir 1983, which contains survey articles on Atwood's novels and poems but omits her short stories, as do VanSpanckeren and Castro 1988; Rao 1993; Staels 1995; Mycak 1996; and Cooke 2004.
3. See Nischik 1991b, 1993c, 1994, 1994a; diverse articles (by Meindl, Suarez, and Keith) in Nicholson 1994; Howells, Cooke, and York in York 1995; Manley and Arnold Davidson in Wilson, Friedman, and Hengen 1996; Roth 1998; Ljungberg 1999; Stein 1999; and Sturgess 2000/02.
4. Reviews appeared within days of the publication in September 2006 in the *New York Times* (20 September), the *Boston Globe* (20 September), the *London Free Press* (9 September), and the *Globe and Mail* (two reviews, 6 and 9 September).
5. See, e.g., Thompson 1981; and Sturgess 2000/02.
6. "Two-Headed Poems, xi" (1978), in *Eating Fire* (1998, 227).
7. "The Grave of the Famous Poet" (1972), in *Dancing Girls* (1977, 84).
8. "Under Glass" (1972), in *Dancing Girls* (1977, 76).
9. Laing continues: "Such a person is not able to experience himself 'together with' others or 'at home in' the world, but, on the contrary, he experiences himself in despairing aloneness and isolation; moreover, he does not

experience himself as a complete person but rather as 'split' in various ways, perhaps as a mind more or less tenuously linked to a body, as two or more selves and so on. ... [T]here is a comprehensible transition from the sane schizoid way of being-in-the-world to a psychotic way of being-in-the-world" (1965, 17).

10. See "Polarities" (1971) alongside the short stories "The War in the Bathroom" (1964), "Under Glass" (1972), and "A Travel Piece" (1975), all in *Dancing Girls*, as well as the novels *The Edible Woman* (1969), *Surfacing* (1972), and *Lady Oracle* (1976).

11. For a more detailed analysis of the polarities in the communication structure, and of Morrison's frequent indirect speech acts, see Nischik 1994c.

12. This tallies with the authentic comments of schizophrenics; see Laing 1965. In a more general context, see Grace on Atwood's attempts at synthesization in "Articulating the 'Space Between,'" in Grace and Weir 1983, 1–16.

13. "The cracked mind of the schizophrenic may *let in* light which does not enter the intact mind of many sane people whose minds are closed" (Laing 1965, 27).

14. See also the metaphors of conquest and destruction applied to Morrison in the context of his relationship with Louise: e.g., "a defeated formless creature on which he could inflict himself like a shovel on earth, axe on forest, use without being used" (62).

15. See, e.g., Mathews 1969.

16. See the classic statement on this in Atwood's short story "A Travel Piece" from *Dancing Girls*: "for those who are not responsible, for those who make the lives of others their transient spectacle and pleasure. She is a professional tourist, she works at being pleased and not participating; at sitting and watching" (152).

17. For a detailed interpretation of "Significant Moments in the Life of My Mother," see Nischik 2007.

18. Modality is a grammatical category that expresses the attitude of a speaker toward realization of the speech act expressed in his or her utterance. Modalities, then, would include possibility, certainty, necessity, obligation, hope, desire, intention, etc.

19. See also Davey 1986: "The juxtaposition of these kinds of narrative creates recurrently surreal effects. Many of the characters, particularly the women, live psychologically in the hidden story, while functioning physically in the official story. They dream and think in the language of symbols but they speak in cliché. They trivialize their inner lives in order to live a life of conventional fiction. Almost all of Atwood's couples remain

strangers to each other because of this failure to declare the hidden story" (12–13).

20. The one portrayed in "Hairball," in contrast, is among the most superficial in the entirety of Atwood's work and ends disastrously.

21. See, in this context, Atwood's well-known statement in the afterword to *The Journals of Susanna Moodie:* "We are all immigrants to this place even if we were born here: the country is too big for anyone to inhabit completely, and in the parts unknown to us we move in fear, exiles and invaders" (1970, 62).

22. "She takes a pill every day, for a chemical imbalance she was born with. That was it, all along. That was what made the bad times for her. Not my monstrousness at all. I believe that, most of the time" (48).

23. For two useful treatments of the Browning poem, referring also to the Duchess's covert opposition to the Duke, see Miller 1989; and Heffernan 1996.

24. Considering first separate publication of individual early stories.

4

"Nomenclatural Mutations"
The Development of Forms of Address and Reference for Female and Male Characters in Atwood's Novels

Names were not just labels, they were also containers.

MARGARET ATWOOD, *The Robber Bride*, 298

INTRODUCTION

Historically one of the first areas to be investigated by scholars interested in institutionalized gender differences was language. From the 1970s onward, North American, British, and German scholarship in particular revealed the extent to which the English and German languages tend toward systematic gender discrimination. Sexism in gender-inflected language based on gender oppositions mirrors social structures as well as individual consciousness concerning the roles of women and men: "Not to address someone under particular circumstances, not to address someone adequately, to overlook, to leave out, to forget her/him, represents an offense. If such acts are systematically oriented towards a particular target group, one speaks of discrimination. If the discriminating behaviour is systematically oriented towards women, one speaks of sexism" (Trömel-Plötz 1980, 193, here translated into English). Sexist and non-sexist language can thus be a linguistic signal pointing to the particular "mind style" of a person or fictional character. "The concept of mind style refers to that specific aspect of (unconscious or conscious) verbalization that—like style in general—is less concerned with aesthetic, functional, situational-contextual, generic, and similar determinants, but rather, more specifically, with attitudes, opinions, values, world views, psychological states, that is, mental (cognitive and emotional) 'sets' or states of the characters" (Nischik 1991b, 3, here translated into English). Roger Fowler introduced the term "mind style" into literary criticism:

> We may coin the term "mind-style" to refer to any distinctive linguistic presentation of an individual mental self. A mind-style may analyse a character's mental life more or less radically; may be concerned with relatively superficial or relatively fundamental aspects of the mind; may ... display preoccupations, prejudices, perspectives and values which strongly bias a character's world-view but of which s/he may be quite unaware. These different discourse structures call upon a variety of linguistic techniques for their expression. (1977, 103)

We may thus ask, in the present context, whether a character systematically avoids sexist language or reflects existing asymmetrical oppositions in the representation of gender. Does the fiction investigated display differences in language use influenced by the sex of the speaker?

One highly informative linguistic area concerning mind style and the relationship between the sexes is the form of address or reference chosen for women and men. Linguists have investigated language phenomena such as the "generic" use of nouns and personal pronouns as well as asymmetrical semantic polarities concerning the representation of gender.[1] The latter will be of particular relevance to an analysis of forms of address and reference in Margaret Atwood's novels since these formulas are often connected with the perpetuation of female stereotypes that work toward a mystification of the image of women. "Mystification" in this context goes back to Betty Friedan's book *The Feminine Mystique* (1963). This groundbreaking publication (which is often credited with launching feminism's second-wave movement) unmasks postwar conventions of femininity as a stifling myth assuming that women find ultimate bliss and fulfillment in the role of suburban homemaker and devoted mother ("the trapped American housewife" [21]). As a result of this image, or "mystique," Friedan finds a "schizophrenic split" ailing the women of her time: "a strange discrepancy between the reality of our lives as women and the image to which we were trying to conform" (7). Critics have distinguished several kinds of stereotypes working toward a mystification of the image of women, such as idealization, demonization, and trivialization.[2] *Trivialization* occurs when adult women are referred to as "girls," whereas men of the same age are referred to as "men." The asymmetrical semantic principle of *demonization* appears in dichotomies such as "playboy" versus "whore" ("bachelor," too, has far more positive connotations than "spinster"). An example of *idealization* in referring to women is the use of "ladies" in contexts where "men" is the equivalent; such allegedly deferential references often function as mere compensations ("ladies first," for instance, mainly applies in trivial contexts, such as who enters a room first), a fact that becomes clear in literary contexts as well.

Numerous asymmetrical semantic tendencies in referring to women and men appear in everyday language. Their analysis with respect to individual speakers is part of the investigation of mind style, since the argument that these linguistic phenomena belong to the language system—internalized by the individual speaker and thus without any characterization potential—no longer holds. There is sufficient awareness today of the imbalance implied in such usage that often discriminates against the so-called weaker sex. A systematic adherence to sexist language in literature tells us that the speaker is either oblivious of the implied discriminations (or does not want to be conscious of them) or intentionally conforms to them. Likewise, an obvious attempt to avoid sexism in language may mirror the willingness of the speaker to conceive of the relationship between the sexes on more equal terms.

In this chapter, I will show to what extent Atwood works with such tendencies in her novels and how she employs them for figural characterization and for the delineation, in miniature, of particular character relationships. Such a lexical analysis in the context of mind style, figural characterization, and character constellation is particularly rewarding concerning the genre of the novel (and that of drama): first due to the number of featured characters, which enables, for instance, the composition of illuminating contrastive character constellations, and second due to the textual lengths of novels, which may be a precondition for significant changes of lexical choice over represented time, going hand in hand with changes in mentality over time. This kind of linguistic approach will indeed prove highly telling in connection with Atwood's novels, nine of which I will subject to detailed scrutiny. My reading here according to the chosen critical methodology will in fact unearth important aspects and developments concerning the representation of gender not only *within* the novels but also— equally significant—*between* them, showing in a nutshell interesting evolutions of gender representation in Atwood's novels over some four decades.

THE EDIBLE WOMAN

Atwood's first novel, *The Edible Woman* (1969), was written in 1965, at a time when feminist thinking in social as well as literary contexts was about to emerge as a consistent movement (see chapter 1). As Atwood wrote in her foreword to an edition of the novel published in 1979, "I myself see the book as protofeminist rather than feminist: there was no women's movement in sight when I was composing the book in 1965, and I'm not gifted with clairvoyance, though like many at the time I'd read Betty Friedan and Simone de Beauvoir behind locked doors" (8). In *The Edible Woman*, Atwood critically uses asymmetrical forms of address, mirroring those social conventions that were to be analyzed by linguists in the years to come. The protagonist Marian MacAlpin, in her mid-twenties, is usually addressed by her first name by her friends. Her stuffy landlady ("the lady down below") chooses the conventional form of address for unmarried women: "'Good morning, Miss MacAlpin,' she said. ... 'I do wish you would tell Miss Tewce [Ainsley] to try not to make so much smoke in future'" (12). For her bosses, too, Marian is "Miss MacAlpin" (a crude case of asymmetrical semantic polarity when compared with "Mr."). The non-sexist alternative "Ms." does not crop up in the novel; in better-known usage today, the form was not yet in use in the 1960s.

Compare in this context, however, the following dialogue from *Lady Oracle* (1976), Atwood's third novel, in which the author plays with the varieties of address and reference to women that were available in the 1970s, only one decade later. In this transitional period of usage, the male character in this passage, an interviewer, has considerable problems grappling with the options available. The protagonist, Joan Foster, for her part, seems to be just as undecided on this point as the interviewer, whose volubility betrays his underlying insecurity:

> The interviewer was a man, a young man, very intense. ...
> "Welcome to *Afternoon Hot Spot.* Today we have with us Joan Foster, author, I guess that's author*ess,* of the runaway bestseller *Lady Oracle.* Tell me, Mrs. Foster—or do you prefer to be called *Ms.* Foster?"
> I was taking a drink of water, and I set it down so quickly I spilled it. ... "Whichever you like," I said.
> "Oh, then you're not in Women's Lib."
> "Well, no," I said. "I mean, I agree with some of their ideas, but ..."
> "Mrs. Foster, would you say you are a happily married woman?" ...
> "Well," said the interviewer. "Thank you very much for being with us this afternoon. That was the lovely Joan Foster, or should I say Mrs. Foster—oh, she'll get me for that one!—*Ms.* Joan Foster, authoress of *Lady Oracle.*" (264–65)

The Edible Woman is not yet haunted by "Ms." and "authoress," but Atwood's awareness of the basic problems involved in such forms of address and reference is unmistakable also in this early text. At the beginning of the novel, we are presented with a social panorama of Toronto in the 1960s as Marian conducts interviews for Seymour Surveys, the firm for which she works. Atwood records interviews with three men in which they choose forms of address for Marian that match their overall behaviour toward her and probably display their stance toward women in general:

> When we finished and I ... got up, and began to thank him, I saw him lurching out of his chair towards me with a beery leer. "Now what's a *nice little girl* like you doing walking around asking men all about their beer?" he said moistly. "You ought to be at home with some *big strong man* to take care of you." (47; emphasis added)

Asymmetrical semantic polarities are juxtaposed in a clichéd and self-serving manner in the discourse of this male character: a "nice little girl" would better suit his purposes than a "big strong woman." The priest, too, who grasps the opportunity for a paternalistic lecture, makes use of the trivializing "girl": "'I'm not going to chastise you personally because I can see you are a nice girl and only the innocent means to this abominable end'" (46).

Another major character in the novel, narcissistic Duncan, uses only one form of reference during his first meeting with Marian on the occasion of the beer interview, and it is also clichéd and trivializing. He reduces Marian to a single attribute suggesting child-like femininity, a trait, ironically, she does not even possess: "'Fish,' he said ... , 'this is Goldilocks.' I smiled rigidly. I am not a blonde" (55).

Marian's fiancé, Peter, for his part, sometimes addresses his twenty-five-year-old bride-to-be as "girl." (It goes without saying that Marian does not in turn address him as "boy.") Once they have decided to get married, Peter explains his plans in the following manner: "'It'll be a lot better in the long run for my practice too, the clients like to know you've got a wife.' ... 'I know I can always depend on you. Most *women* are pretty scatterbrained but you're such a sensible *girl*'" (91; emphasis added). This statement is paradoxical in more than one way: Peter suggests that he is getting married to a "girl," not a woman. "Women," in turn, are characterized as "scatterbrained," whereas Marian is classified as a "sensible girl," but then it is Marian, after all, who is in fact repeatedly acting in a "scatterbrained" manner, as one would expect from young "girls." Peter's wavering, illogical argumentation betrays his insincerity concerning Marian: He wants to get married to her for professional reasons—relating to social status—rather than for love.

The extent to which such patronizing forms of expression tend to reflect specific attitudes and forms of behaviour toward women becomes clear in the following quotation. Peter behaves like a master, and Marian's overt reaction is to comply, but in fact she resents his arrogant demeanour:

> "I could use another drink," Peter said; it was his way of asking her to get him one. The ashtray was removed from her back. She turned over and sat up, pulling the top sheet off the bed and

wrapping it around her. "And while you're up, flip over the record, that's a good girl."

Marian turned the record, feeling naked in the open expanse of the living room in spite of the sheet and the venetian blinds; then she went into the kitchen and measured out Peter's drink. (212–13)

Like "a good girl," she gives in to his paternalistic demands, while his sexist behaviour (e.g., using her naked body as a "table" for his ashtray) has its correlative in her own immature behavioural pattern of seeking approval and acting to please.

As the novel opens, Marian and Peter have been lovers for some time, so it is striking that in the first third of the novel, until their decision to get married, they address each other exclusively by their first names. There is not a single nickname or term of endearment in their communication with each other. To be sure, Marian addresses Peter once—on account of his reckless and inconsiderate behaviour in the car—with the somewhat aggressive phrase "'You maniac!'" (82) and briefly afterward with "'You big silly idiot'" (92). Yet the extreme underlexicalization[3] of positive and emotional forms of address between the alleged lovers is a linguistic indicator of the distance, the emotional chill, between them, against which Marian, in the course of the plot, increasingly reacts.

Even more indicative of the quality of their relationship is the fact that Peter's forms of address for Marian change drastically after their decision to get married. The husband-to-be suddenly addresses her exclusively as "darling" or, less often, as "honey." He uses his formerly preferred address, "Marian," only once more until the cake scene toward the end of the novel, an event that seals their separation. It is obviously the formal decision to get married, and not a deep emotional commitment to Marian, that prompts Peter to suddenly use terms of endearment. Neither his feelings nor his imagination seems to play a role. Indeed, he seems to be fulfilling a norm ("darling" and "honey" are highly conventional, of course), talking as he thinks a lover, soon to be married, ought to talk. As Marian says of her fiancé, "He was ordinariness raised to perfection" (62).

This conclusion is supported by a contextual investigation of Peter's use of "honey" and "darling." Peter often applies them in verbal contexts that in fact negate their connotations, that is, in situations where he runs roughshod over Marian's interests and only considers his own. These terms thus compensate for his lack of emotion and regard (to say nothing of love) for Marian:

> Peter's voice was terse. "Hi honey how are you? Listen, I really can't make it tonight."
> ... "Tomorrow then?"
> "Look darling," he said, "I really don't know. It'll really all depend, you know how these things are, I'll let you know, okay?" (116)

A similar discrepancy between lexical meaning and pragmatic use applies to those speech acts in which Peter comments on Marian in a paternalistic manner: "'Darling, you don't understand these things,' Peter said. ... 'But I've seen the results, the courts are full of them, juvenile delinquents'" (151). Terms of endearment are used deviously here, allowing Peter to dominate Marian's behaviour[4] to the point where patterns of communication between the couple are, in fact, reminiscent of a father-daughter relationship. Peter eventually uses "darling" so often and indiscriminately that it becomes an empty term (easily dropped, as becomes clear toward the end of the novel): "'Take your coat into the bedroom, darling,' he said, 'and then come on out to the kitchen and help me get things ready. ... Darling, you look absolutely marvellous'" (234–35).

Marian's forms of address for Peter as well as other people are quite different. Marian addresses her friends, with whom she has a relatively unproblematic relationship, simply by their first names (Ainsley, Len, Clara, even—less often—Duncan, who in turn repeatedly calls her "girl"). Strikingly, however, Marian hardly ever addresses her boyfriend Peter (in the whole novel only seven times) and almost never through terms of endearment—a fact clearly indicative of the problematic, asymmetrical relationship between the two. An address represents a relatively direct approach to communication by the interlocutor, yet Marian's increasing insecurity with Peter complicates such a direct approach; in fact, her behaviour around him hardly reflects her authentic personality any longer:

"When do you want to get married?" he asks, almost gruffly.

My first impulse was to answer, with the evasive flippancy I'd always used before when he'd asked me serious questions about myself, "What about Groundhog Day?" But instead I heard a soft flannelly voice I barely recognized, saying, "I'd rather have you decide that. I'd rather leave the big decisions up to you." I was astounded at myself. I'd never said anything remotely like that to him before. The funny thing was I really meant it. (92)

Peter's increasingly egocentric demeanour seems to be sanctioned by Marian's dependence on his decisions and opinions. Unsure of herself, self-estranged, even self-effaced, Marian can hardly bring herself to confront her landlady ("I suppose ... [I have] what they call a mental block about it" [11]), let alone Peter.

Only twice does Marian take over Peter's standard form of address, "darling," during their engagement phase. In the first example, she merely echoes Peter: "'Darling, where are you?' Peter called from the kitchen. 'Coming, darling,' she called back" (236). In the second example, Marian, proving herself to be a docile pupil, uses the verbal form of endearment as a type of appeasement, as Peter habitually does. She is afraid that he might be annoyed because she has, at the last minute, invited her somewhat peculiar friends Duncan, Ainsley, and the "office virgins" to their first party: "'Darling,' she said in a casual tone when they had reached the fifth floor ... , 'something came up and I've invited a few more people. I hope you don't mind.' All the way in the car she had been pondering how she would tell him" (232).

Apart from her outbursts "'You maniac!'" and "'You big silly idiot'" (in a context where Peter endangers her physically rather than psycho-logically), Marian directly addresses him only by his first name. In all four cases, the situation is similar. Either she longs for attention, or her address signals a need to get through to Peter and not be put off, as she often is, by his immature behaviour: "'*Peter*, why can't you be *serious*? You're just an overgrown adolescent'" (83). In the other examples, Marian, for a change, considers her own desires and interests. Significantly this occurs toward the end of the novel and at crucial points in the development of the couple's relationship: "'Too bad we don't have time to hop into bed,' he said, 'but I wouldn't want to get you all mussed up.' ... 'Peter,' she said, 'do you love me?'" (237). Shortly afterward, when Marian feels increasingly cornered by her fiancé's way of "hunting" her with the camera, she stutters: "'Peter, ... I don't think ...'" (237). She is not yet in a position to verbalize her opposition to his behaviour toward her. By the end of the novel, she is able to say politely, yet with determination, "'Please, Peter, ... I just hate talking about things like that over the phone'" (274). Shortly before Marian presents her fiancé with an "edible woman" as a symbolic substitute for herself—and thus ends their relationship—she says purposefully, "'Peter, why don't you go into the living room and sit down? I have a surprise for you'" (278). In contrast to earlier dialogues in which Marian seems to be insecure and dependent, she now behaves in a self-possessed, determined manner.

Her self-confidence toward the end of the novel is all the more striking since Marian does not address Peter at all throughout large parts of the novel. His verbal behaviour, in contrast, develops precisely in the opposite direction. In the latter part of the novel, after Marian has fled their party, Peter is annoyed and stops addressing her as "darling" and "honey" just as suddenly as he took up these forms of address in the first place. While Marian, now more at ease with him (and herself), uses his first name, he addresses her only once more, again as "Marian." The insincere "darlings" and "honeys" are dropped: the slightest deviation from conventional patterns of behaviour on her part completely does away with his conventionalized forms of address for her.

The analysis of the forms of address used by Marian and Peter reveals a good deal, then, about the quality and development of their relationship, their attitudes toward each other, and how they conceive of their roles in this relationship. The variation in forms of address throughout the novel is systematic to an extent, so it offers an important key to our understanding of the relationship that is central to the novel.[5]

This relationship seems to be highly conventional and at first glance not really detrimental to Marian. Indeed, Peter's sexism is "nicely packaged" (as Ainsley characterizes Peter [150]) from a linguistic point of view. For the most part, Peter uses neutral or even positively connoted forms of address and almost never loses control of himself. Taken out of context, his terminology in fact seems to characterize him as a "loving" ("darling") and "caring" man, though always bordering on the paternalistic ("'you really can't hold your liquor, can you darling,'" [251]). The inconsistent and often derogatory use of these words becomes clear only when seen against their context: his sexism is not obvious; it works indirectly, covertly. Marian is given hardly any direct opportunities to criticize Peter, who on the surface behaves in a socially conformist way. Yet the contradictory nature of his verbal and non-verbal behaviour toward her contributes significantly to the deterioration of her psychological condition (for which Marian herself, with her victim mentality and attitudes, is also responsible, of course).

SURFACING

Atwood's second novel, *Surfacing* (1972), was written at a time when the "second wave" of the Women's Movement had just about come into existence, at least in North America. In *Surfacing*, in contrast to *The Edible Woman*, patterns of sexist behaviour are presented more drastically, especially in the character of David.

David, Anna's husband, humiliates women whenever he can and does not even bother to conceal this behaviour in socially sanctioned ways. He views women almost exclusively in terms of their sexuality and repeatedly attempts to establish sexual contact with them. This attitude is mirrored in the forms of address and reference he uses. A relatively mild example of sexism is his use of generically polite forms of address, such as "lady," in an abusive manner and/or context: "'Hey, lady, wanna buy a dirty book?'" (32). Seen from a pragmatic point of view, that is, considering how such supposedly idealizing forms of address appear in context, their compensatory function and their artificiality become clear. In the following passages, the semantic asymmetry ("lady" versus "man") and the implied sexism degrading women are clearly exposed: "'Hey, lady,' he said, 'I see your woodpile's gettin' low. You could use a handyman'" (93). And "Behind me someone came into the room, it was David. 'Hey lady,' he said, 'what're you doing in my bed? You a customer or something?'" (110). His lewd reactions stigmatize women either as deficient, if they do not have "a man," or as prostitutes. In view of its combination with "lady" in the same utterance, the last sentence is thus a classic literary example of the "Madonna/Whore syndrome" described by Mary Ritchie Key (1975, 57). David's remark is all the more impertinent as the communication takes place in the cabin of the protagonist's father, in which David is the guest (thus, the protagonist is not really lying on his bed at all). Yet because of his use of the interrogative form, a semantically "polite" form of address, it is difficult for the protagonist to react immediately to the impudent implications of the utterance. As a result, she reacts at this point in a highly defensive manner, again letting David get away with it: "'Sorry,' I said" (110).

The barely veiled sexism in David's use of "lady" becomes evident in the episode in which David forces Anna, at first verbally then also physically, to undress in front of the protagonist and her boyfriend Joe for a take in their amateur film:

"Come on, take it off," David said; his light-humor voice.

"I wasn't bothering you." Anna was muted, avoiding.

"It won't hurt you, we need a naked *lady*." ...

"Oh for Christ's sake," Anna said. She picked up her murder mystery again and pretended to read.

"Come on, we need a naked *lady* with big tits and a big ass," David said in the same tender voice; I recognized that menacing gentleness, at school it always went before the trick, the punchline. ...

"It's token resistance," David said, "she wants to, she's an exhibitionist at heart. She likes her lush body, don't you? Even if she is getting too fat." " ... You're trying to humiliate me."

"What's humiliating about your body, *darling*?" David said caressingly. "We all love it, you ashamed of it? That's pretty stingy of you, you should share the wealth; not that you don't." Anna was furious now, goaded, her voice rose. "Fuck off, you want bloody everything, don't you, you can't use that stuff on me."

"Why not," David said evenly, "it works. Now just take it off like a *good girl* or I'll have to take it off for you. ... Okay, *twatface*," he said, "is it off or into the lake?" ...

"Bottoms too," David said *as though to a recalcitrant child*. Anna glanced at him, contemptuous, and bent. "Look sexy now, move it; give us a little dance." ...

"Get that?" David said mildly over his shoulder.

"Some of it," Joe said. "Maybe you could order her to do it again." ...

I could hear Anna splashing and then stumbling below on the sand point; she was really crying now, her indrawn breaths rasping. (158–61; emphasis added)

The supposedly idealizing forms of address and reference stand in stark contrast to David's degrading remarks and callous behaviour calculated to humiliate his wife. In the quoted passage, David also makes use of the principle of trivialization ("like a good girl"; "David said as though to a recalcitrant child"). Trivialization also occurs in several other passages of the novel:

"Good girl," he [David] said, "your heart's in the right place. And the rest of her too," he said to Joe, "I like it round and firm and fully packed. Anna, you're eating too much." (117)

He [David] opens his packsack and gropes around inside, and Anna says "What a dumb place to put them [joints], it's the first place they'd look."

"Up your ass," David says, smiling at her, "that's where they'd look first, they grab a good thing when they see one. Don't worry, baby, I know what I'm doing." (45)

David refuses Anna's justified criticism of his impudent behaviour in a paternalistic, dismissive manner by his repeated reduction of Anna to a sexual object or to a child who cannot possibly give a grown man advice.

In the scene in which David tries to conquer the protagonist sexually, his forms of address reveal the will to trivialize and demonize, combined with his suggestion that to a dominant man a woman is constantly available for sex. He behaves as rudely as in the film-shooting scene, even calling his wife "that cunt on four legs" (177). His reduction of Anna to her sexual organ and the animalistic implications of his statement represent the lowest point of his sexist behaviour in the novel. When the protagonist is entrapped and refuses his sexual advances in an apparently cool and self-possessed manner ("There must be a phrase, a vocabulary that would work. 'I'm sorry,' I said, 'but you don't turn me on,'" [178]), for once she makes (mild) use of his own weapons by negating the sexual attraction David thinks he radiates. He immediately loses his self-control. Deeply hurt and unsettled in his supposedly virile self-dramatization, he viciously "demonizes" the protagonist, again in highly degrading, animalistic, and sexual metaphors: "'You,' he said, searching for words, not controlled any more, 'tight-ass bitch'" (178).

In *Surfacing*, then, David uses forms of address for women in a manner that corresponds to the three strategies of communication of sexist reference to women differentiated above (trivialization, demonization, idealization), forms indicative of his sexist, dismissive attitude toward women in general. David is Atwood's most overtly sexist character, and he is presented almost as if to illustrate the sexist tendencies in communication with and about women that were analyzed and criticized by linguists in the 1970s and 1980s, that is, largely *after* Atwood conceived of *Surfacing*.

CAT'S EYE

Atwood's fifth novel, *Cat's Eye* (1988), shows a further development in her writing, not least with respect to the use of forms of address and reference to women. *Cat's Eye* is concerned with the communication *between women* rather than that between women and men. Women are less prone in general to place and/or evaluate their interlocutors in spoken discourse than men have been. And indeed forms of address that characterize the speaker's evaluation of and attitude toward her or his interlocutor feature far less frequently in this novel (and, when they do, are mainly used, significantly, by male characters). Then, too, when symptomatic forms of address for women are used, they are more or less explicitly commented on in the novel itself (by the narrator and the characters), demonstrating a higher awareness of the problem in this novel of the late 1980s than was the case in the 1960s and 1970s. One might describe this phenomenon as a shift from illustration to analysis. Last but not least, *Cat's Eye* conveys a strong consciousness of the general significance of names and naming[6] as well as of forms of address for the individual and her or his communication with others.

Although earlier Atwood novels also tackle the issue,[7] it is particularly foregrounded in *Cat's Eye*:

> I also have two daughters, by now grown up. Their names are Sarah and Anne, good sensible names. ... I am a believer ... in sensible names for children, because look what happened to Cordelia. (15)
> Cordelia's two older sisters are Perdita and Miranda, but nobody calls them that. They're called Perdie and Mirrie. ... (76)
> Cordelia ought to be Cordie, but she's not. She insists, always, on being called by her full name: Cordelia. ... "It was Mummie's idea," she says.
> All three of them call their mother Mummie. (77)

The use of idealization, trivialization, and demonization in referring to women also appears in *Cat's Eye*, if less frequently than in Atwood's earlier novels. Elaine Risley and other female characters in *Cat's Eye* are far more conscious of the implications of such strategies of communication than are Marian and other earlier characters. (The protagonist of *Cat's Eye* is in her forties, whereas the female protagonists of *The Edible Woman* and *Surfacing* are in their twenties.) In contrast to *The Edible Woman, Surfacing,* and *Lady Oracle*, men barely get away unscathed in this novel when they openly depreciate women:

> One newspaper sends a photographer, in advance, who says, jokingly, "Come on, *girls*, burn a few bras for me," while he is taking our pictures.
> "Pig," says Carolyn in a low voice.
> "Cool it," says Jody. "They love it when you freak." (370; emphasis added)

Whereas criticism in this instance is obvious, it works by mere implication in the following examples, which again demonstrate a systematic use of semantic irregularities in referring to women and men:

> "Mr. Banerji, *sir*," he [my father] says. He always calls his students *Mr.* and *Miss.* ... (137; emphasis added)

"A little off the sternum, *sir*?" my father asks him, and
Mr. Banerji brightens at the word. (138; emphasis added)

Beautiful Mr. Banerji from India is with him [my father]. He
smiles nervously at me and says, "How are you, *Miss*?" He always
calls me *miss*. (181; emphasis added)

When the *boys* come to pick me up, my father ... assesses them
with his shrewd, twinkly, ironic little eyes and calls them "*sir*," as
if they're his graduate students. (255–56; emphasis added)

It must be a strange world, indeed, from the perspective of the female
protagonist, for while the East Indian man, male graduate students,
and Elaine's boyfriends are aggrandized in her father's discourse by
being addressed as "sir," Elaine is deflatingly addressed as "miss." But
in contrast to Marian in *The Edible Woman*, Elaine is fully aware of the
gender discrimination involved in such discrepancies and resents it.

Another sequence that shows the enhanced consciousness and
explicitness of the novel about the significance of forms of reference
pertains to women in a professional context:

Marjorie and Babs go home. They have husbands, and are not
taken seriously. The *boys* call them "*lady* painters."

"If they're *lady* painters, what does that make me?" I say.

"A *girl* painter," Jon says, joking.

Colin, who has manners of a sort, explains: "If you're bad,
you're a *lady* painter. Otherwise you're just a painter." They don't
say "artist." (297; emphasis added)

In *Cat's Eye*, such instances of prejudice against women tend to be
commented on not only in dialogue form, as shown above, but also and
fairly extensively by the perceptive female protagonist and first-person
narrator. That is, illustration of sexist attitudes is followed by analysis
and/or criticism:

In any case they are *boys*, not *men*. Their pink cheeks and group
sniggering, their good-*girl* and bad-*girl* categories, their avid,
fumbling attempts to push back the frontiers of garter belt and
brassiere no longer hold my attention. ...

When they've had several beers they might talk about women. They refer to their girlfriends, some of whom live with them; these are called "my *old lady*." Or they make jokes about the models in Life Drawing, who change from night to night. They speak of going to bed with them, as if this depends only on their inclination or lack of it. There are two possible attitudes to this: lip smacking [idealization or, rather, trivialization—men smack their lips as a sign of lust, often for easy women] or nauseated revulsion [demonization]. "A *cow*," they say. "A *bag*." "What a *discard*." (279, 298; emphasis added)

Other instances of demonization of women are commented on and analyzed by the narrator in a more explicit manner:

I know things about *boys*. ... I know what kind of talk goes on among them as they horse around. ... *Stunned broad, dog, bag* and *bitch* [emphasis in original] are words they apply to *girls*, as well as worse words. I don't hold these words against them. I know these words are another version of pickled ox eyes and snot-eating, they're prove-it words *boys* need to exchange, to show they are strong and not to be taken in. (254–55; emphasis added)

I don't think any of these words apply to me. They apply to other girls, girls who walk along the high school halls in ignorance of them, swinging their hair, swaying their little hips as if they think they're seductive, talking too loudly and carelessly to one another, fooling nobody; or else acting pastel, blank, daisy-fresh. And all the time these clouds of silent words surround them, *stunned broad, dog, bag* and *bitch* [emphasis in original], pointing at them, reducing them, cutting them down to size so they can be handled. (255)

Just as analytical and perceptive is the narrator's following comment on an instance of idealization of women and the varied uses of the term "lady":

When I get up even, I see that this person is a woman. She's lying on her back, staring straight at me. "Lady," she says. "Lady. Lady."

That word has been through a lot. Noble lady, Dark Lady, she's a real lady, old-lady lace, Listen lady, Hey lady watch where you're going, Ladies' Room, run through with lipstick and replaced with Women. But still the final word of appeal. If you want something very badly you do not say *Woman, Woman*, you say *Lady, Lady*. As she is saying now. (162)

"Here," I say. I fumble in my purse, find a ten, crumple it into her hand, paying her off. ... "God bless you lady, Our Lady bless you." (163)

THE ROBBER BRIDE

In Atwood's eighth novel, *The Robber Bride* (1993), hardly any explicit, evaluative forms of address for women (or for men) are used. The largest part of dialogue scenes takes place between two or more of the four female protagonists—Roz, Tony, Charis, and Zenia—and most of the time these women address each other neutrally by their first names. The only exception is Roz, who uses the term of endearment "sweetie" repeatedly and rather indiscriminately for Charis and Tony, her girlfriends, and for Mitch and Larry, her husband and her son. It is striking that, whereas this term of endearment is used by Roz in a generally positive, supportive manner for her girlfriends, in one of the few instances when she uses "sweetie" and "honey" for her beloved husband she does so in a wary, distanced, and compensatory manner (she is alert and suspicious because for once Mitch wants to take her out for lunch, not one of his lovers; see 293, 300 versus 301, 302).

Other, rather conniving, terms of endearment are used by women for other women in *The Robber Bride*. When Tony's mother leaves her husband and little daughter for another man, she writes her daughter a misleading note: "Darling, you know I would like to take you with me but I can't right now. ... Your Mother who loves you very much" (150). As in *Cat's Eye*, an analytical comment on the inauthentic use of "darling" follows: "Tony kept this note, and marvelled over it later, when she was grown up. As an explanation it was of course inadequate. Also, nothing in it was true. To begin with, Tony was not *darling*. The only people who were *darling*, for Anthea [Tony's mother], were men, and sometimes women if she was annoyed with them" (150). Another deceitful, compensatory sense of "darling" is used by Zenia after she has come between Tony and her beloved husband, West, so that West eventually leaves Tony for Zenia; when Zenia in turn runs away from the desperate West, she writes him this note: "*My darling, I am not worthy of you. ... I will love you till I die. Your loving Zenia*" (175). And when she has the nerve to show up again, after many years, she addresses Tony innocently as "Tony darling" (181) before snatching West away from her a second time. The deceptive use of terms of endearment, which is integrated in a more subtle and more extensive manner in *The Edible Woman*, thus reappears sporadically in Atwood's later novel. In *The Robber Bride*, however, such devious "misuse" of language is predominantly voiced by female characters.

Only a slight residue of the derogatory forms of address for women found in earlier Atwood novels can be detected in this later work. Again, as in *Cat's Eye*, comments on such uses follow in the novel itself:

> "Listen *lady*, you want a hot dog or not?" says the vendor.
>
> "What?" says Charis, startled.
>
> "*Crazy broad*, shove off," says the vendor. (198; emphasis added)
>
> As she's trying to decide what to do next, a bicycle courier starts swearing at her for no reason at all. *Jesus lady, watch the fuck out!* ... Although she's not sure why, she minds being called *lady* even more than she minds being called *crazy broad*. Why is this word so offensive to her? (199)

Since there are only a few instances of such subtly but effectively discriminatory terminology in *The Robber Bride*, one is tempted to refer the question to the reader of earlier Atwood novels who knows that "lady" is often used by (male) speakers as a compensatory semantic element in an offensive pragmatic context (see also "On the whole she fares better with the men, if they can work their way past the awkward preliminaries; if they can avoid calling her 'little lady'" [22]).

Two further developments can be observed in *The Robber Bride* concerning the use of forms of address and reference for both women and men. For one thing, female characters tend to follow suit and call young men "boys," just as young women have often been called "girls" (e.g., "Bernice called them 'boys'" [213]; "She has to make a conscious effort to stop herself from calling her students 'my boys,'" [23]). Imbalanced systems of address thus appear in this novel as an aspect of power structures that in effect over-rule gender relationships—at least to a certain extent—in contrast to the apparent co-extensiveness of power and gender in earlier novels. Thus, the top manager Roz greets her employees, female and male, by their first names, whereas she herself is addressed by her employees as Ms. Andrews. (Yet gender differences remain: "It's complicated, being a woman boss. Women don't look at you and think *Boss*. They look at you and think *Woman*, as in *Just another one, like me, and where does she get off?*" [88]).

The central form of power displayed in *The Robber Bride*, however, is the attraction that beautiful, clever, mysterious Zenia exerts over men and women alike, winning the admiration and trust of her girlfriends and then robbing them of their male partners. Since Zenia accomplishes this in a deviously indirect and obscure manner, power structures are not made obvious in her communication. For the most part, they tend to appear subtextually. Thus, she remains the only one who occasionally calls Tony "Antonia," the name by which Tony's difficult, indeed traumatizing, mother called her. Then, too, Zenia repeatedly calls Charis, against her will, by her former name Karen, a name that Charis, a victim of child abuse, has consistently avoided since her "nomenclatural mutation"[8]—that is, her (futile) attempt to overcome her deeply rooted despair through a new identity, a new name. Addressing her girlfriends by their former first names, Zenia confronts them with their traumatic pasts, forcefully opening the entrances to their troubled existences.

In the brief but revealing scenes in which Zenia discloses a few bits and pieces of the "Zenia mystery," she eventually calls her girlfriends nasty names to their faces. Even then her heavily betrayed but still fascinated, non-aggressive female friends do not follow suit. It is only in their imaginations that the betrayed Roz and Charis dare to address Zenia drastically as "bitch" (78, 86).

Hence, in *The Robber Bride*, where most of the communication that is represented takes place among women, most of the forms of address are neutral: symmetrical as to gender representation, non-evaluative, not particularly denigrating. If terms of endearment are used at all, they are used either in a sincere manner for men and women or in a compensatory, inauthentic manner by women mainly for other women, who now come up (or down) to what only male characters do in earlier Atwood works. There are a few signs of a more balanced system of gendered reference (see "boys") and of forms of address being geared to power irrespective of gender. Nevertheless, even the powerful female characters in this novel communicate differently—largely on equal terms, in a neutral, non-evaluative manner, with both gender groups—compared with the earlier male characters in Atwood's novels. But then, too, the male characters in *The Robber Bride* have given up denigrating women through particular forms of address (there are a few such instances left outside the circle of the main characters). In this novel, it is, after all, no longer the male characters who control and define social relationships but a female character who acts and to whom everyone reacts, largely in the ways she intends them to. This gradual shift in gender roles over the course of Atwood's oeuvre is mirrored in the systems of address used in the novels: from categorizing (trivializing, idealizing, or demonizing) women in the earlier novels to neutral, non-evaluative terms (denigrating or aggrandizing neither women nor men if, in the case of Zenia, often used cunningly and deviously so) in *The Robber Bride*.

THE LATER NOVELS: *ALIAS GRACE, THE BLIND ASSASSIN, ORYX AND CRAKE, THE PENELOPIAD*

As I have shown, Atwood's novels from her early and middle creative periods up to *The Robber Bride* are predominantly set in the present time (with the exception of her first dystopian novel, *The Handmaid's Tale* [1985]; see chapter 5) and largely show a development from gender asymmetrical, at times highly evaluative, gendered forms of address and reference to more gender symmetrical, non-denigrating ones. This kind of development is not kept up, however, in her more recent novels from *Alias Grace* onward. Most novels of Atwood's later creative period are exclusively or mainly set in the past—encompassing events that span the twentieth century in *The Blind Assassin* (2000), probing the nineteenth century in *Alias Grace* (1996), and moving even further back, to antiquity, in the case of her rewriting of the Odysseus-Penelope myth in *The Penelopiad* (2005). In contrast, her second dystopian novel, *Oryx and Crake* (2003), is set in the near future of the twenty-first century. Accordingly, with her general pronounced awareness of the relevance of forms of address for the structuring of communication and human relationships, Atwood carefully adapts these linguistic choices to the historical contexts established in her novels.

Alias Grace is her fictional treatment of the historical double murder of Thomas Kinnear and his mistress Nancy Montgomery in the 1840s, for which the beautiful Grace Marks is found guilty along with James McDermott. The latter is hanged, and Grace spends some thirty years in prison and in an insane asylum before eventually being released for lack of clear evidence of her involvement. Considering the setting of the events around the middle of the nineteenth century, there are no particular surprises about the handling of forms of address in this novel. The social norms of the time and the differences between the social classes and the sexes are mirrored in the forms of address. Grace, a former servant, is usually addressed by her first name, both by characters belonging to similar social strata, such as Mary Whitney and Nancy Montgomery, and by characters socially above her, such as Dr. Jordan, MacKenzie, and Kinnear. Grace, in turn, only addresses characters of her own standing by their first names, such as Mary Whitney and James McDermott. She approaches her superiors mostly with "Sir" or "Ma'am." A substantial part of the book, especially toward the end, is made up of exchanges of letters—a format in which the chosen forms of address are even more prone to conform to social norms.

As for gender differences, it is, again, mainly female characters who find themselves in an inferior position simply due to their sex. The cases where men are discriminated against on these grounds are few and far between and relatively harmless. As Grace, for instance, says of men in general,

> Men such as him [Dr. Jordan] do not have to clean up the messes
> they make, but we have to clean up our own messes, and theirs into
> the bargain. In that way they are like children, they do not have
> to think ahead, or worry about the consequences of what they do.
> But it is not their fault, it is only how they are brought up. (214)

Women, in contrast, have to face harsh denigrations, usually of a sexual kind. They are readily referred to as "whores" or "sluts" (see, e.g., McDermott about Nancy [255]); the prison keepers even claim that "Women should be born without mouths on them, the only thing of use in them is below the waist" (240). When Nancy and Grace quarrel about their common crush on Kinnear, Grace sticks to her usual form of address "Ma'am" for Nancy, yet Nancy calls Grace a "common slut" (275). Quite illogically so, McDermott, in love with Grace, calls her a "slut" even when she refuses to have sex with him (331). Since he cannot fulfill his physical desires with her, he keeps on demonizing her by calling her "hot bitch" (335), "damned slut," and, literally, "a demon" (336). The apparent commonness of reducing women to their bodies, supposedly always sexually available to any man, is stressed by the fact that even Grace's father dismisses his daughter as an "ungrateful slut" (127) and "a slut and a whore" (129). Their common denigration is also shown to have infiltrated the female characters' own minds in the book: Grace herself, when under hypnosis, calls Miss Lydia a "little slut" (400), and in one of her nightmares she dreams of a man (perhaps McDermott) calling her "you dirty little girl" (297), thereby combining trivialization with demonization of women.[9] Indeed, at the same time as McDermott uses demonizing terms, he also uses trivializing forms of reference for Grace when she refuses to have sex with him, such as "my girl" (331) and "a good girl after all" (335).[10] The asymmetrical social conventions concerning husband and wife at the time are mirrored in the book when Grace calls Jamie Walsh by his first name before their marriage but "Mr. Walsh" afterward, whereas Jamie before and after marriage calls Grace by her first name.

Women's status in the middle of the nineteenth century, the novel underlines, was secondary, if not inferior, restrictive, essentialized, and thereby precarious. In their frequent reduction to their bodies, women tended to be seen as representatives of their sex rather than as individuals. As Grace states about the ruling interchangeability of women at the beginning of the novel, "It is not always the same wife, as they change them around according to the politics" (21). Although Atwood presents Grace as an individualized, cunning trickster figure, highly talented in her knack for telling stories (by which she eventually secures her release from prison), the social context Atwood draws in *Alias Grace* is a men's world, where chances, opportunities, and reputations are unequally distributed according to gender (and class). Even Grace's defence counsel in court regards Grace, unhelpfully and misleadingly, as an "idiot" (23).

Finally, there are several passages in the book where intelligent characters show their acute sense of the social and communicative significance of the chosen form of address. When Grace applies for a new position, for instance, she points out that "I remembered to say Ma'am" (128). The ambivalent relationship between Nancy and Grace becomes apparent when Grace comments on the phenomenon she calls "Ma'am-ing" (224). Dr. Jordan refers to his landlady as "she" but then considers that this "sounds too intimate" (323).[11] He then calls her "Rachel," rather than "Mrs. Humphrey," when they enter into a sexual relationship, only to revert to "Mrs. Humphrey" in letters after they split up (419, 420). How much the social status of the interlocutors, rather than their individual relationships with each other, determines the chosen forms of address in the novel also becomes clear when Grace starts to call Jeremiah no longer by his first name but by "Sir" after it turns out that he is Dr. DuPont (305, 306). Moreover, questions pertaining to social status correlate with an essentializing or at least strongly generalizing view of gender: for instance, "that is what the ladies are like" (22); "young girls were often weepy" (163). As Atwood states in one of her essays in *Second Words* (see chapter 6 in this volume), referring to a late-twentieth-century context, "Perhaps it is time to take the capital W off Woman" (1982, 227).

Atwood's Booker Prize-winning and intricately structured novel *The Blind Assassin* (2000) is presented mostly from the perspective of the first-person narrator, Iris Chase Griffen, an eighty-two-year-old woman who writes some kind of journal in the hope that it will be read by her granddaughter Sabrina after her death. The narrative includes several newspaper clippings about the Chase family, following their history over decades. It also incorporates a novel by Laura Chase, Iris's sister, posthumously published as *The Blind Assassin*, which gives its title to Atwood's book. The Chase sisters grow up in the period between the two world wars, and the climax of the novel is set several days after the end of the Second World War. Atwood describes the social and political context in detail: the optimism of the 1920s, the fear and tumultuousness pervading the Great Depression, the political insecurity until the late 1940s. Again the forms of address used in the book are adapted to the historical period. The newspaper clippings refer to the Chase family members in the conventional formats of the time, marking unmarried women (but not men, of course) as such ("Miss Chase") and sometimes referring to married women in a de-individualizing manner with their husbands' full names ("Mrs. Richard E. Griffen" [3] yet also "Mrs. Iris (Chase) Griffen" [14]). Similarly, as in *Alias Grace* (yet now adapted to the higher social classes), Captain Chase looks down on his daughters Iris and Laura. In a stereotypical manner, he refers to girls in general as being "dumb as a stump ... specially the blondes" (289), and he seems to take a real interest in Iris only when he is about to arrange her marriage with Richard Griffen. When his lover Callista tells Captain Chase that he is too strict with his two daughters, his negative prejudice against women becomes obvious: "'You're being too hard on the kiddies,' said Callista. 'They're not boys.'—'Unfortunately,' said Father" (159). Mr. Erskine, the teacher hired to educate the two sisters, refers to the girls' brains derogatorily as "the brains of insects or marmots" (161). And when Iris tells her husband that she is pregnant, he addresses her in a trivializing, paternalistic manner: "I waited until the end of October to tell Richard that I was pregnant. I said I'd wanted to be sure. He expressed conventional joy, and kissed my forehead. 'Good girl,' he said. I was only doing what was expected of me" (426). The form of address "good girl" appears repeatedly in the novel, in similar functions as in *Alias Grace*, both as derogatory and compensatory forms of reference. Thus, Iris's lover, Alex Thomas, a communist and political activist, sarcastically calls her "good girl" (213) after an unsuccessful attempt to seduce Iris. Obviously, sexist language cuts across social classes, even for those who seek to abolish them.

Direct communication/direct speech (at least for the main plot of the novel) occurs predominantly between the *female* characters; the chosen forms of address are mostly neutral, non-evaluative, and particularly non-denigrating. They nevertheless also mirror emotional closeness or distance. Iris addresses beloved women directly with their first names ("Laura," "Sabrina," "My dearest Liliana"), yet she never employs such direct forms to address a man. She makes use of her husband's first name only when she talks *about* him, not when she talks *to* him. Hence, like

Atwood's previous novels, *The Blind Assassin* shows the personal and especially social modulation of forms of address.

Whereas Atwood's earlier dystopian novel *The Handmaid's Tale* takes gender differences and a heavily essentialist view of women as its central theme (see chapter 5), her later dystopia *Oryx and Crake* (2003), unusually so for Atwood, does not seem to be particularly focused on issues of gender. This cautionary narrative about a near-future world[12] involves genetic engineering, a climatic catastrophe, and a global epidemic. The largest part of the dialogue scenes in the book take place between the narrator—now called Snowman, known as Jimmy in the time before—and the people in his past and now lost world. There is hardly any opportunity for dialogue on the present time level since Snowman, over the larger part of the novel, appears to be the only human survivor after a global catastrophe (see, however, the open ending of the novel, which suggests that there are at least three more human survivors). Snowman lives up in a tree in order to avoid wolvogs, genetically mutated creatures generated from dogs and wolves. He considers himself the shepherd of a group of humanoid creatures called "Children of Crake" and recalls the bygone world in flashbacks. The devastated postcatastrophic world conceived by Atwood with her sharp intellect and dark humour has been caused by company compounds, killer viruses, gene splicing, bioterrorism, pollution, global warming, and volatile weather conditions, whereas the former world recalled by the protagonist is one of social inequality, where "ordinary folks" are kept outside the gated towns built by biotech companies for their employees. Jimmy, although bright as well as amusing and sexy, did not belong to the leading minds of this society, but his best friend, Crake, definitely did, with severe consequences on a global scale. Crake intervened in the biological processes of human life with his project that "create[s] totally chosen babies that would incorporate any feature, physical or mental or spiritual, that the buyer might wish to select" (304).

The results of his genetic experiments are the "Children of Crake," who are, significantly and perhaps symbolically, presented as sex- and genderless: sex and gender, it seems, have been neutralized in this world. The creatures' ignorance of socioculturally predetermined gender roles is already suggested by the prevailing use of the term "children" in referring to them, which signals a stage in human development before the final adoption of gender roles. A consideration of Judith Butler's theoretical formulation of the performative character of gender proves to be relevant in this context:

> there is neither an "essence" that gender expresses or externalizes nor an objective ideal to which gender aspires, and because gender is not a fact, the various acts of gender create the idea of gender, and without those acts, there would be no gender at all. Gender is, thus, ... the tacit collective agreement to perform, produce, and sustain discrete and polar genders as cultural fictions. (1990, 190)

According to Butler, the binary-coded category sex is similarly performative as gender, and in transferring this perspective of sex and gender onto the Children of Crake it can indeed be said that they possess neither gender nor sex because they do not have any culturally preconceived notions of a gendered cultural order or prescribed norms of sexuality. They do not perform gender because the concept of gendered behaviour has been programmed out of their brains. As Jimmy puts it, the Crakers are "hard-wired"—that is, genetically programmed—for dreaming and singing only (352); all other human activities such as art or courtship behaviour have been deleted from their brains. Their only concern is reproduction. The females of the species come into heat at regular intervals and celebrate a mating feast with three sexual partners of their choice, completely devoid of such concepts as love or jealousy, which ends as soon as pregnancy is ensured. The fact that Jimmy changes his name to "Snowman" stresses his view of the present situation and context: short for "The Abominable Snowman" (7), the new name stresses his isolation, his concern with survival in a world that has been made (by humans) unfit for human life, and his view of his present life as approaching that of an animal.[13]

It is not surprising, then, that most forms of address used in this novel occur in Snowman's flashbacks to his former life. In contrast to Atwood's previous novels, however, the forms of address used in Jimmy's family or in the love triangle between Oryx, Crake, and Jimmy are at first sight unremarkable: for instance, they do not express any denigration according to gender (thus, the lovers mainly address each other by their first names or by conventional terms of endearment such as "honey"). In this sense, then, the tendency detected up to, and especially in, *The Robber Bride* is prolonged into the future: gender is, by and large (see, however, Oryx's pornographic past as a child), not a central issue in this book concerned with physical survival, and relationships between gender groups are usually designed on equal terms—if gender is of relevance at all (see the sexless "Children of Crake"). Arguably, this disregard of gender differences might be the one hopeful sign in an otherwise gloomy view of the future. On the other hand, on an even gloomier note, it might also be regarded as a sign that humanity itself might be on the wane once this important feature, sex (and gender) difference, has more or less vanished from all maps of reference, especially since sexuality counts as the natural means of ensuring the survival of the species, now replaced by nefarious technologies.

Like the three previous novels, *The Penelopiad*[14] seems to step out a little from my line of argument since the historical context presented in the book is not our present time. As with Atwood's hilarious short dramatic monologue "Gertrude Talks Back" (*Good Bones*), which renarrates Shakespeare's *Hamlet* from Gertrude's perspective (see chapter 2), *The Penelopiad* re-envisions the Odysseus-Penelope myth from Penelope's point of view. Atwood notes in "The Myths Series and Me: Rewriting a Classic Is Its Own Epic Journey" that the hanging of the twelve maids, "slaves, really, ... at the end of *The Odyssey* seemed to me unfair at first reading, and seems so still" (2005), which apparently gave her the impetus to set the record straight.

For the two main characters of the original myth, Odysseus and Penelope, there is hardly any opportunity to talk to each other in this novel (similar in this respect to *Oryx and Crake*) since Odysseus is gone for most of the time (twenty years), fighting in the Trojan War. When Penelope speaks about him, she refers to him, unsurprisingly, as "Odysseus" (88), "my husband" (84), and "my beloved husband" (89). Odysseus, in contrast, addresses her paternalistically as "my poor duckling" and "precious girl" (48). More interesting in our context is the relationship between Penelope, the maids, and the many lustful and greedy suitors chasing her (or, rather, her money). In this book, going far back in time, we see again the "time-honoured" principles of trivialization and demonization of women. As to trivialization, Penelope herself refers to the maids as "girls" (116) and "pleasant girls" (113), whereas she refers to the suitors, who are of a similar age as the maids, as "men" (117). Similarly Eurycleia, Odysseus's former nanny, somewhat illogically addresses Penelope as "my child" (130) or "dear child" (148), whereas she refers to Odysseus, her former charge, as "the master" (148).

In this book, however, which incorporates today's ways of approaching gender in a more balanced manner, the tables are also turned. Thus, Penelope speaks of the suitors in a trivializing attitude as "mannerless young whelps" (109) and "noble puppies" (110), and she says about Telemachus that "Boys with their first beards can be a thorough pain in the neck" (170; see also 129). Helen calls the men who have a crush on her "poor lambs" (155). As to demonization, the suitors refer to Penelope among themselves as "the old bitch" (105) or "the old cow" (105)—according to information given in the story, Penelope must be twenty-six or twenty-seven years old at the time. The suitors directly and authentically make her into a financially coveted object by calling her "the prize" (106) of the ongoing bridal race. In a similar manner, they speak of Telemachus as "the little bastard" (105). Then, too, in this book—picking up trends from *Alias Grace*—female characters, like men, not only trivialize but also denigrate women. Thus, Eurycleia conforms to the unfortunate convention of double-faulting women who have become victims of men, as if the perpetration done to them was their own fault: she refers to the maids who were raped by suitors as "notorious whores" and, in a combination of demonization and trivialization, as "impertinent girls" (160). As in *Alias Grace*, this negative orientation is taken even further by the maids' apparent internalization of this denigrating and often sexually grounded view of women, albeit stated in an ironic manner—they call themselves "naughty little jades" (151), "sluts" (152), and "poxy little scuts" (152).

CONCLUSION

Concerning forms of address and their way of representing gender, we see a development in Atwood's novels from the late 1960s to the late 1980s and early 1990s and beyond. Atwood has moved from subtle (*The Edible Woman*, 1969) as well as drastic (*Surfacing*, 1972) illustrations of sexist attitudes—which are largely not discussed and remain, in part, apparently unperceived by the female protagonists in the early novels—toward an explicit awareness of the communicative relevance of forms of address in Elaine Risley's comments in *Cat's Eye* (1988). In this novel, perceptive analysis characterizes the illustration of sexist tendencies in referring to women. The female characters in *Cat's Eye* do not acquiesce in discrimination against women, as Marian and the nameless first-person narrator largely do in *The Edible Woman* and *Surfacing*; they also do not ridicule men as Ainsley does in *The Edible Woman*. Instead, they shrewdly observe sexist tendencies, sensibly analyze and verbalize them, and speak out against the implied negative stereotyping of women. In *The Robber Bride* (1993), where most of the communication represented takes place between women, most of the forms of address are neutral, symmetrical in terms of gender representation, and in any case geared to power rather than gender.

In her later novels from *Alias Grace* (1996) onward, Atwood chooses non-present time frames, in one case going back as far as antiquity, in another moving into the near future of the twenty-first century. The two novels dealing with the early twentieth century and the nineteenth century, *The Blind Assassin* (2000) and *Alias Grace*, predictably display a traditional system of reference that reflects its time, with men regarded as superior to and ready to trivialize and denigrate women. In the future time frame of *Oryx and Crake* (2003), gender no longer plays a remarkable role in terms of address and reference. Concerning *The Penelopiad* (2005), one could argue that Atwood blends traditionally unbalanced with more symmetrical forms of address in that the male characters are featured as the socially much more valued gender group, while at the same time the female characters tend to see the men critically and show it in the forms of reference chosen for them—not going as far as demonization, as the men do with the women, but trivializing the men occasionally, just as the men readily do with the women. As to demonization, female characters in this recent novel repeatedly denigrate their own gender group, an interesting turn in the development of systems of address in her novels, though we have to keep in mind that this book is set furthest back in time.

This analysis has demonstrated Atwood's keen and observant sensibility regarding the communicative problems and literary opportunities involved in forms of address. Atwood systematically chooses specific options in the characters' communication with the other gender group in *The Edible Woman, Surfacing, Alias Grace, The Blind Assassin, Oryx and Crake,* and *The Penelopiad.* These options, as well as the comments made by Elaine in *Cat's Eye* and by the female protagonists in *The Robber Bride,* show the general importance of forms of address when judging the characters' stances toward one another (and, in the final analysis, toward themselves in relation to others). The chosen forms of address suggest the attitudes of the speakers toward their interlocutors and show in particular the relevance of the systematic use of sexist forms of address for the creation and/or perpetuation of prejudice and stereotyping in connection with women:

> These are not trivialities that may be shrugged off as lexical surface phenomena. ... By means of the form of address the whole interaction is often controlled and the reality of the relationship defined. ... Thus, dominance relationships develop, and thus the negative stereotype of woman develops. By the use of asymmetrical forms of address and pejoratives, the prejudice is strengthened and perpetuated. (Trömel-Plötz 1980, 195)

As has become clear from the analysis of nine of Atwood's twelve novels to date, Atwood has been fully aware of such inter-relationships throughout her writing career, from her earliest through to her most recent works. By exemplary, circumspect, artful presentation of prejudice against and stereotyping of women, she has contributed significantly to the long and wearisome process of realizing, acknowledging, and eventually, one hopes, overcoming such prejudice and stereotyping particularly in connection with women. The development in her novels over the decades—which points toward an increasing equality between women and men and reflects this in the chosen forms of address (i.e., the "nomenclatural mutations")— mirrors to some extent corresponding social, extraliterary developments. *The Robber Bride,* Margaret Atwood's latest novel to deal primarily with contemporary times, is at the same time her first novel in which forms of address and reference to women and men are used in a largely non-evaluative, symmetrical manner. And perhaps we might interpret it as a hopeful sign in this context that gender no longer seems to be such a problematic issue in the near-future world presented in *Oryx and Crake* and that the following comment in *The Robber Bride* is made in retrospect, looking back on a bygone time: "Names were not just labels, they were also containers" (265).

NOTES

1. See Hook 1974; Key 1975; Kolodny 1975; Kramer 1975; Lakoff 1975; Thorne and Henley 1975; Nilsen et al. 1977; McConnell-Ginet 1978; McConnell-Ginet et al. 1980; Nilsen 1990; Nischik 1991b, chapter 2, 7.1.; Spender 1980; Trömel-Plötz 1980; Whitcut 1980; Cameron 1985; Cannon and Roberson 1985; Braun, Kohz, and Schubert 1986; and Henley 1987.
2. This differentiation is made by German scholar Würzbach 1985, 196–97. Fowler in his analysis of *Language in the News: Discourse and Ideology in the Press* (1991) includes chapters on "Discrimination in Discourse: Gender and Power" and "Terms of Abuse and of Endearment," and he speaks, for instance, of "diminutive and juvenile forms to refer to or address woman" (96). He, too, comes to the conclusion, after his wide-ranging investigation of language in the news, that "Linguistic usage is sexist, responding to the ideological paradigms in discourse which assign women special, deviant status in certain respects" (97).
3. "*Underlexicalization* is lack of a term or a set of terms. ... *Overlexicalization* is ... the opposite process: the availability, or the use, of a profusion of terms for an object or concept" (Fowler 1986, 152, 154).
4. On this and on the general question of how the particular speech act types systematically used by a speaker may characterize his or her attitude toward his or her interlocutor, see Nischik 1993c. One may well argue in the present context that Atwood provides us with many examples of a linguistic kind not yet systematically analyzed by literary critics. See also chapter 3 concerning Atwood's short story "Polarities."
5. Just as indicative of their relationship is the very different distribution of speech act types systematically used by Marian and, particularly, by Peter.
6. For a survey of the significance of names and naming in the novel, with particular reference to the Canadian novel, see Kroetsch 1989; and Nischik 1991a.
7. See, e.g., the interview scene in *Lady Oracle* quoted above or several passages in *Bodily Harm* (1981), for instance the following power game played by

police officers: "'They look at your driver's licence. Then they use your first name. Not *Miss* or *Mrs.* or anything, your first name, and you've got no way of knowing any of their names at all'" (93).

8. "Her name wasn't Charis then, but plain Karen. (It changed sometime in the sixties, when there were a lot of nomenclatural mutations)" (117).

9. In such usages, too, the novel is true to its represented time. Throughout the nineteenth century, gender-related notions of propriety prevailed in Britain and its empire, and unless women strictly adhered to these standards they quickly ran the risk of being branded by sexually grounded forms of denigration. See Hall 2004.

10. Kinnear also belittles Grace by calling her "a good girl" (256), playing down her status from that of a woman to that of a child.

11. "'Where is she?' says Simon. He shouldn't have said *she*; it sounds too intimate. *Mrs. Humphrey* would have been better" (323).

12. Although Atwood does not give any exact dates, not surprisingly considering her narrative principles, Coral Ann Howells's suggestion that the present time of the book must be around 2025 is plausible; see Howells 2006a, 163.

13. The abominable snowman, also known as yeti, is a legendary ape-like figure said to live in the Himalayas.

14. As we have come to expect with Atwood's works, critics are uncertain how to classify this book generically: some call it "novel" (e.g., the *London Review of Books*), some "novella" (e.g., the *Washington Post*), some simply "story" (the *Guardian*), "tale" (the *Washington Times*), and "retelling of a myth" (the *National Post*).

5

How Atwood Fared in Hollywood
Atwood and Film (Esp. *The Handmaid's Tale*)

ATWOOD'S WRITING AND ITS INVOLVEMENT WITH THE VISUAL MEDIA, ESPECIALLY FILM

Margaret Atwood is a strikingly intertextual and intermedial writer, constantly involved in probing and intermingling different textual formats and media. She frequently discusses and even incorporates other media, especially the visual arts, into her writing: photography ranks the highest (see Nischik and Breitbach 2006), yet Atwood also integrates painting,[1] television,[2] and film. Her use of these media in her literary texts ranges from brief references, through motivic elaboration, to extended metafictional comment—such as deceptive surfaces; the difference between looking and seeing; the subjectivity of perception, interpretation, and meaning; problems of representation; or how the (mass) media may colour our perceptions and self-conceptions as well as prestructure our actions.[3]

A case in point for the latter is Atwood's untitled poem beginning with "You take my hand" (from *Power Politics*, 1971). The poem establishes a parallel between a love affair and the cinema, which conventionally serves as the site of "romantic" encounters, both on and off the screen. The lyrical I recognizes the received and repetitive plot patterns of Hollywood romances in her life, feeling as if she were part of "a bad movie" (2), with love falling prey to stale clichés (see stanza 2). At the same time, she confesses to being "addicted" to the romantic idea(l)

of love as perpetuated by the plot formulas of Hollywood. The cinematographic, highly visual subtext of the poem shows that "life imitates
(popular) art," that couples tend to re-enact the stock situations dissem-
inated by the "culture industry." Atwood thus addresses the lure as well
as the intricacies of romantic love (see chapter 1), and, in accordance
with contemporary research on the sociology of love, she sarcastically
shows even this supposedly highly individual emotion to be a plotted
cultural production. Mediated by the mass media, love is drenched
in stereotypical, here ironically rendered, situations: the exchange of
prefabricated lovers' talk ("an air stale with aphorisms" [6]), the "endless"
staging of stealthy meetings in the artificial pastoral of "potted palms"
(7), and dramatic climbings "through the wrong windows" (8). Gender
roles are equally predictable: the male partner is the agent, leading the
"waltz," the female lyrical I is passive yet responsive ("You take my hand
and // I'm suddenly in a bad movie" [1–2]).

The sense of entrapment in a commodified film/life script, seemingly
robbed of any authentic, individualized emotions and situations, results
from the lyrical I's peculiar position of knowing better and playing
dumb at the same time, being appalled spectator and brain-washed
actress in the same person. This paradox is the real tragedy of gender
relations. The unattainable ideal of romantic love has made the lyrical I
a slave to love's promises despite her experiences of a reality that forever
falls short of a false dream. In the poem, a virulent layer of "smoke and
melted/celluloid" (15–16) clings to her naked body in the bathtub and
has to be peeled off (14), perhaps a reference to acts of purification
following involuntary sexual intercourse. Here and elsewhere the
cinematographic frame and language Atwood employs not only vividly
"picture" the abstract realm of gender relations but also pay tribute to
their historical context by critically commenting on the perversion of
realistic love through a manipulative cultural ideology of mass-media
productions.

Not only has Atwood successfully integrated various media discourses
into her literary writing, but she has also lent her hand repeatedly
to productions outside the writer's solitary chamber. She wrote, for
instance, the libretto for an opera (*Inanna's Journey*, based on Inanna, an
ancient Sumerian goddess), produced by the Canadian Opera Company
in 2004. Several of her fictional texts, such as the novel *The Edible*

Woman or the short-fiction collection *Good Bones*, have been turned into theatre performances by others.[4] July 2007 saw Atwood's professional debut as a dramatist when her drama adaptation of *The Penelopiad* premiered with the Royal Shakespeare Company in association with Canada's National Arts Centre at the Swan Theatre in Stratford-upon-Avon.[5] An opera based on *The Handmaid's Tale* premiered in Denmark in March 2000.

The medium of film (produced both for TV and the cinema) has crossed Atwood's path in several different ways and instances. As for her direct involvement and contact with film in connection with her literary works, there have been few film adaptations of her novels, although practically all of them have been optioned for this purpose at one point or another (see Walker 2001). One general reason for this striking lack of adaptations of her fiction may be related to Alfred Hitchcock's statement that the best movies are made from the worst books and the other way around, though there are many exceptions, of course (e.g., *The English Patient*). Atwood's artful foregrounding of language and the challenging structural intricacies of her novels are hard to transfer to the screen,[6] as is her frequent use of psychological realism, with a focus on the inner lives of her characters. In the latter context, Atwood quotes Oscar Lewenstein, British would-be producer of a film version of her first novel, *The Edible Woman*, as saying, "'You know, Margaret, an awful lot of the good part of your book takes place in this girl's [Marian MacAlpin] head. How can we show that?' Then one day, he said, 'I have a solution, we could have voice balloons. Like comic strips.' I said, 'no, I don't think so'" (Lorinc 2000). Then, too, Atwood's long-time critical focus on female characters and their specific problems and plights may have failed to capture the interest of many mainstream (and largely male) producers and directors. A case in point is *The Handmaid's Tale*. As the discussion of Volker Schlöndorff's adaptation of the novel will show, its feminist perspective considerably hindered realization of the project.

Finally, and probably partly also in connection with the other potential reasons put forward, there are the imponderabilities of collaborative production in the film business. *The Edible Woman* (1969), for instance, "had been passed through a number of hands, including those of John Kemeny and Oscar Lewenstein, Sir Tony Richardson, and British television director Alan Cooke. Atwood had written two screenplays of the novel: one with George Kaczender in 1970, another with Tony Richardson in 1971. But the film was never made" (Cooke 1998, 301). Atwood herself points out (in Walker) that "'I had tonnes of fun working on the first script that I ever wrote, *The Edible Woman*, which was with (British director) Tony Richardson. It was just a lark from beginning to end.'" But then Richardson and the producer had a falling-out, and the film was not realized. A similar fate met the plans to adapt *Lady Oracle* (1976). The book had been optioned by producer Margot Kidder, "who, while in love with the book, was never satisfied with the scripts she received—including Atwood's. The project was finally derailed by these script problems—and by Kidder's desire to write, produce, direct, and star in the film herself" (Cooke 1998, 301). Plans to make movies of *Life before Man*, *Bodily Harm*, and *Cat's Eye*— which involved well-known personalities such as Atom Egoyan, Helen Shaver, Anne Cameron, and Peter Pearson—similarly came to nothing (see Cooke 1998, 301–02, 306–07).

The earliest film version of an Atwood text goes back to the early 1970s, namely, the 16 mm black-and-white film *The Journals of Susanna Moodie* (1972), a drama with a run of fifteen minutes. The film is based on Atwood's eponymous poetry cycle, and Atwood herself wrote the screenplay together with Marie Waisberg. The second film also derived from her poetry, Paul Quigley's six-minute visual interpretation of Atwood's poem "Progressive Insanities of a Pioneer,"[7] which in its second version (*Poem as Imagery*) was issued with a teacher's guide for educational purposes. Two TV productions followed for which Atwood wrote the screenplays: the CBC production *The Servant Girl* (1974) and *Snowbirds* (1981, dir. Peter Pearson). *The Servant Girl* is, interestingly, Atwood's first fictional treatment of the life of Grace Marks, a story to which Atwood returned some two decades later in her novel *Alias Grace* (1996).

The beginning of the 1980s saw the first adaptation of an Atwood novel for the big screen, Claude Jutra's *Surfacing* (1981), based on Atwood's eponymous second novel from 1972, which still counts as one of her most difficult novels. The project ended disastrously and surely must have made Atwood wary of the film world. Quebec filmmaker Jutra (1930–86), a critically acclaimed director, took over the film project after another director stepped down. Yet at this stage it was "too late to change either the script or the casting—in other words, there was no longer leeway to improve the film in measurable ways" (Cooke 1998, 301). To make things worse, Jutra was in the early stages of Alzheimer's disease, as became clear in retrospect, and thus often overtaxed:

> Financial problems with the production meant that the producers had to keep bringing in new investors, all of whom wanted to tinker with the screenplay. Nor did they know the director was in the early stages of Alzheimer's. She [Atwood] recalls that a crew member told her later on, "We just thought he was on drugs. We would say, 'The scene's ready to be shot.' He'd say, 'what scene?'" (Lorinc 2000)

Given all these problems, it is not surprising that the finished product did not even come close to the quality of Atwood's novel—the film was an artistic failure.[8]

After another, this time highly successful, collaboration with Peter Pearson on the CBC production *Heaven on Earth* (1987)—a six-part documentary on the "Barnado children," for which Atwood wrote the final version of the screenplay (see Cooke 1998, 306–07)—her best-known film adaptation to date was tackled by German director Volker Schlöndorff in *The Handmaid's Tale*, released in 1990. (This venture will be dealt with separately and in greater detail in the following section of this chapter.) More than ten years passed after the release of Schlöndorff's (and Atwood's) first "Hollywood film" before Atwood returned to the screen with *The Atwood Stories* (2003), a six-part series on CBC Television, which adapted six of her short stories (from her first three collections: "Polarities," "Betty," "The Man from Mars," "Death by Landscape," "Isis in Darkness," and "The Sunrise").

The third adaptation of an Atwood novel that was actually accomplished is the CBC Television production of *The Robber Bride* (March 2007). Again Atwood herself refrained from writing the screenplay (the credits go to Tassie Cameron). Rumours/announcements are that films of Atwood's novels *Alias Grace* and *The Blind Assassin* are being worked on, but with so many abortive attempts to adapt her novels to the screen these plans should clearly be taken with a grain of salt.[9]

This survey of Atwood's direct involvement with collaborative productions once again shows her variable creativity. Atwood has tackled libretti for operas, scripts for documentary films, a script for a theatre play (a drama adaptation of one of her novels), and screenplays for two of her novels. Neither of her screenplays, though, made it to the production stage, for various reasons. In this context, it is also worth noting that the only major genre Atwood has hardly become involved with is stage drama.[10] It can be argued that a writer such as Atwood who places a strong focus on language—with an extraordinarily wide range of stylistic variants at her disposal—and who likes to explore her characters' *inner* lives, is not predisposed to write drama/film dialogue. The latter, due to the almost exclusive use of spoken language, might be somewhat too restrictive for Atwood in terms of literary structure, language, and style. It is not surprising, then, that only three of her twelve novels (and six of her numerous short stories, in one production) have been adapted to film (TV and cinema) to date.

All in all, it is fair to say that the liaison between Atwood and the film world has not been a particularly productive and successful one so far. Although her first attempt at a screenplay (for *The Edible Woman*) was apparently a lot of fun for her, she learned a lesson, even with this earliest venture, about the difference between single and collaborative production—a lesson that many writer-colleagues working for the film industry had to learn the hard way.[11] The relationship between writers and film(makers) has largely been a strained one; Atwood pointedly formulates the major reasons for this problematic relationship:

> You're much more at the mercy of fate when you're making a movie. When you are writing a novel, you're at the mercy of the circumstances on the inside of your head, not of what's inside other people's heads—until you publish it. ... You have to understand that making movies is a social occasion. If you don't get on with those people, it's hell. If you do get on with them, it's a riot. ... Whereas if you're a novelist, you're in a room by yourself. You

have your piece of paper and whatever you're using to make marks on it and that's it. ... Nobody talks back. ...

On the other hand, you don't get to toss the ball around, either. ... If you enjoy that kind of multiperson, unpredictable activity, then movies are the thing for you. If you like to be totally in control of the product, you better stick to novels. (cited in Lorinc 2000)[12]

With a writer like Atwood, who sets such great store by language (and who even tends to design the covers of her books herself), it is clear on which side she stands. After her first two failed attempts, she seems to have given up writing screenplays. She also seems to have abandoned interest in partaking in the productions based on her literary works: "She's chosen to stay out of the process because she finds it too time-consuming and not always enjoyable" (Lorinc 2000). About the more recent film production, the TV adaptation of *The Robber Bride*, it is known that "she was on the set one day"[13]—not necessarily a sign that her interest has revived significantly. And the severe twisting of her novel in this adaptation, too, may serve as an explanation for both Atwood's and Atwood scholars' lack of enthusiasm for adaptations of her work.[14]

Another crucial experience for Atwood, after the failure of Jutra's attempt at *Surfacing*, must have been the film production of *The Handmaid's Tale*, still the best-known adaptation of her works. In the following analysis, I will look first at the dystopian gender system established in Atwood's novel before investigating what became of the book, and especially of its gender representation, in Schlöndorff's film version.

According to Linda Hutcheon, an adaptation is an "extended, deliberate, announced revisitation of a particular work of art" (2006, 170). I am fully aware that adaptations also exist in their own right, as works in dialogue with, not in hierarchical relationship between, original source text and later re-creation, often in another medium. Thus, while I am certainly not a supporter of the outmoded "fidelity rhetorics" of film adaptation, it is my particular interest in this chapter to explore, compare, and evaluate the respective treatments of gender aspects in Atwood's novel and its adaptation to the screen by Volker Schlöndorff and Harold Pinter.

GENDER AND GENRE IN *THE HANDMAID'S TALE*

When Atwood's sixth novel, *The Handmaid's Tale*, appeared in 1985, I was so fascinated that I immediately wrote an analytical response. The article, entitled "Back to the Future: Margaret Atwood's Anti-Utopian Vision in *The Handmaid's Tale*," opens as follows:

> Margaret Atwood's latest novel ventures into grounds Atwood has not moved in before. *The Handmaid's Tale* is a dystopia, a negative utopia, which extrapolates negative trends of the past and present, radically plays them through to their consequences, and thus presents a shocking image of the immediate future. The novel encompasses a wealth of topical themes, weaves them into an ingenious, almost perfect plot, and fascinates the reader by dazzling feats of imagination as well as the skill with which past, present and future are intertwined. The style is quintessential Atwood, condensed but eloquent, and in this novel particularly well suited to content and theme. The reader may be shattered, even repelled by the social and personal conditions presented in the novel, but also be forced to admire it: *The Handmaid's Tale* is Atwood the novelist at her best. It may well prove to be a kind of *Nineteen Eighty-Four* of the 1980's. ...
>
> With the Orwellian 1984 just safely behind us, Atwood offers us another vision of the future. It is her most political novel, also her most topical, and the one which paints the fate of women in bleakest colours. (Nischik 1987, 139, 145)

This immediate response to the novel has stood the test of time. The book became an international bestseller and signalled Atwood's definitive international breakthrough, especially in the United States: "*The Handmaid's Tale* was on the *New York Times* best-seller list for 23 weeks, and it cemented Atwood's reputation on the international scene, breaking the sound barrier in terms of mainstream popularity for her work" (Cooke 2004, 135; German readers, incidentally, had been avid Atwood readers even before *The Handmaid's Tale*).[15] Americans in particular were fascinated and stirred by Atwood's graphic depiction of a futuristic Gilead, forcefully established by police power in a bygone

United States. Readers were concerned about the trends Atwood saw in contemporary America and the Western world, pointedly visualized in the story of Offred, Atwood's female protagonist and narrator. Offred is one of Gilead's child-bearing slaves, instrumentalized in a Christian totalitarian theocracy for the procreation of the ruling classes—due to the widespread sterility of the Gilead population in the wake of ecological catastrophe and a postnuclear state of scarce natural resources. In my recent interview with Atwood, when asked about potentially different reactions to her (works) in Canada and the United States, she answered by drawing attention to the crucial significance of *The Handmaid's Tale* in this context:

> RN: If you, as a Canadian celebrity writer, go to the United States, do you have the feeling that you're approached differently there than in Canada?
> MA: Somewhat. People in the United States think that I have a window into the future. ... Because of *The Handmaid's Tale*, and now increasingly because of *Oryx and Crake*. So they're going to be asking me more questions like "What's going to happen?" That happened as soon as *The Handmaid's Tale* was published. People in England said, "Jolly good yarn." ... Canadians, being a nervous group of people, said, "Could it happen here?" And Americans *immediately* said, "How long have we got?" (see chapter 8)

In fact, today *The Handmaid's Tale* is probably more frequently read and treated than Orwell's *1984* (1949), also because Atwood's novel, though even more outrageous in its statements, feels closer to the present world than Orwell's novel does. *The Handmaid's Tale* is, in any case, Atwood's most widely read book at the university level[16] and has been included in international school curricula.

Atwood's vision of Gilead based on gender, class, and religious segregation may seem to be glaring in its particular imaginative concoction, yet, as Atwood points out in an earlier interview (reprinted in *Moving Targets*, 2004), "in *The Handmaid's Tale*, nothing happens that the human race has not already done at some time in the past" (102)—be it with regard to scriptural precedence in the Old Testament (e.g., the procreational ceremonies), technological innovations (e.g., the "compuchecks"), political systems and events (e.g., totalitarian mono-theocracy, police state, civil war), social regulations (e.g., class and gender segregation, food rationing, homophobia), or ecological phenomena (e.g., air and water pollution). In what follows, I want to concentrate on the book's statements and implications concerning gender.[17]

One of the crucial motifs of *The Handmaid's Tale* is vicarious reproduction (see also today's artificial insemination or so-called surrogate mothers), which, as the first of three epigraphs illuminates, goes all the way back to Genesis in the Old Testament:[18]

> And when Rachel saw that she bare Jacob no children, Rachel envied her sister; and said unto Jacob, Give me children, or else I die.
>
> And Jacob's anger was kindled against Rachel; and he said, Am I in God's stead, who hath withheld from thee the fruit of the womb?
>
> And she said, Behold my maid Bilhah, go in unto her; and she shall bear upon my knees, that I may also have children by her.
>
> Genesis 30:1-3

The monthly ceremony of procreation—the Handmaid lying on her back with her head between the wife's spread legs, the Commander trying to impregnate her, and the whole household watching—for the greater part of the book divests sex of any positive emotions, to say nothing of love. It also brings the differences between the sexes to the extreme, stressing the one thing that men cannot accomplish: that is, bearing a child, which is being postulated officially as the supreme value of women ("We are two-legged wombs, that's all: sacred vessels, ambulatory chalices" [146]). In a complete backlash to prefeminist times, biological determinism and an utterly essentialist view of the sexes have come full circle. The society of "The Republic of Gilead"[19] (projected by Atwood probably into the late 1990s)[20] is thoroughly obsessed with religion and the "religion" of giving birth—the prescribed greeting formulas between the Handmaids are "Blessed be the fruit" and "May the Lord open."

Gileadean gender politics and the concomitant class differences have also defined the uniform naming system, accompanied by colour coding. Both methods further serve to reduce individuality and to stress allocation in groups. Handmaids have been robbed of their individual names and are identified by way of a patronymic, a combination of the possessive preposition "of" and their respective Commander's first name ("Commander" is the official functional name of the male characters at the top of the social hierarchy). The female protagonist is called "Offred" (i.e., Of Fred, her Commander)—her former first and family names are never mentioned in the novel. Offred's temporary companion is referred to as "Ofglen," whereas the former Janine mutates to "Ofwarren" and then to "Ofwayne." The Handmaids' social and personal dependence on men could hardly be shown more concisely and emphatically than in such a drastic patronymic naming system. In addition, Handmaids may only wear red clothes (signalling, probably, blood, birth, life, and— here ironically so—love). The Commanders' "Wives," such as Offred's mistress, the former Serena Joy, are to stay in the house, directing their attention to their husbands. Their pastime is knitting, and many of them tend to little gardens, as if to compensate for their loss of professional influence and, often, the ability to bear life and nurture children: "It's something for them to order and maintain and care for" (22). The Wives wear blue (standing for authority, respectability, serenity). The "Aunts," dressed in brown, have kept some amount of power in society, yet it is used exclusively for the indoctrination of future Handmaids and for the general control of women—Aunts are the female arm of the government, using electric cattle prods for indoctrination if need be. The "Marthas"[21] do the housework and wear green only (workforce). The degraded "Econowives" are Wives of the poorer men and own no colour of their own ("These women are not divided into functions. They have to do everything; if they can" [34]). "Unwomen," finally, whose very name divests them of their sexual identity, are women who have confronted state ideology (e.g., by their way of dressing) and/or are considered infertile and therefore packed away to the feared "colonies," where they soon die ("Give me children, or else I die"[22]). A social hierarchy exists for men, too, but being male still ensures a certain status in Gilead. Thus, only men can become "Guardians (of the faith)" and "Eyes," who are the watchforce of the social system, or "Angels," that is, soldiers and other important social representatives.

Atwood also shows how modern technology may be put to use for systematic gender discrimination. Thus, on the day of the political coup, all computer cards with an "f" code number (for "female") are declared invalid by the new regime. This simple implementation means total expropriation of all women, since all money transactions have long been computerized. Women also lose their jobs instantly ("I started doing more housework, more baking" [189]), thus becoming economically dependent on men. The regressive state of Gilead becomes particularly obvious with the retroactive status of women (not exclusively, though, since men also suffer under this repressive system): women's options are completely regulated according to their function for society. The *raison d'être* of the Handmaids is to give birth. Thus, they must take daily walks "to keep [the] abdominal muscles in working order" (36). These walks are strictly supervised: Handmaids cannot communicate outside their "family," apart from in regulated situations such as when buying food or exchanging greetings in the prescribed formula. They wear nun-like habits and must avert their gaze when talking to people; when outside, they must even wear "wings," which hamper their peripheral vision. Women must also be uneducated and hold no jobs other than those of the Marthas and the Aunts. Significantly, to read is to commit a crime: "Our big mistake was teaching them to read" (320). Unfairly so, childlessness is always ascribed to a woman's infertility; it is a crime to suggest that men, too, may be sterile (and it turns out that Offred's Commander *is* sterile, while Offred has to take the blame for this, which endangers her life).

In spite of such drastic gender hierarchies and total oppression of women, Atwood remains level-headed in her presentation of female and male characters in the book. *The Handmaid's Tale* is definitely not a feminist tract—in fact, it was criticized by feminist hardliners due to the conflicting feminist ideologies the book presents. Thus, the radical feminism of the narrator's determined mother (see her participation in burning pornographic books) is sarcastically shown by Atwood to be somewhat imbalanced too ("Mother, I think. ... You wanted a women's culture. Well, now there is one. It isn't what you want, but it exists" [137]). Then, too, Moira, the narrator's best friend, turns out to be the bravest character in the novel. She applies the determination and consistency with which she leads the life of a woman who has "decided to prefer women" (180) in her political behaviour as well; she emerges as a sane, flexible, and clever character, admired by the weaker, more timid narrator.

The Handmaid's Tale is far from being an apotheosis of women in general. Rather, the book is Atwood's reaction to the rise of the fundamentalist Christian right in the United States, particularly since the 1970s and 1980s. Atwood warns that the Gilead theocracy could come to power because of widespread indifference and ignorance ("Nothing changes instantaneously: in a gradually heating bathtub you'd be boiled to death before you knew it" [66]). She warns against any kind of absolutist approach, be it in politics, religion, or the relationship between men and women. *The Handmaid's Tale* shows the devastating effects of political, sexual, and mental despotism as well as the manipulability and malleability of the individual ("I have failed once again to fulfil the expectations of others, which have become my own" [83]). Atwood views fundamentalist religion and the relationship between the sexes in combination, demonstrating how political power structures endanger the group as well as the individual if the ruling ideology is made absolute. As Atwood said in an interview about her novel in 1985,

> This is a collective nightmare, and the thing about writing it out is that then you can see it. You can see where this or that might lead. ... This is a pretty crucial time, and the way women are treated in a society determines the shape of the society. It determines to a great extent what choices are available to men as well.[23]

MAKING THE HOLLYWOOD MOVIE *THE HANDMAID'S TALE*

It is not surprising that this provocative novel—with its fascinating plot and remarkable imaginative range—soon caught the attention of the film world. The eventual producer, Daniel Wilson, met Atwood as early as 1986 when she was promoting the novel in New York. Atwood sold the film rights to Wilson (for "not an unsubstantial amount of money," Wilson said; cited in Teitelbaum 1990, 19), not least because he had chosen Harold Pinter to write the screenplay.[24] Dramatist and scriptwriter Pinter, with a long list of successful screenplays to his credit,[25] seemed to be the ideal person for the purpose; as Atwood herself said,

> Pinter's very good at writing scenes which play against the dialogue: in which what people are saying is not what's happening in the scene. That was very much required for this film. And there are so many silences in his plays, and I thought that would be necessary for this as well. There are a lot of pauses in the book. (cited in Cooke 1998, 302)

In an interview with Geoff Hancock (1986), Atwood had similarly praised Pinter's suitability for adapting this book to film: "If anybody can do it, he can. One of his specialties is scenes in which people don't say very much, but convey meaning anyway" (in Ingersoll 1990, 217).

Atwood could not have known that in this case Pinter's script would eventually turn out to be "his" least good, diverging so much from his original version—due to changes by others during the production process—that Pinter hardly recognized the end product. As Steven H. Gale states,

> The final cut of *The Handmaid's Tale* is less a product of Pinter's script than any of his other films. He contributed only part of the screenplay: reportedly he "abandoned writing the screenplay from exhaustion." Although he tried to have his name removed from the credits because he was so displeased with the movie (in 1994 he told me that this was due to the great divergences from his script that occur in the movie), his name remains as the screenwriter. (2003, 318)

Small wonder under the circumstances that Pinter never published his original filmscript of *The Handmaid's Tale* (though he did so with almost all of his other screenplays); he was also afraid of copyright problems since the original and the script used in the movie are too different (Gale 2003, 319).[26] The constant revision had come about with a change of directors. Producer Daniel Wilson had originally hired British Czech director Karel Reisz, sixty-three years old at the time, who had worked together with Pinter very successfully on the film version of John Fowles's *The French Lieutenant's Woman* in 1980 (released in 1981). Reisz and Pinter seemed to get along well with the new project too.[27] Pinter consulted Reisz about the screenplay and completed his first draft, "with considerable input from Reisz," in September 1987 (Teitelbaum 1990, 19). Everyone concerned with the film—director, producer, and Atwood herself—liked Pinter's script very much. As Wilson reports,

> What Pinter did—and he did this brilliantly, was to take these [Offred's] thoughts and transform them into dramatic scenes. He winnowed the book into its essence, and he didn't waste a comma doing so. ... Pinter simply had the right intellect and style for the material. We solicited Atwood's comments about the script, and she loved it. ...
>   I naively thought that with a best-selling author like Atwood, a screenwriter like Pinter, and a director like Reisz, any studio would want to finance the production. ...
>   Boy, was I wrong. (cited in Teitelbaum 1990, 19)

After the successful completion of Pinter's screenplay, which was to everybody's liking, fate turned against the film. Practically all film studios approached by Wilson declined the project. They obviously also shied away from the gendered statements and feminist concerns of the story, which shows women reduced to their biological sex and the purpose of procreation. Hollywood in the 1980s was apparently not yet ready for such a radical statement on gender politics: "During the next two and a half years, Wilson would take the Pinter script to every studio in Hollywood, encountering a wall of ignorance, hostility, and indifference" (Teitelbaum 1990, 19). Reasons given for the refusals were, among others, "that a film for and about women ... would be lucky if it made it to video" (19).

The project thus languished until the spring of 1988, when American actress Sigourney Weaver read a copy of Pinter's script and expressed an interest in playing the lead role of Offred. After director Karel Reisz had had to retreat from the project due to other commitments because a production studio for the filming of *The Handmaid's Tale* could not be found for years, this interest by a star actress with a certain guarantee for the box office gave the project a new boost, and a small New York film studio, Cinecom, agreed to produce the film. A new director was found, Germany's renowned Volker Schlöndorff (known particularly for his successful literature adaptations, such as Nobel Prize winner Günter

Grass's *The Tin Drum*, 1979),[28] who had resided in the United States for five years by that time and was looking for a way to make it into the American film market.[29] Once again things seemed to be looking up for the halted project. Yet a month after preproduction had begun and less than three months before the scheduled beginning of the shooting of the film, Weaver had to retreat from the project at her doctor's advice because she was pregnant (rather a remarkable twist considering the film's story). Again the project was close to folding up. Schlöndorff is reported to have approached almost every American actress to take over the part of Offred, stepping in for Weaver, yet every one of them declined: "No one wanted to play Kate" (Teitelbaum 1990, 20; the film invents "Kate" as the former name of the novel's anonymous protagonist). Some actresses thought it would be "a feminist art-house film" and did not want to offend their fans (20). Again the oppressive gender politics and depressing setting of the novel/script seemed to hinder realization of the film. After much hassle, Schlöndorff was eventually able to recruit two British actresses[30] for two of the leading female roles (Natasha Richardson for Offred/Kate and Victoria Tennant for Aunt Lydia), though Richardson, too, had taken her time deciding: as Teitelbaum notes, "Richardson was not without qualms about the project. ... Her boyfriend, said Schlondorff [sic], never stopped warning her that the role would ultimately harm her career" (22). With relatively high sums of money offered to the renowned actors Robert Duvall (Commander) and Faye Dunaway (his wife, former Serena Joy), the project came together at the last minute after all.

SCHLÖNDORFF'S REMASCULINIZATION OF ATWOOD'S FEMINIST DYSTOPIA

Hiring Schlöndorff as the new director had major consequences for the conception of the film. He wanted revisions to the screenplay even after the shooting had started and approached Pinter to do them, but Pinter declined, claiming to be "absolutely exhausted" (cited in Gale 2003, 319). Pinter told Schlöndorff to get Atwood to do the revisions,[31] but Atwood is said to have spent only one day on the set, and Nathalie Cooke states that "her involvement with the film was minimal—she attended some preliminary meetings; she commented on the script, mainly suggesting small vocabulary changes" (1998, 302).[32] Thus, the major changes to Pinter's script probably have to be put down largely to Schlöndorff himself (and partly to the actors and many others involved)[33] during the production process. Such a scenario is in line with William Goldman's (somewhat sarcastic) general description of a finished film "as the studio's adaptation of the editor's adaptation of the director's adaptation of the actor's adaptation of the screenwriter's adaptation of a novel that might itself be an adaptation of narrative or generic conventions" (cited in Hutcheon 2006, 83). Interestingly in this context, even the latter claim is true since Atwood's novel *The Handmaid's Tale* "adapts" the traditionally male-oriented conventions of the literary dystopia by rendering the events from a female, marginalized perspective, with clear consequences for both content and form of the book.

When Schlöndorff first read the Pinter screenplay and afterward Atwood's novel, he did not like either of them very much. He repeatedly said, even after completion of filming, that he did not buy the political premises of the work, which Atwood, in contrast, took seriously. Schlöndorff envisioned the movie mainly as a *thriller*, thereby not only shifting the medium from book to film but also undermining Atwood's choice of genre. He saw the Commander as "the villain" yet also the one who is liked most in the film (Teitelbaum 1990, 22)—quite a remarkable statement for a movie based on a first-person narration by a woman utterly oppressed by the outrageous gender politics of Gilead. Such statements point to a severe reorientation by Schlöndorff that twists Atwood's statements and concerns in the book and that is largely responsible for the lack of success of his first attempt at a "Hollywood movie." In fact, one may even argue that Schlöndorff, in his desire to create an American film for an American audience, over-Hollywoodized the film, thus partly wrecking the shrewd statements and warnings in the novel. Ironically, while the focus on gender of the underlying story hindered the project's inception in the first place, the main reason for the film's eventual lack of success must indeed be seen in Schlöndorff's traditional view and downplaying of gender issues as well as his overly Hollywoodized ending. Not surprisingly, these major changes disappointed the group of knowing viewers who saw the adaptation *as adaptation.* Yet the reduced thriller plot of the film also failed to raise the interest of a larger new audience, who had not read Atwood's novel before watching the movie. Indeed, the changes to the Atwood plot in the film are so severe that the move from the telling mode to the showing mode effected a change not only in media but also in genre— from a (feminist) dystopia to a (Hollywood) thriller (cf. Hutcheon 2006, 45). As Schlöndorff himself said, unwittingly admitting his slanted reduction and sensationalist Hollywoodization of Atwood's novel, "I wanted the film to be extremely blunt and straightforward. ... Margaret Atwood's world struck me as uniquely surreal, like a naked woman with a veil on her face" (cited in Teitelbaum 1990, 61).[34]

Arguably, Schlöndorff's wife at the time, German filmmaker Margarethe von Trotta, could be imagined to have accomplished a more sensitive adaptation—lifting the veil from the woman's face and at the same time putting clothes on her body, to extend Schlöndorff's metaphor. Rita Kempley similarly wrote in the *Washington Post* that "Schlondorff [sic] seems as uncomfortable in this feminist nightmare as a man in a lingerie department. ... And one can't help but wonder why a woman didn't direct this movie about women being dominated by men."[35] As Linda Hutcheon observed in general terms,

> the creative transposition of an adapted work's story and its heterocosm is subject not only to genre and medium demands ... but also to the temperament and talent [and, we might add in the present context, experiences related to his or her sex/gender group] of the adapter—and his or her individual intertexts through which are filtered the materials being adapted. (2006, 84)

Atwood replied to the question why this particular novel was entrusted to an essentially male crew for production that "she had received no offers from women producers, directors, or screenwriters during the six months before the deal was signed" (Cooke 1998, 300). Apart from this, there seem to be no written statements by Atwood on this film, which is perhaps telling in itself.[36] I was at one of Atwood's readings in Germany around the time when the film was released. Atwood was bombarded with critical questions about the film and how she liked it. Somewhat annoyed, she refused to comment on the film. However, the film definitely helped to further increase her international fame.

The Handmaid's Tale was shot in and around Durham, North Carolina (the Duke University campus and the Sugar Mountain Ski Resort) between February and May 1989 (see Teitelbaum 1990, 16), with the relatively small budget of $13 million. The film, released in 1990, did not have a long run. The reviews were lukewarm, non-committal, or negative, such as "Mr. Schlondorff [sic], not known for a light touch, has come a surprisingly long way toward making the film version work strictly on the level of popular entertainment. ... The film's ending ... is a mistake."[37] Or "German director Volker Schloendorff (working in a foreign language) and screenwriter Harold Pinter scoop the surface aspects of Margaret Atwood's novel carefully, but leave her darker implications about ... fundamentalist-type beliefs and individual freedoms swinging in a facile, finger-wagging wind."[38] A list of review titles of the film fills more than four pages (see Wydra 1998, 293–97). Some of these titles, especially the German ones, are quite telling and harsh: "Zuletzt blieb nur Schlöndorff übrig" [Finally Only Schlöndorff Was Left], "Männliche Kopfgeburt" [A Male "Cerebral Birth"], "Eine dumme Männerphantasie" [A Stupid Male Fantasy], "Happy End für Hollywood," "Ein ratloses Werk" [A Helpless Work], "Plumpe Antiutopie" [Heavy-Handed Anti-Utopia], "The Filmmaker's Tale."[39]

Altogether the film and its audience reception thus may not be called a great success. But then it was certainly a tough task to make a film of a brilliant, intricately structured novel such as Atwood's, which features little direct action. In general, film adaptations have to face the difference between the telling and the showing modes, having to translate words into pictures. Also, as Hutcheon points out, "a novel, in order to be dramatized, has to be distilled, reduced in size, and thus, inevitably, complexity" (2006, 36). Any film adaptation of *The Handmaid's Tale* would thus have to face the following specific challenges, among others: how to deal with the overall narrative situation in the novel, in which an oppressed female, who is not even allowed to communicate, speaks her thoughts onto some thirty tapes; how to cope with the discontinuous time structure of the novel and its technique of montage; how to handle the metafictional aspects of the book and its many passages in which Offred ponders and analyzes her condition; how to treat the partly poetical, always elaborate language that Offred uses in her "tale"; how to deal with the "Historical Notes" at the end of the book. Again I agree in principle with Hutcheon that "multiple versions of a story in fact exist laterally, not vertically" (2006, 169), and with her general challenging of the major clichés about the problems of adaptation, which traditionally supported prose narrative's place at the top of a hierarchy.[40] Although I believe that *The Handmaid's Tale*'s general and specific challenges would in principle be translatable in showing and perhaps even interactive[41] modes, the Schlöndorff adaptation in the final analysis victimized the Atwood novel and did not live up to its qualities, as I will elaborate in the following.

Since Schlöndorff opted to make—in his own words—a "straight-forward, blunt," Hollywood "thriller," he streamlined the complexity of the book into an easily consumable film. Thus, the elaborate narrative situation of the book is completely lost in the film, more so than would have been necessary in the transfer from the novel's narrator Offred to the film's "narrating" camera. Offred, though important, seems to be one character among several in the film. The Hollywood movie offers hardly any correspondences for the rich thoughts and emotions revealed in the book. Natasha Richardson, the actress playing Offred, often seems to be rather detached and uninvolved. Only rarely are attempts made to externalize her inner life, such as when she has tears in her eyes talking to Nick about her daughter, or when she sees Moira again in Jezebel's (the high-class nightclub/brothel for the men of the ruling class), or, most strongly, after she has killed the Commander (a glaring invention of the film that is not supported by Atwood's text). The discontinuous time structure in the book is changed into a chronological, dramatically climaxing time line in the film, with very few and brief flashbacks (when Offred repeatedly visualizes the scene in which she lost her daughter during her family's attempt to escape to Canada). The metafic-tional aspects of the book are not at all mirrored in the film by any metarepresentational, self-reflective techniques. The same applies for the last two challenges distinguished above: namely, Offred's elaborate language[42] and the "Historical Notes." Offred/Kate does not come across as a particularly educated character in the film; Richardson's rather bland style of acting is one of several reasons why the film fails to fully grip the audience emotionally. Atwood's futuristic view of the Gilead system in the "Historical Notes"—by means of a conference held in the year 2195, long after Gilead has ceased to exist—is completely omitted in the film.

Schlöndorff decided to distill the external action from Atwood's novel for his "straightforward, blunt thriller." If we do not adhere to the outmoded "fidelity principle" of film adaptation—which regards the degree of correspondence between novel and film as the sole criterion for judging the quality of the film adaptation—but view the film in its own right, Schlöndorff indeed came up with what he had intended to do: that is, to produce a "thriller" (and the film is particularly effective in its mass scenes).[43] Atwood, too, is far from applying a biased fidelity principle to her appreciation of film adaptation in general and is aware of the differences between the two media, including the difficulties a film has with viewers who have read and appreciated the novel and who come to the film expecting a satisfying "mixture of repetition and difference, of familiarity and novelty" (Hutcheon 2006, 114):

> It's the nature of the media. When you are reading a work of fiction, you are your own screenwriter, you are your own sound-effects person, you are your own costume designer. Movies are sounds and pictures, that's it. A novel and a movie are two completely different things, so you're not changing your book. You're making something different, which has to stand on its own. (Atwood in Lorinc 2000)

Indeed, the general characteristics of Schlöndorff's adaptation could partly be put down to the necessity of a Hollywood film, made to capture the interest of multitudes rather than that of film (or literature) connoisseurs. Nevertheless, one may ask to what extent a film director is legitimized to twist essential statements of the source book in his attempt to "popularize" the book for film. One may argue that an artistically successful film adaptation depends on the degree to which it retains what is *essential* in the novel. It can be either "style" or "the 'spirit' of a work or an artist" that a successful adaptation captures and conveys. However, the majority of adaptation theories agree "that the story is the common denominator, the core of what is transposed across different media and genres" (Hutcheon 2006, 10). In the case of *The Handmaid's Tale*, Schlöndorff also "streamlined" important aspects of the gender representation—so much at the core of Atwood's novel— by twisting her take on gender in an unsympathetic, slanted manner, which makes the film altogether much less moving and virulent than the novel. Students, for instance, who have read the novel and have seen the film, understandably state that they find the book "gripping" but the film "flat" in comparison.[44]

The film's biggest mistake is the Hollywoodized happy ending. Mary Kirtz calls it "a complete capitulation to Hollywood's insistence on a happy ending" (1996, 145). Linda Hutcheon describes the substitution of the ending by director Volker Schlöndorff and screenplay writer Harold Pinter as an attempt "to mute tragedy or horror ... in their 1990 film adaptation of Margaret Atwood's dark, dystopic narrative" (2006, 37), which, indeed, may be a suitable approach for a Hollywood film. Yet particularly for anyone knowledgeable about Atwood and her writing, who views the adaptation *as adaptation*, the mawkish film ending is not only "unhappy" but also outright annoying. For one thing, Atwood typically opts for open endings in her fiction and does so effectively in *The Handmaid's Tale*. The final chapter (before the coda of the "Historical Notes") concludes as follows:

> The van waits in the driveway, its double doors stand open. The two of them ["two men" (306)], one on either side now, take me by the elbows to help me in. Whether this is my end or a new beginning I have no way of knowing: I have given myself over into the hands of strangers, because it can't be helped.
>
> And so I step up, into the darkness within; or else the light.
> (307)

The novel thus leaves open whether the two men, who get Offred out of the Commander's house, are friends or foes. They could be state police officers, which would probably mean the death sentence for Offred ("Violation of state secrets" [306]), or they could be working undercover for the underground "Mayday" rescue organization, as Nick whispers to her (305)—in the novel, neither the reader nor Offred knows whether she can really trust Nick, who might be an "Eye," after all.[45] The ambiguity of the ending thus involves readers much more, keeping them wondering and much more aware of the political and social disaster of the Gilead system instead of focusing on Offred's salvation, as the film chooses to do. The "Historical Notes" in the novel do not clear up her fate either: they only tell us indirectly that Offred must have somehow survived, if perhaps only for a short time, or she would not have been able to speak her story onto the tapes—though this method of archiving may also suggest that her survival was still under severe restrictions.

The film closes with a brief shot of a pregnant Offred, who has been rescued by the rebels, as she is waiting for her lover Nick to return and for her baby to arrive. This final scene (Gale states that "the escape to Canada" was Pinter's invention [2003, 318]) also suggests that voice-over might have been an appropriate method throughout the film to introduce Offred's thoughts to the viewer. Unfortunately, Schlöndorff, although otherwise known for his adept use of voice-over, makes use of this technique only in this one scene and thus in what is arguably the film's weakest moment:

> I don't know if this is the end for me or a new beginning. But I'm safe here in the mountains held by the rebels. They bring me food and sometimes a message from Nick. And so I wait. I wait for my baby to be born into a different world. I still dream about Jill [her daughter, unnamed in the novel], about them telling her I don't exist, or that I never existed. But I know we're going to find her. She will remember me. (film soundtrack, 1:39–40 min.)

The scene before this final shot shows the female protagonist during her rescue scene clinging to Nick, who has to leave and is in danger too. The message of the film is clear: Offred loves Nick so much that she does not care for her own life and through her clinging to him unwittingly endangers his life as well. The film thus caters to the romance formula of the helpless emotional woman, passively waiting for her lover to return, and the brave rational man, bound to fight for a larger cause. As Grace Epstein summarizes this final scene, "Hollywood's classic tradition of dealing with women invaded the film ... to reassert the romance plot assaulted by Atwood, and returned the female protagonist—her body and voice—to her objectified position in the classic cinema ...

putting the woman back in her place as the passive part of the couple. ... Tradition dictates this" (1993, 54, 59).

This mainstream trend of the film, which feeds on conventional forms of gender representation, is also shown in many other ways. For instance, the severe oppression and suppression of women in the novel are considerably reduced in the film. In the novel, the Handmaids wear unattractive clothes going down to their ankles and wings around their heads to hamper free sight. The Handmaids' dress in the film is more attractive, less unusual, and less restrictive—the wings are not used, and Richardson's beautiful, lush hair is repeatedly flaunted. "The movie Handmaid's uniform allows her to see and, more important, to be seen. It also allows her to move more freely than the all-encasing nunlike habit described by Atwood" (Kirtz 1996, 144). The novel states that, even when Offred is taken by the Commander to Jezebel's and is provided with extra clothes for the occasion, she feels clumsy and unhappy in these clothes and does not seem to look particularly attractive in them. In the film, in contrast, Richardson looks glamorous, immaculate, and tempting, the "decorative ingredient" and "spectacle for voyeuristic pleasure" that women have tended to be in the Hollywood tradition (van Zoonen 1994, 87). Again the film brings the story closer to the conventional romance formula, in which it is the woman's role to attract men by her beautiful looks.

Another instance in which the film severely deviates from the novel is the Commander's murder by Offred. In the novel, she supposedly imagines such a situation, in connection with the Scrabble scene, but never acts it out:

> I think about how I could take the back of the toilet apart, the toilet in my own bathroom, on a bath night, quickly and quietly, so Cora outside on the chair would not hear me. I could get the sharp lever out and hide it in my sleeve, and smuggle it into the Commander's study. ... I think about how I could approach the Commander, to kiss him, here alone, and take off his jacket, as if to allow or invite something further, some approach to true love, and put my arms around him and slip the lever out from the sleeve and drive the sharp end into him suddenly, between his ribs. I think about the blood coming out of him, hot as soup, sexual, over my hands.

In fact I don't think about anything of the kind. I put it in only
afterwards. Maybe I should have thought about that, at the time,
but I didn't. As I said, this is a reconstruction. (149–50)

In fact, one of the fascinating character and situational aspects in
the book is Offred's ambivalence between oppositional, internalized
protest on the one hand and placid passivity on the other, as Offred
has to adapt, by existential necessity, to a largely inactive, highly re(pro)
ductive role in Gilead. As she is conceived of in the novel, she would
have been incapable of killing the Commander,[46] particularly in the gory
way it is done in the film. Even at the end of her tale, she states in the
novel, "I still have it in me to feel sorry for him" (306). This "feminine"
capacity for sympathizing with the Other—a characteristic supportive
of nurturing, of motherhood—is thrown overboard at the end of the
movie. Although Kate is shown to have qualms about her brutal act,
she nevertheless goes about it. Even worse, the murder is shown in a
close-up, lurid manner, with blood spurting from the Commander's
slashed neck. The oppressed state of women in the book and Offred's
anxiety about making a false step,[47] also drastically shown as one side
effect of social restrictions, are thus considerably relieved in the movie
and translated into mainstream Hollywood's desire for sensationalist
scenes and unambiguous endings. Kirtz points out that Offred's murder
of the Commander in the film may also be a lurid part of the film's
romance plot and criticizes "the inflation of Nick's role" in the film.
The film suggests that Offred's "involvement in the Mayday movement
is largely due to his influence and even her decisive blow for freedom
is traced back to her growing love for her heroic rescuer" (1996, 145).

The complexity and depth of the novel and the comparative
roughness and flatness of the film can also be seen in an exemplary
manner in the Scrabble scene. In the novel, this scene begins with the
tension-raising "I want you to kiss me, said the Commander" (145),
which actually, on the level of the story, happens at the end of this scene
(repeated on 149–50). The reader is thus curious to know what events
have led up to this demand, which is outrageous in the Gilead system.
Before the Scrabble scene, another brief account of the household's
reaction to the birth of a baby in another household is interspersed
(145–46), stressing again the supreme official role of women in Gilead,

which is to give birth. The Scrabble scene then, Offred's first unofficial meeting with the Commander in his room,[48] is prepared for in greater detail by focusing on her emotions—curiosity but mainly trepidation— about the upcoming secret meeting. Offred feels utterly helpless and dependent, like a child.[49] She is aware of the social doctrines for Handmaids,[50] afraid of being found out and eventually having to pay with her life,[51] and she is very much aware of the power structures in Gilead,[52] curious about the Commander's intentions,[53] for to want something means to have a "weakness."[54]

Practically all this rich inner action is lost in the film version. Even more striking is that the "narrating" camera focuses on the male rather than on the female perspective. This can already be seen in the way the Scrabble scene is introduced. Offred and Nick meet in the dark hallway at night, and Nick—who earlier was the messenger to arrange the secret meeting between the Commander and Offred—silently accompanies her toward the Commander's door. Her approach to this door is shown not from her perspective, as it is in the novel ("I raise my hand, knock, on the door. ... I'm told to enter. I open the door, step in" [146–47]), but from Nick's perspective (which is completely absent in this episode in the novel). After this shot from his perspective, the camera immediately jumps into the Commander's room and from there observes Offred entering the room. Via this shift in camera perspective, it appears as if she is handed from Nick to the Commander, a passive object with no gaze of her own in a gendered power game.[55] Thus, not only is her individual voice subdued in the film, but Offred also loses the hegemony of perspective she has in the novel. The Commander seems to be much more at the centre and in charge of the situation than Offred due to his character in the film talking more than in the novel and due to the many camera takes focusing on him. The film does not take up his "sheepishness" as described in the book either—the whole exchange between the two loses a lot of the awkward tension it has in the book; it becomes a much more "normal," less restrictive scene, with even a certain amount of coziness suggested (see the film's addition of the Commander opening a refrigerator and offering Offred strawberries, which she relishes). The frightening emotional impact of the secret meeting on Offred in the novel (e.g., "It's panic. The fact is I'm terrified. I don't say anything" [147]) is almost completely lost

("'Hello,' he says. It's the old form of greeting. ... I think I will cry" [147]). In this scene in the film, Offred never seems to be close to tears, only somewhat insecure and reserved at the beginning. Lifting her veil at the Commander's request and then standing a while with the veil held up comprise an adequate attempt to render the forced nature of the meeting and her fright. At the end of the scene, however, Offred seems to be almost at ease, even evading the Commander's attempt to kiss her, whereas she obeys his "order" to kiss him in the novel.

Offred's emotional turmoil in this scene in the novel also derives from objects in the Commander's room, above all books, which the Commander has saved from "the time before" (before the revolution): "All around the walls there are bookcases. They're filled with books. Books and books, right out in plain view, no locks, no boxes. No wonder we can't come in here. It's an oasis of the forbidden. I try not to stare" (147). Offred's yearning for books—her former job was to transcribe books to disk form, after all—is ignored in the film. The film instead invents one of several dialogues that is again representative of a masculine perspective. The Commander dominates the conversation and comments on Offred's good performance in the Scrabble game, attributing it to her former job as a "librarian."

The Scrabble game as such is totally reconceived in the film, as it is shown from the masculine perspective as a matter of winning or losing. In the film, even Offred is focused on this issue ("I can use my last three letters in one go. I won"), whereas in the novel her interest in the Scrabble game is quite different ("I win the first game, I let him win the second" [149]). The opportunity to play with letters and words after a long time of deprivation is what is truly fascinating for her, not the question of winning a game. Offred feels a sensual joy dealing with the Scrabble counters and displays her high level of education through her inventiveness with words:

> *Larynx*, I spell. *Valance. Quince. Zygote.* I hold the glossy counters with their smooth edges, finger the letters. The feeling is voluptuous. This is freedom, an eyeblink of it. *Limp*, I spell. *Gorge.* What a luxury. The counters are like candies, made of peppermint, cool like that. ... I would like to put them into my mouth. They would taste also of lime. The letter C. Crisp, slightly acid on the tongue, delicious. (149)

The Scrabble scene—like the novel as a whole—puts human desires and needs into perspective, pointing out what human beings can hardly do without: speech/language, communication with others, emotions, love, food.[56] Offred's intense involvement with letters/language in this scene is not transferred to the film, though. Instead, looks between the Commander and Offred are exchanged, and they talk quite a lot compared with the scene in the novel, with Offred taking the reactive part. The Commander's offer of strawberries—in what is arguably a mimicry of a lover's seduction—as well as the diffuse lighting and the background music toward the end of the scene all serve to stress romance patterns that the novel repeatedly undercuts. Again the utter oppression, deprivation, and silencing particularly of women in Gilead are considerably relieved in the film.[57]

It can be argued that the shift to a male perspective in the film can also be detected in the complete omission of the novel's important coda, the "Historical Notes" (311–24), because they point out the masculine, reductive, unsympathetic appropriation of a woman's story. In fact, one can even say that Schlöndorff "replaces" the "Historical Notes" of the book in that the film takes a view of gender matters similar to that of the prejudiced professor commenting on the Handmaid's tapes at the conference. Professor Pieixoto from Cambridge University, England, outs himself at the beginning of his talk by making sexist introductory remarks about the female panel chairperson, who has just introduced him very kindly: "PIEIXOTO: Thank you. I am sure we all enjoyed our charming Arctic Char last night at dinner, and we are now enjoying an equally charming Arctic Chair. I use the word 'enjoy' in two distinct senses, precluding, of course, the obsolete third. (*Laughter.*)" (312). Atwood thus suggests, dishearteningly so, that the reduction of women to their bodies—even while they are acting out a demanding professional, here scholarly, function—is still the same in the year 2195. What is more, the renowned male professor looks at the Handmaid's story, very much a woman's story, from a purely scholarly, detached point of view, brushing away all ethical questions in the name of alleged objectivity and displaying no capacity or will to sympathize with women's fates in Gilead: "In my opinion we must be cautious about passing universal judgment upon the Gileadeans. Surely we have learned by now that such judgments are of necessity culture-specific. ... Our job is not to censure but to understand. (*Applause.*)" (314–15). Even worse, he chastises the Handmaid for providing posterity with a personal rather than a more "scholarly" report, thereby completely ignoring her individuality and the circumstances of her "telling" this story onto tape:

> Many gaps remain. Some of them could have been filled by our anonymous author, had she had a different turn of mind. She could have told us much about the workings of the Gileadean empire, had she had the instincts of a reporter or a spy. What would we not give, now, for even twenty pages or so of printout from Waterford's [the Commander's] private computer! (322)

Clearly the biased[58] professor would have much preferred an official "male" document from the centre of power to the Handmaid's subjective account from the female margin.[59] The professor also speculates longer about the Commander's identity than about the Handmaid's, and his patronizing remarks about women and his overall approach to Gilead draw the audience's applause. As Arnold E. Davidson rightly states, "in crucial ways the epilogue is the most pessimistic part of the book" (in VanSpanckeren and Castro 1988, 120).

Although in a less drastic, more subtle manner than in Gilead, women and their stories are still dismissed at the end of the twenty-second century, even among scholars and intellectuals. Rather than having learned their lesson from their scholarship, Professors Pieixoto and Wade, responsible for assembling the unearthed tapes into "The Handmaid's Tale," are simply interested in a fact-finding reconstruction from a masculine perspective. As Coral Ann Howells points out,

> That story is lost for two hundred years and when it is rediscovered and published by the male professor from Cambridge, his version threatens to erase its significance as thoroughly as Gilead had tried to erase her identity. The professor is not interested in her personal memoir except as evidence for his grand impersonal narrative of a fallen nation's history, and readers are left with the challenge of Offred's unfinished story. Do we understand more about the past (or is it the future?) from her story or from official history? (2006a, 169)

For the perceptive reader of the novel, the answer is clear, yet Schlöndorff nevertheless has followed the male view of (this) history.

CONCLUSION

Although a change in medium, such as from novel to film, inevitably brings along a shift in audience expectation, and although "the adapted text ... is not something to be reproduced, but rather something to be interpreted and recreated, often in a new medium ... a reservoir of instructions ... that the adapter can use or ignore" (Hutcheon 2006, 84), these tenets of contemporary adaptation theories in my view do not fully legitimize Schlöndorff's drastic changes to Atwood's (or her text's) intentions/story/spirit, especially considering gender representation. It can be said that the Schlöndorff film makes rather a "his-story" of Atwood's "her-story"—Atwood warns us in her "near-future novel" or "speculative fiction" (Howells 2006a, 161, and Atwood 1989, 103) about potential consequences of the political, social, religious, and ecological trends in the United States, particularly from a female perspective and focusing on women's stories. By this shift in gender perspective, the film "remasculinizes" the traditionally masculine dystopian genre, which Atwood precisely complemented in her novel by rendering the events from a female and, at the same time, marginal as well as largely internal perspective. As Howells perceptively states,

> Atwood gives us a dissident account by a Handmaid who has been relegated to the margins of political power. This narrative strategy reverses the structural relations between public and private worlds of the dystopia, allowing Atwood to reclaim a feminine space of personal emotions and individual identity, which is highlighted by her first-person narrative. ... By an irony of history, it is Offred the silenced Handmaid who becomes Gilead's principal historian when that oral "herstory" is published two hundred years later. (2006a, 164, 165)

Just as the historians in the "Historical Notes" can only see the world from a masculine point of view and thereby once again refuse to recognize and appreciate Offred's "her-story," so too the film unfortunately "mainstreams" Atwood's revisionist text as to genre and gender. Again gender issues considerably stamp the design of the genre (here dystopia) as a whole, with Atwood transcending traditional generic boundaries and Schlöndorff, in the mass medium of film, pushing back the focus to a traditional view of genre and gender, here mainly in the context of a Hollywood thriller.

Thus, Atwood's first (and, to date, last) venture to Hollywood has not been particularly successful by any account—even considering Hutcheon's proposal that "knowing audiences have expectations—and demands. It may be less, as Béla Balázs tried to insist, that 'a masterpiece is a work whose subject ideally suits its medium' and therefore cannot be adapted ... than a case of a 'masterpiece' being a work a particular audience cherishes and resists seeing changed" (2006, 122). With a highly intellectual, critical, and elaborate writer such as Atwood, chances are that her works will not fare too well in *mainstream* Hollywood films in the future either. After the disappointment of Atwood connoisseurs (and film critics) over the film version of *The Handmaid's Tale*, and probably Atwood's own disenchantment with the adaptation, it will be interesting to see whether another attempt at an Atwood (Hollywood) film version will see the light of day.

In a sense, any discussion of a film adaptation takes up an important thematic thread of Atwood's novel *The Handmaid's Tale*, namely, the constructivist tenet that any kind of representation is of necessity a reconstruction. This "offer" by Atwood's novel is, again, completely omitted in the film. What Offred metafictionally considers in the novel, focusing in retrospect on the nature of her story and the medium in which it is told, language, or onto which (tapes) it is told, is also highly resonant in the light of film adaptation:

> This is a reconstruction. All of it is a reconstruction. It's a reconstruction now, in my head. ... [I]f I'm ever able to set this down, in any form, even in the form of one voice to another, it will be a reconstruction then too, at yet another remove. It's impossible to say a thing exactly the way it was, because what you say can never be exact, you always have to leave something out, there are too many parts, sides, crosscurrents, nuances; too many gestures,

which could mean this or that, too many shapes which can never
be fully described, too many flavours, in the air or on the tongue,
half-colours, too many. (144)

Ironically, this metafictional passage in the novel precedes the Scrabble
episode analyzed above. The passage also harmonizes with Margaret
Atwood's statement about film adaptation that "a novel and a movie
are two completely different things, so you're not changing your book.
You're making something different, which has to stand on its own"
(in Lorinc 2000). Nevertheless, in view of my analysis of Schlöndorff's
action-packed Hollywood film and particularly the way it severely
twists the adapted text's gender perspective and gender representation,
one may also sympathize with Offred's more fundamental statement
in the novel and transfer it, *mutatis mutandis*, to this particular film
adaptation: "I try to remember if the past was exactly like this. ... I know
it contained these things, but somehow the mix is different. A movie
about the past is not the same as the past" (247).

NOTES

1. See her poems "Manet's Olympia" from *Morning in the Burned House*
   (1995) and "Quattrocento" from *Interlunar* (1984), the short story "Death
   by Landscape" from *Wilderness Tips* (1991) as well as the novel *Cat's Eye*
   (1988).
2. E.g., in the poem "Heart Test with an Echo Chamber" from *Interlunar*
   (1984) or in *The Handmaid's Tale* (1985).
3. Her most unusual forays into the dynamics of intermedial relations are,
   arguably, the sophisticated comics Atwood has produced throughout her
   career (see chapter 7).
4. Dave Carley, after having first adapted *The Edible Woman* for a radio play,
   then supervised the theatrical adaptation of the novel in a co-production
   for the Vancouver Playhouse and Toronto's CanStage (see Walker 2001).
   Good Bones saw its German debut performance in Frankfurt in 1996 by
   the German group E9N (Ensemble 9. November).
5. See Martin Morrow at www.cbc.ca/arts/theatre/atwood.html [consulted
   20 July 2007].

6. See Cooke 1998, 307, on the structural difficulties of adapting *Cat's Eye* to the screen.

7. *Reflections: Progressive Insanities of a Pioneer* (Cinematics Canada, 1972; Universal, 1974).

8. Treatment of this film, which is hardly ever mentioned in Atwood criticism, may be found in Kirtz 1996, 141–43; and Dickinson 2007, 62–69.

9. In April 2009, the National Film Board of Canada optioned the film rights for a documentary based on Atwood's non-fiction book *Payback: Debt and the Shadow Side of Wealth*: see www.onf-nfb.gc.ca/eng/news/index.php?id=1951 [consulted 12 May 2009].

10. Excepting her recent debut as a dramatist in connection with her adaptation of *The Penelopiad*. And Atwood facetiously claims that she had "another whole theatrical career" in high school and at university when she acted as a puppeteer and wrote and acted in plays.

11. Consider, e.g., the painful experiences of F. Scott Fitzgerald, which he integrated in his last novel, *The Last Tycoon*, or, more recently, Sam Shepard stepping down as a screenplay writer during his first attempt of the kind, with Antonioni's movie *Zabriskie Point* (1969). Shepard, though, has always kept up his involvement with the film world in various ways.

12. Linda Hutcheon summarizes collaborative production as follows: "There is an increasing distance from the adapted novel as the process moves from the writing of the screenplay to the actual shooting (when the designers, actors, cinematographer, and director move in) and then to the editing when sound and music are added and the entire work as a whole is given shape. The script itself is often changed through interaction with the director and the actors, not to mention the editor. By the end the film may be very far from both the screenplay and the adapted text in focus and emphasis" (2006, 83).

13. See Melissa Hank, "Margaret Atwood's *Robber Bride* Becomes TV Movie," www.entertainment1.sympatico.msn.ca/Bell.Sympatico.CMS [consulted 9 March 2007].

14. Ted Sheckels, editor of the journal *Margaret Atwood Studies*, explained his disappointment over this adaptation in scholarly terms in a paper given at an ACCUTE session at the Congress of the Humanities at the University of British Columbia in Vancouver in May 2008.

15. It has been stated repeatedly that German readers have been among Atwood's earliest and most faithful audience. In the earlier stages of her career, more books of hers were sold in Germany than in any other country (including Canada itself). For potential reasons, see Oeding and von Flotow 2007.

16. Thus reports Shannon Hengen after a survey; see Wilson, Friedman, and Hengen 1996, 108.

17. For a more comprehensive treatment of this rich novel, see Nischik 1987; in comparison with Atwood's later dystopia *Oryx and Crake*, see Howells 2006a.

18. For the relevance of these three epigraphs, see Cooke 2004, 132–33.

19. Gilead in the Old Testament circumscribes the area of ancient Palestine east of the Jordan River, corresponding to the modern northwestern Jordan; to Gilead, which is first mentioned in Genesis 30:21, 23, there is no definite boundary. Cf. *The Handmaid's Tale:* "This is the heart of Gilead, where the war cannot intrude except on television. Where the edges are we aren't sure, they vary, according to the attacks and counterattacks. ... The Republic of Gilead, said Aunt Lydia, knows no bounds. Gilead is within you" (33)—an unsettling thought indeed. In the Bible, Gilead, significantly, was the home of the prophet Elijah.

20. Coral Ann Howells claims that the novel's scenario occurs "around 2005" (2006a, 163). Although the novel is ambivalent about the date references it gives, and although Howells's choice could be supported, by detective reckonings, with Offred's comments about the documentary (154), there are more clues in the book that would point to the late 1990s as the time of Offred's experiences in Gilead. One clear clue is Professor Pieixoto's research, which classifies Gilead as a "Late-Twentieth-Century Monotheocrac[y]" (312).

21. In the Bible, Martha, sister of Mary, receives Jesus in her house and serves him; see Luke 10:38–42.

22. From Genesis 30:1–3; see the novel's epigraph page.

23. In *Quill and Quire* 51.9, September 1985, 67.

24. "'What I think convinced her to deal with me was my suggestion that Pinter do the screenplay.' ... Wilson did not think to offer Canada's Queen WASP raconteur a crack at adapting her own novel, nor, apparently, did she ask for one" (Teitelbaum 1990, 19).

25. See Nischik 1993b; and www.haroldpinter.org/films/index.shtml [consulted 25 June 2007].

26. See also Gale's report (319–21) on Pinter's endeavours with this script and Pinter's proud statement in 1997 that, of the twenty-two screenplays he had written to date, seventeen had been filmed exactly as he had written them (365).

27. Most of the facts of the production given here are based on Teitelbaum 1990, the best, most detailed report on the filming of *The Handmaid's Tale.*

28. Other well-known literature adaptations by Schlöndorff include *Der junge Törless* (1966; *Young Torless*), *Die verlorene Ehre der Katharina Blum* (1975; *The Lost Honour of Katharina Blum*), *Un amour de Swann* (1984; *A Love of Swann*), *Death of a Salesman* (1985), and *Homo Faber* (1991; *Voyager*).

29. As production designer Tom Walsh stated, "'Volker ... was completely frustrated by his inability to get a number of other projects he had been working on off the ground. With Sigourney Weaver's connection to the project at the time, it seemed that here was finally a picture that actually could get done'" (cited in Teitelbaum 1990, 21).

30. "'That's what I admire about the Brits,' said [production designer] Walsh. 'They dive in with equal energy whether they are playing a positive or negative character. They are there to act, whereas American actors and actresses want to be loved—especially if that's what they are successful at'" (cited in Teitelbaum 1990, 22).

31. "Whether Pinter ran out of steam or simply could not get a handle on the essence of the novel, in the end *The Handmaid's Tale* was a bad experience for him" (Gale 2003, 321).

32. "Atwood further insists that she did not influence the promotion of the film" (302).

33. See this reference by Pinter in Gale 2003, 319. See also Gale's comment: "As it turned out, not only did Atwood make changes, but so did many others who were involved in the shoot" (318). The degree to which she was involved in the film adaptation of her novel is described differently in different sources. Cf. also Schlöndorff's statement "Margaret Atwood worked more on this picture than Pinter did" (in Denicolo 1990, 22); or "Atwood was heavily involved in overseeing the book-film translation" (Hewitt 1996, 111); or "Volker Schlondorff [sic] modified portions of Pinter's original screenplay. Following several digressions, including talks with Margaret Atwood and additions by the cast, Schlondorff [sic] comments that the filmscript ended up 'as straight and lean as Pinter's original'" (Epstein 1993, 59n2).

34. Maybe Schlöndorff was inspired here in his choice of metaphor by a passage in Atwood's novel: "At neck level there's another sheet, suspended from the ceiling. It intersects me so that the doctor will never see my face. He deals with a torso only" (70). In the film version, there is indeed Offred with a transparent veil on her face (no sheet from the ceiling); her face can still be seen, and her body is covered by a sheet. The arrangement in the book is the more powerful one, more fitting to the novel as a whole, whereas Schlöndorff perhaps wanted to avoid showing a naked woman's body in the film.

35. See www.washingtonpost.com/wp-srv/style/longterm/movies/videos/ thehandmaidstalerkempley_a09ffb.htm [consulted 11 June 2008].

36. See also Glenn Willmott: "Atwood's response to having seen Pinter's translation on film remains unrecorded" (1995, 188n6).

37. Janet Maslin in the *New York Times* on 7 March 1990.

38. Desson Howe in the *Washington Post* on 9 March 1990. See also "The film received generally poor reviews" (Willmott 1995, 188n7).

39. Cooke reports a chorus of boos by fellow German directors to Schlöndorff after *The Handmaid's Tale* premiered at the Berlin Film Festival (1998, 303). I do not think Cooke is right to explain this response as envy on the part of the German directors, at Schlöndorff's working in the United States. Schlöndorff has been productive after *The Handmaid's Tale*, directing a film almost every year, such as *Homo Faber* (1991) and *Palmetto* (1998), his second American movie (his earlier American productions, *Death of a Salesman* [1985] and *A Gathering of Old Men* [1987], had been made for TV, then released theatrically in Europe). At the beginning of the 1990s, he returned to Germany, where he is still busy directing films and teaching at film academies in Berlin as well as in Saas Fee, Switzerland. For a good survey of Schlöndorff's oeuvre, see Moeller and Lellis 2002.

40. These clichés can be briefly summarized as follows: (1) "Only the telling mode" can truly render "intimacy and distance in point of view" (Hutcheon 2006, 52); (2) interiority is best handled by the telling mode (56); (3) only the telling mode can handle relations between past, present, and future (63); (4) "only telling (in language) can do justice to such elements as ambiguity, irony, symbols, metaphors, silences, and absences" (68).

41. E.g., computer games or hyperfiction.

42. For the intricacies of the language used by Offred in the novel, see Deer 1994.

43. Cf. Hutcheon: "If we do not know that what we are experiencing actually *is* an adaptation or if we are not familiar with the particular work that it adapts, we simply experience the adaptation as we would any other work" (2006, 120).

44. Of course, this does not have to be the case or could be the other way around—the history of film adaptations of novels knows many examples of all kinds.

45. The "Historical Notes" state that he was, indeed, an "Eye" (322).

46. See Cooke 2004, 125–26, in greater detail on Offred's passivity. Epstein calls Kate "hesitant and nearly catatonic" (1993, 58).

47. Offred, for instance, refuses to let the doctor help her out by inseminating her due to her fear of being found out and put to death.

48. "This forbidden room where I have never been, where women do not go. Not even Serena Joy comes here, and the cleaning is done by Guardians. What secrets, what male totems are kept in here?" (146–47).

49. "I stand outside it [his door], feeling like a child who's been summoned, at school, to the principal's office. What have I done wrong?" (146).

50. "We are for breeding purposes: we aren't concubines, geisha girls, courtesans. On the contrary: everything possible has been done to remove us from that category. ... We are two-legged wombs, that's all" (146).

51. "If I'm caught, it's to Serena's tender mercies I'll be delivered. ... After that, reclassification. I could become an Unwoman" (146).

52. "But to refuse to see him could be worse. There's no doubt about who holds the real power" (146).

53. "So why does he want to see me, at night, alone?" (146).

54. "But there must be something he wants, from me. To want is to have a weakness. It's this weakness, whatever it is, that entices me. It's like a small crack in a wall, before now impenetrable. If I press my eye to it, this weakness of his, I may be able to see my way clear" (146).

55. I find Stephanie Barbé Hammer's reference to a popular gothic romance structure even more appropriate for the film than for the novel: "In such stories the heroine, like Offred, is often made a helpless prisoner by an evil and sexually desirous male force, until she is finally liberated by the romantic hero" (cited in Cooke 2004, 133).

56. See also "The minimalist life. Pleasure is an egg. ... If I have an egg, what more can I want? In reduced circumstances the desire to live attaches itself to strange objects" (120).

57. For a good analysis of the Scrabble scene from a different angle, see Willmott 1995, esp. 175–79.

58. See also his remarks on tale/tail or his calling "The Underground Femaleroad" the "Underground Frailroad" (313). See also Cooke: "Taken together, these barbs suggest that men's attitudes toward women are dismissive and hostile in the year 2195" (2004, 129).

59. See also "Anything from the man's office would have been preferable to the woman's story she actually leaves. Once again, a woman is rendered invisible and worthless within her own story" (Kirtz 1996, 144). Willmott formulates more/too reservedly: "One might suspect some masculinist distortion of values in this totalitarian overdetermination, drained of its heroine's reflections" (1995, 189n16).

6

"On Being a Woman Writer"
Atwood as Literary and Cultural Critic

ATWOOD AS CRITIC

For such a prolific writer of fiction and poetry, Margaret Atwood has an astonishingly large output of expository prose on diverse literary, cultural, and political issues to her credit. She is a *poeta doctus* if ever there was one. Her expository prose extends from reviews of literary texts and introductions to her own works and those by other authors, via statements on politics such as US-Canadian relations and human rights, to lecture series on the myth of the North in Canadian literature and culture, on the concept of debt in human history and culture, as well as on writing and the position of the writer.

By now, her literary and cultural criticism encompasses seven books ranging over four decades. With the best-selling *Survival: A Thematic Guide to Canadian Literature* (1972), Atwood catapulted CanLit and, as it turned out, herself onto the literary map. Written in the vein of Northrop Frye's myth criticism, the often-quoted survey of Canadian literature is an important document of thematic criticism. *Second Words: Selected Critical Prose* (1982) is the first of two collections of critical prose, this one covering the period from 1960 to 1982. The second such collection, *Moving Targets: Writing with Intent 1982–2004* (2004), picks up the thread from the earlier collection and covers the following two decades into the twenty-first century. In between, Atwood published three critical books with unified themes: *Strange Things: The Malevolent*

North in Canadian Literature (1995), *In Search of Alias Grace: On Writing Historical Fiction* (1997), and *Negotiating with the Dead: A Writer on Writing* (2002). Her latest book in this genre, also devoted to a unified theme, is *Payback: Debt and the Shadow Side of Wealth* (2008).

Considering the range of Atwood's critical oeuvre and her status and influence, rather little significant criticism has so far been published on her expository prose, with critical responses mainly framed in reviews of the individual works or briefly scattered in books and articles. The most useful of the few more extensive contributions are those by Walter Pache (2000/02)—the most substantial and up-to-date evaluation—and by George Woodcock (1981), as well as the relevant chapters in Jerome H. Rosenberg (1984) and Barbara Hill Rigney (1987), though they date back more than twenty years. So does a review by William Keith (1983), which is mainly negative in its evaluations of Atwood as critic, partly also because Keith does not seem to appreciate her sense of humour in serious analytical contexts. Neither does he give her the benefit of the doubt when Atwood herself has insisted that she is, by her own choice, first and foremost a writer of literature and a critic only from necessity or, rather, from moral and "national" obligation. In the four-page introduction to *Second Words*, she ruminates on her motivations for turning to criticism in the first place, which she calls a "rescue operation" in Canada at the time:

> When I began writing and first discovered that there were other people writing in Canada, it was fairly clear that unless some writers reviewed Canadian books, some of the time, they wouldn't get reviewed at all. That has changed a great deal, but ... occasionally I may review a book, still, just to get it reviewed, or, because I feel it's been badly treated or misunderstood. ... Book reviews seem to me one of the dues you pay for being a writer, especially in Canada. (12)

Atwood also claims that her gender has been a reason for people inviting her to write critical prose, be it in the form of reviews, essays, or speeches: "Even in the 1980's I'm still being approached by groups who say I just have to do it because this or that august body has never had a woman before (as they're fond of putting it). ... Sometimes it's a writer, and sometimes, even and especially in Canada, it's a Canadian.

Sometimes it's all three" (13). Other motivations for her critical activities are what can be called self-expressive and self-educative, even self-revelatory: "I began as a profoundly apolitical writer, but then I began to do what all novelists and some poets do: I began to describe the world around me" (15). Atwood calls book reviews "the most difficult form for me" and characterizes the critical essay as "more like talking to yourself. It's a way, too, of finding out what you really think" (13).

In the introduction to *Moving Targets*, written more than twenty years after the introduction to *Second Words*, Atwood reviews her critical practices and confirms them. She produces most of these "pieces written for special occasions" (1) on invitation, rarely on her own initiative. She states that these texts feel "so much like homework" (3) to her that she shelves them for as long as possible and writes them mostly from a sense of duty: "Those who are reviewed must review in their turn or the principle of reciprocity fails" (3). Increasingly, at this later stage in her career (in which she has advanced from "being world-famous in Canada to being world-famous, sort of, in the way that writers are" [5]), she has written these texts for worthy causes such as fundraising: "I have a difficult time resisting such lend-a-hand appeals" (1). It again becomes obvious that Atwood much prefers her literary writing and that her much-sought-after critical activities are dutiful, obliging tasks done on request. And it is obvious that a writer with the intellectual, verbal, and personal appeal of Atwood must have turned down many more offers than she has accepted. Being free to choose—"It's a great luxury not to be a professional full-time reviewer: I'm at liberty to close books that don't seize hold of me" (4)—she speaks or writes only on issues truly relevant to her: "Why *Moving Targets?* ... One, ... I can't write about subjects for which I feel nothing. Thus *moving*" (5). The other meaning of "moving" in the context suggests that the subjects of her critical writings are not stationary, even if, as she claims, "my interests have remained fairly constant, although I like to pretend their scope has broadened somewhat" (3).

ATWOOD'S CRITICAL WRITING AND GENDER

One of these "fairly constant interests" and nevertheless a "moving target" for her critical pursuits has been the issue of gender, especially the role of women in both society and literature and the significance of being a woman writer. On all these aspects, Atwood writes with her usual wit, humour, and gift for language, her astute mind, and, of course, her first-hand experience.

I will start my thematic analysis of the relevance of gender in Atwood's expository prose with *Second Words* since—though published ten years after *Survival*—its initial thirteen selected contributions of Part I (1960–71) first appeared in print in the years before *Survival*. They go back to her student years at Victoria College at the University of Toronto, where Atwood co-edited and contributed to *Acta Victoriana*, the literary journal of Victoria College: "A handful of us, all in black, not only edited the magazine but practically wrote the whole thing, under pseudonyms and otherwise" (19). In this early phase of her critical activities, she reviewed Canadian books exclusively (see the quotation above concerning criticism as a "rescue operation"). Any potential naive prejudice about Atwood as a woman writer being partial to books written by women is thwarted right from the beginning—in her early phase, the vast majority of the books she reviewed were written by male authors. Her earliest critical activities may concern practically the only books she reviewed on her own initiative, yet even then, after her first successes as a poet and a writer of fiction before the publication of *Survival* in 1972, she wrote reviews at the request of the editors of *Alphabet*, *Canadian Literature*, and *Poetry*.

Of the thirteen texts of Part I of *Second Words*, only two are of some interest to a gender-conscious reading of Atwood's criticism: the earliest review (of 1961) on the collected poems by Margaret Avison, written for *Acta Victoriana*, and an article of 1970 on Gwendolyn MacEwen's poetry, written for *Canadian Literature* (then edited by George Woodcock). The earlier text refers to Avison the poet repeatedly as "Miss Avison," a gender-asymmetrical kind of address that came to be criticized by the Women's Movement in the following decade (see my analysis of such forms of address and their development in Atwood's novels in chapter 4). Atwood also addresses one of the best-known gender clichés (still) around, the housewife accomplished only at non-expert, non-demanding activities: "If one praises a poet's descriptive powers, one risks conveying the image of a housewife cooking up a poem ... by applying adjectives to an object like icing to a cake, with the same result: if one swallows much of it, one feels a little ill" (22). If in these early few instances Atwood shows herself to be a product of her times, rather than working against problematic mainstream phenomena, as she tends to do later on, we need to remember that this review was written by a twenty-two-year-old student literarily already accomplished if not precocious. In her article on MacEwen's poetry for *Canadian Literature*, "MacEwen's Muse," Atwood explains to what extent MacEwen's "muse" is clearly a male one. Atwood herself, in contrast, when asked in 1993 whether her muse was male or female, replied: "Oh, she's a woman" (cited in Sullivan 1998, 37; on this, see also Nischik 2007).

The seventeen reviews and articles of Part II of *Second Words* were first published in the four years between 1972 and 1976, 1972 being the year in which *Survival* appeared. As Atwood herself explains in *Second Words*,

> Having written an expository work *about* Canadian literature, I was suddenly called upon to produce yet more expositions of my exposition. ...
>
> This was also a period in which I was asked to review a number of books by women ... "women" had now become a *subject*. I began to get worried about the possibility of a new ghetto: women's books reviewed only by women, men's books reviewed only by men, with a corresponding split in the readership. It wasn't what one had in mind as a desirable future for the species.
>
> It's in this period too that I began to get requests for reviews from publications other than Canadian ones. (105–06)

Indeed, in this period, as many as nine of the eleven books reviewed by Atwood were written by female authors, most of them American: Adrienne Rich (three book reviews), Audrey Thomas (two book reviews), Erica Jong, Kate Millett, Marie-Claire Blais, and Marge Piercy; in the following period, the years 1977–82 of Part III of *Second Words*, the ratio was still more than half in favour of female writers, again most of them American: Atwood reviewed books by Anne Sexton, Tillie Olsen, Sylvia Plath, Ann Beattie, Jay Macpherson, and Nadine Gordimer. These writers, of course, may be counted as more or less gender-conscious authors and, with the exception of Plath, as part of or sympathetic to the Women's Movement, which was making itself heard at the time against centuries-old traditions of male voices.

It was also in these ten years between 1972 and 1982 that several essays by Atwood on the special problem of being a woman writer in Canada first appeared, which may be regarded as classic statements on the issue: "On Being a 'Woman Writer': Paradoxes and Dilemmas," "The Curse of Eve: Or, What I Learned in School," and "Writing the Male Character."[1] In an immediate review of *Second Words*, John W. MacDonald (1982) rightly calls these three essays "real masterpieces of essay writing—thoughtful, wise and witty ... filled with illuminations of a very serious kind."

"On Being a 'Woman Writer': Paradoxes and Dilemmas" (1976) starts out by focusing on Atwood's own aversion to writing on this topic and indeed derives "illuminating" thoughts from this aversion. Atwood states first of all the drawbacks of writers' involvement in political movements of any sort (including the Women's Movement): "Their involvement may be good for the movement, but it has yet to be demonstrated that it's good for the writer" (190). Pleading for the writer's independence from any such allegiances, she goes on to comment on the individual female writer's potential stances toward the Women's Movement: those female writers who had made it by that time (e.g., Atwood) might feel "grudging admiration, tempered with envy" (191), because they had had to fight against earlier sexual/gender discrimination practically on their own. Atwood also mentions the memory of guilty feelings and the (self-)indictment of gender "abnormality" (191) when they tried to set aside time for their writing (by necessity often at night), thereby acting against the essentialist, biological view of women that restricts them to the role of wife, mother, homemaker. She concludes that "These writers, if they are honest, don't want to be wrongly identified as the children of a movement that did not give birth to them. Being adopted is not the same as being born" (192). As a third kind of reservation against being incorporated into the Women's Movement, Atwood mentions her dread of implied restrictions on the writer's imaginative creativity, potentially postulated as a one-dimensional conformity to a particular ideological position by which writerly achievements might be judged. Atwood adds perceptively, "However, a feminist criticism need not necessarily be one-dimensional. And ... no matter how narrow, purblind and stupid such a criticism in its lowest manifestations may be, it cannot possibly be *more* narrow, purblind and stupid than some of the non-feminist critical attitudes and styles that have preceded it" (192).

Another stance adopted by women writers that Atwood observes is the "phenomenon of the member of a despised social group who manages to transcend the limitations imposed on the group, at least enough to become 'successful,' ... to dissociate him/herself from the group and to side with its implicit opponents" (192). Evidence of this may be the claims of successful women that they have never had any career hindrances based on gender. Atwood concludes that "Such a woman tends to regard herself, and to be treated by her male [and, one might add, sometimes also female] colleagues, as a sort of honorary man. ... 'You think like a man,' she is told, with admiration and unconscious put-down" (193). Being accepted on false terms in such a context implies denigration not only of the individual but also of the whole group she is part of and helps to define. Atwood puts her finger on the "traditionally incompatible notions of 'woman' and 'good at something'" (193); one might also think of the still almost insurmountable, deeply ingrained hindrances established for highly competent female politicians who grasp at positions of important leadership, with the truly denigrating statements clearly attached mainly or even exclusively to the female sex.[2]

Atwood eventually turns to an analysis of gendered reviewing practices that she noticed over the years, based in part on a project she was involved with at York University in 1971–72. Her findings are, among others, that in many reviews of books authored by women, the author's sex is made an issue of, as in comments "on the cute picture of the (female) author on the cover, coupled with dismissal of her as a writer" (199). A further "essentializing" is the frequent attribution of a "feminine" style to women writers, considered to be "vague, weak, ... 'subjective,' ... 'confessional,' ... 'personal,' or even 'narcissistic' and 'neurotic'" (197). A crasser form of what one might call a biological or even sexual approach to reviewing occurs when works by male writers are appreciatively described as having "balls." Atwood counters provocatively: "Ever hear anyone speak admiringly of work by a woman as having 'tits'?" She sarcastically continues: "*Possible antidotes:* Development of a 'good/female' vocabulary ('Wow, has that ever got Womb ... ')" (198). And, as so often, after such a sarcastic challenge, she clinches the argument in a serious manner: "preferably, the development of a vocabulary that can treat structures made of words as though they are exactly that, not biological entities possessed of sexual organs" (198).

Other gendered strategies that put down the writing of female authors are the focus on and the diminishment of their supposed "domestic themes," while ignoring other themes in the book ("when a man writes about things like doing the dishes, it's realism; when a woman does, it's an unfortunate feminine genetic limitation" [199]), or an exclusive attention to content, eclipsing the aesthetic quality of the writing. With regard to interviews and media stereotypes about female writers, the results are similar. Interviewers, Atwood finds at the time, tend to be more interested in the author's life than in her work, in the idea of writing as a hobby rather than a serious profession for women; they assume that female writers are "crazy freak[s] ... Suicidal Sylvia" (201, 200) or that they are mere spokeswomen for a movement—such as Women's Lib or Canadian nationalism—not inventive, independently thinking writers in their own right. Drawing the sums of her observations first published in 1976—in the decade that saw a blooming of writing by women in North America—Atwood feels bound to conclude that "The woman writer, then, exists in a society that, though it may turn certain individual writers into revered cult objects, has little respect for writing as a profession, and not much respect for women either. If there were more of both, articles like this would be obsolete. I hope they become so" (204).

Because of its yet more fundamental orientation, "The Curse of Eve: Or, What I Learned in School" (1978) is probably even more topical today than the previously discussed essay, which focuses mainly on gendered principles and prejudices in reviewing and interviewing. "The Curse of Eve" could/should be required reading not only in literature classes interested in gender differences but also in political science or sociology classes or in any contexts in which the status of woman and man is at stake.[3] Atwood in this essay traces different evaluative patterns concerning women and men back to gender-biased socialization and to the deeply ingrained ways gender has been handled in literature over the centuries, by both male and female writers.

Atwood again begins by pointing out that, when she grew up, the public sphere was clearly reserved for men, the domestic sphere for women ("I was asked by one of my professors whether I really wanted to go to graduate school ... wouldn't I rather get married?" [215]). She then turns to the question of representation of women and men in literature: "When writing about women, what constitutes success? Is success even plausible? Why, for instance, did George Eliot, herself a successful female writer, never compose a story with a successful female writer as the central character?" (218). The answer, of course, is that female writers, too, are part of their cultural context and upbringing as well as victims of a kind of indoctrination from their social context ("the media, books, films, radios, television and newspapers, from home and school, and from the culture at large, the body of received opinion" [219]). This "body of received opinion" essentializes women into fixed entities, with women usually getting the negative or at least non-dynamic end of the contrastive gender definitions:

> Passive helpless men are aberrations; passive women within the range of the norm. But powerful, or at any rate active, heroes ... are seen as the fulfillment of a *human* ideal; whereas powerful women, and there are many of them in literature, are usually given a supernatural aura. They are witches, Wonder Women or Grendel's mothers. They are monsters.[4] They are not quite human. (223)

Powerful women, because they do not match their received gender roles, are considered not only "not quite human" but also non-feminine. Wonder Woman, the female comic-book creation of male cartoonists, loses her "superhuman" strength when kissed by her boyfriend (223, 224). That, for a woman, being good at something often involves the sacrifice of "femininity" can be seen with many female writers of the nineteenth and twentieth centuries. Atwood ironically suggests the received opinion in connection with Jane Austen, Emily and Charlotte Brontë, George Eliot, Christina Rossetti, Emily Dickinson, Elizabeth Barrett Browning, Sylvia Plath, or Anne Sexton: "These women were writers, true, but they were somehow not women, or if they were women, they were not *good* women. They were bad role models, or so their biographies implied" (225). Having to choose between professional writing and personal happiness, between being successful at work and being allowed to keep up one's gender identity, is a choice presenting itself only to female, not male, writers. Atwood concludes that

> It *is* more difficult for a woman writer in this society than for a male writer. But not because of any innate mysterious hormonal or spiritual differences: it is more difficult because it has been made more difficult, and the stereotypes still lurk in the wings, ready to spring fully formed from the heads of critics, both male and female. ... Women are still expected to be better than men, morally that is, even by women, ... and if you are not an angel, if you happen to have human failings, as most of us do, especially if you display any kind of strength or power, creative or otherwise, then you are not merely human, you're worse than human. You are a witch, a Medusa, a destructive, powerful, scary monster. (226)

Atwood argues that women, just like men both inside and outside literature, "must be allowed their imperfections" (227), without this resulting in their general damnation. They must also be regarded as individuals, just as men are, rather than first and foremost as typical representatives of their (downgraded or idolized) gender: "Perhaps it is time to take the capital W off Woman" (227). Atwood realizes along the way that she herself is, of course, part of these social gender negotiations: "Even I may judge women more harshly than I do men; after all, they were responsible for Original Sin, or that is what I learned in school" (228).

In "Writing the Male Character" (1982), Atwood again shows such prejudiced treatment and evaluation of the two sexes at work in her own metier and according to her own experiences: "We're handing out black marks for what male critics (and, to be fair, some female ones) consider to be unfavourable depictions of men by female authors" (418). She argues that men are not better human beings than women and that it is therefore not objectionable if the female novelist "depicts men behaving the way they do behave a lot of the time" (419). She also argues that, both with male and with female characters, those with pronounced weaknesses or moral stains are the most challenging and interesting characters for writers to construct and that the most obnoxious male characters have been created by male writers:

> Is *Hamlet*, for instance, a slur on men? Is *Macbeth*? Is *Faust*, in any version? How about the behaviour of the men in *Moll Flanders*? Or *Tom Jones*? Is *A Sentimental Journey* about the quintessential wimp? [The list goes on.] Please note that all these characters ... were the creations of men, not women; but nobody, to my knowledge, has accused these male authors of being mean to men. ... If a man depicts a male character unfavourably, it's The Human Condition; if a woman does it, she's being mean to men. ... Woman authors have historically been easier on men in their books than male authors have. (421–22)

Again Atwood redresses the gender imbalance, pointing out prejudiced, slanted evaluations of the writer's craft based on gender.

Her second collection of criticism, *Moving Targets* (2004), covers a selection of her critical writings first published in the years 1982–2004. In this period, some of Atwood's great novels foregrounding gender appeared: *The Handmaid's Tale* (1985), *Cat's Eye* (1988), *The Robber Bride* (1993), and *Alias Grace* (1996). In her critical works of these two decades, there seems to be less focus on gender issues than in the earlier period covered by *Second Words*. Then, too, the book reviews accepted by Atwood during the later period are rather balanced between books written by male and female writers.[5] Yet there are also a few essays in *Moving Targets* that are specifically involved with gender. In fact, gender does remain an issue sprinkled throughout the book, and the broadening of Atwood's range throughout the decades becomes apparent also in her statements on gender issues in this collection of her expository prose.

An important, illuminating contribution is Atwood's autobiographical essay "Great Aunts" written for the book *Family Portraits: Remembrances by Twenty Distinguished Writers* (see Anthony 1989). This essay can be read as a non-fictional companion piece to Atwood's resonant short story "Significant Moments in the Life of My Mother" (which I analyzed elsewhere; see Nischik 2007) in that it makes clear the dominant female family impact on Atwood in the formative period of her life, extending from grandmother to aunts. Although the Atwood inner family circle consisted also of grandfather, father, and two uncles, they are only briefly and factually mentioned: it was Atwood's mother and grandmother and, according to this essay, especially her two aunts who had the most important influence on the budding writer. The mother, as in "Significant Moments," is the model narrator, mainly of family stories, for the daughter: "They [the aunts] were even more alive in my mother's stories, for, although she was no poet, my mother was a raconteur and deadly mimic. The characters in her stories about 'home' became as familiar to me as characters in books" (76). Her mother's stories were also Atwood's first lesson in reading between the lines (78), indirectly teaching her the art of omission and suggestion.

In her relationship with the world outside the family, especially the writer's world, her two aunts seem to have been important mediators. Aunt J. (Joyce Barkhouse), author of five books and children's stories, took the eighteen-year-old Margaret to her first writers' conference (by the Canadian Authors Association in 1958). The aunts also took Atwood on a "literary outing" (80) to visit Canadian writer Ernest Buckler in the early 1970s—that is, around the time when Atwood was already becoming better known than Buckler was. Indeed, the aunts always seem to support her: "'That was something! He said you had a teeming brain!'" (82). Together with the mother's sometimes unconventional behaviour ("'Do what you think is right, no matter what other people think,'" [83]), the aunts provide an alternative model to received notions of womanhood such as modesty and politeness ("If you can't say anything nice, don't say anything at all" [83][6]) or marriage as women's only, practically compulsory, life option (79). They introduce a culture of writing into their family ("The three sisters wrote one another every week, and my mother read these letters out loud" [75]) and encourage Atwood in her early writing endeavours in various ways: "Aunt J. showed me his [an English professor's] letter, beaming with pleasure. This was my first official encouragement" (73). Aunt J., the literary minded, is indeed the one young Atwood showed her poems to, not her mother, and the aunt took her ambition seriously ("She read them and did not laugh" [73]). Aunt K. was the one "who had told me something everyone else had forgotten, including myself: that I had announced, at the age of five, that I was going to be a writer" (81).

The end of the essay forms the climax of Atwood's expression of gratitude toward her two aunts. The virulence of gender-role socialization even in the context of such a relatively unconventional family becomes apparent when Atwood, upon the appearance of her "first real book" (83), dreads disapproval by her family:

> I suppose any person, but especially any woman, who takes up writing has felt, especially at first, that she was doing it against a huge largely unspoken pressure, the pressure of expectation and decorum. This pressure is most strongly felt, by women, from within the family, and more so when the family is a strong unit. ... I didn't worry much about my father and mother, who had gracefully survived several other eccentricities of mine. ... Instead, I worried about my aunts. (83)

This singling out of the aunts probably occurs because they seemed to be more into writing than Atwood's parents and therefore in a better, more accepted, position to judge her literary product. The end of the essay is particularly moving, not only brilliantly conceived and written but also with noteworthy indirect comments on gender roles and the importance of a female supportive family network for Atwood's development and self-esteem as a writer:

> To my surprise, my aunts came through with flying colours. Aunt J. thought it was wonderful—a real book! She said she was bursting with pride. Aunt K. said that there were certain things that were not done in her generation, but they could be done by mine, and more power to me for doing them.
>
> This kind of acceptance meant more to me than it should have, to my single-minded all-for-art twenty-six-year-old self. (Surely I ought to be impervious to aunts.) However, like the morals of my mother's stories, what exactly it meant is far from clear to me. Perhaps it was a laying-on of hands, a passing of something from one generation to another. What was being passed on was the story itself: what was known, and what could be told. What was between the lines. The permission to tell the story, wherever that might lead.

> Or perhaps it meant that I too was being allowed into the
> magical static but ever-continuing saga of the photo album. Instead
> of three different-looking young women with archaic clothes and
> identical Roman noses, standing with their arms around each other,
> there would now be four. I was being allowed into *home*. (84)

This ending might also serve to support John W. MacDonald's claim
(1982) that no contemporary writer in Canada writes better non-fiction
prose than Atwood does.[7]

In "The Public Woman as Honorary Man" (1989), Atwood's
three-page review of Antonia Fraser's analysis of powerful female leaders
entitled *The Warrior Queens*, we see again how the age-old gender
ideology has twisted the tradition of successful females, confirming
Atwood's earlier arguments, here in the context of women's agency in
politics and the military. Atwood finds that these female leaders'

> styles vary enormously, but they have one thing in common: All
> were instantly mythologized. ... They are aberrations, and as such
> are thought to partake of the supernatural or the monstrous:
> angels or devils, paragons of chastity or demons of lust, Whores
> of Babylon or Iron Maidens. ... Women leaders, it seems, find it
> difficult to be life sized. For good or ill, they are gigantic. (100–01)

Atwood also discovers in Fraser's analysis what she herself calls the
"honorary male" syndrome, with successful women distancing themselves from their sex group. She comments, sarcastically, "If you're
playing boys' games, you need to be one of the boys" (101).

With "Spotty-Handed Villainesses: Problems of Female Bad
Behaviour in the Creation of Literature," a lecture delivered in 1993
on the occasion of the publication of *The Robber Bride*, Atwood returns
to what she calls "practical" (162) writerly problems in connection with
gender representation. This text may be regarded as a companion to her
earlier essay "Writing the Male Character" in that Atwood now defends,
indeed calls for, the presentation of morally stained female characters
in literature: first because such women obviously also exist in real life,
second because "women have more to them than virtue. They are fully
dimensional human beings; they too have subterranean depths; why

shouldn't their many-dimensionality be given literary expression?" (172). Atwood also stresses that the Women's Movement significantly contributed to opening up whole new areas for the writer's exploration, whereas more traditional plot patterns, such as "the Cinderella happy ending—the Prince Charming one" (164), have lost their matter-of-course quality. In more general terms, "The tendency of innovative literature is to include the hitherto excluded, which often has the effect of rendering ludicrous the conventions that have just preceded the innovation" (164–65)—with the "conventions" here referring to the female character as either a paragon of virtue or a whore, according to the Madonna-Whore Split, denying women multidimensionality.

In her more recent book survey "Resisting the Veil: Report from a Revolution" (2003), Atwood ventures into the Iranian Islamic world, pointing out how the Iranian mullah regime systematically suppresses women, "forced into the veil, deprived of most of their autonomy. Their fate reminds all women of the fragility of their so-called rights and freedoms, for, under the rule of the Iranian mullahs, the female body itself was transformed into a highly charged symbol, a vehicle for projections and religious fantasies" (368). Through Atwood's discussion of largely autobiographical texts by Marjane Satrapi and Azar Nafisi, as well as of a novel by Farnoosh Moshiri, we see the dismal consequences of this allegedly religiously legitimized political system for Iranian women. As Atwood stated elsewhere, and indirectly in her own version of a theocratic society that acts on women's bodies (*The Handmaid's Tale*), the liberality of a social system may be detected in the kind of rights it grants—or does not grant—to women. Atwood ends on a pessimistic or, one may fear, realistic note: if vice is socially supported, she argues, "that licence will be used to the full. ... Unfortunately, although we continue to dream of heaven, we aren't very good at creating it. We're so much better at hell" (371). One function of literature is to counteract such tendencies with warnings—the precious value of freedom of thought and expression also becomes clear in Nafisi's high esteem of Western literature, considered absolutely essential by her in a social context of oppression such as exists in Iran.

The fifty-first and final contribution in *Moving Targets*, "Mortification" (2003), also shows the continuing problems, challenges, and often "mortifying" relevance of gender in relationships and identification

processes, here eventually prolonged from exterior to interior mortifications. Atwood structures this three-page piece episodically into three
parts, early, middle, and modern periods (of her writing life). The earliest
episode goes back to 1969, with Atwood having just published her first
novel, *The Edible Woman*, and struggling to become a recognized writer.
Her publisher arranged her first-ever book signing in the Edmonton
Hudson's Bay Company department store (a disillusioning experience
Atwood keeps returning to), where the signing table was set up in the
men's sock and underwear department (possibly because of the resonant
title of the novel)—no wonder that Atwood sold only two copies of the
book on this occasion. The second episode, from the late 1970s, is about
her appearance on an American TV talk show, where Atwood was placed
after a group from the Colostomy[8] Association, with the result that no one
seemed to be particularly interested in her, to say nothing of her creative
art: "'What did you say your name was? And tell us the plot of your book,
just in a couple of sentences, please'" (408). These two episodes show
Atwood's long-time experiences with a social context and particularly a
media circus ignorant of the value and essentials of literature (see also her
treatment of this issue in her autobiographical comics, chapter 7).

The most recent episode rendered in the text, from a TV show in
Mexico, continues along the same line but moreover shows patterns of
personal, sexist assumptions, which Atwood, also in her capacity as a
writer, keeps being confronted with—and keeps putting her finger on.
The interview proceeded pleasantly enough until the male interviewer
"hit me with the F-question. The do-you-consider-yourself-a-feminist
question." Even worse, "'Do you consider yourself *feminine?*' he said"
(408). Even in the twenty-first century, sexist prejudices persist: a female
writer presenting her stories from a woman's perspective is branded a
"feminist," whereas a male writer doing the same from a male perspective
is simply the norm and is not branded a "masculinist" writer. A successful
female writer, the second question suggests, loses, or at least jeopardizes,
her femininity, high achievement and success apparently still being outside
the female gender role in many quarters. Atwood reacted shrewdly in the
awkward situation by turning the sexist undercurrent of this offensive
question inside out: "'You really shouldn't be asking *me*. You should be
asking the men in my life. ... Just as I would ask the women in *your* life
if you are masculine. They'd tell me the truth'" (409). Atwood's retort,

clever and effective as it may have been in the situation, runs counter to one of the maxims of her childhood concerning the education of girls, however (see "Great Aunts"): "If you can't say anything nice, don't say anything at all." As a result, the conflict became internalized, her adequate tit-for-tat behaviour in the situation troubling her for days. With gender issues, "mortifications never end" (406), it seems, even with a literary icon such as Atwood, who was reduced to her sex/gender by the interviewer. This incident shows the deep-rootedness and persistence of essentialist, trivializing views of women—even her stardom does not protect Atwood from what we may call the sexist fallacy, even in the twenty-first century.

In her four thematically unified critical books so far, Atwood turns to predominant themes in CanLit (*Survival*, 1972), the theme of the North in Canadian literature and culture (*Strange Things*, 1995), writing and the position of the writer in general (*Negotiating with the Dead*, 2002), and the highly topical examination of the concept of debt as a human construct (*Payback*, 2008). None of these four books is thus explicitly devoted to gender, but Atwood's gender awareness nevertheless shines through again and again. Concerning *Survival: A Thematic Guide to Canadian Literature*, the hotly debated best-selling book of literary criticism on CanLit (by 1980, within eight years, it had sold over 70,000 copies; see Rosenberg 1984, 135), the famous victim positions—which Atwood claims to be of relevance for CanLit as a whole in connection with its supposed main theme, survival—can also be linked to the position of women. Atwood herself establishes this connection early on in her presentation of the four victim positions:

> *Position Two:*
> *To acknowledge the fact that you are a victim, but to explain this as an act of Fate, the Will of God, the dictates of Biology (in the case of women, for instance), the necessity decreed by History, or Economics, or the Unconscious, or any other large general powerful idea.* (37)

In chapter 10 of *Survival*, Atwood surveys the predominant views of women in Canadian literature, according to her point of view[9] ("Ice Women vs Earth Mothers: The Stone Angel and the Absent Venus"), and concludes that "most of the strong and vividly-portrayed female characters in Canadian literature are old women[10] ... , and a tough, sterile, suppressed and granite-jawed lot they are" (199).

In *Strange Things: The Malevolent North in Canadian Literature*, Atwood shows that the Canadian North, inhabited primarily by men in Canadian literature, has usually been personified as a "savage but fascinating female ... hostile to white men, but alluring; ... it would drive you crazy, and, finally, would claim you for its own" (18–19). Again and again the North is negatively rendered as a giant female, "icy, connected with madness, and destructive" (26). As in *Survival*, Atwood devotes one chapter mainly to women, asking what happens to the representation of the North when it is rendered from the perspective of women. She starts out by giving interesting potential answers to the question of why there are so many Canadian women writers (89–93);[11] in fact, there are not more than "men writers," but even this rather balanced state of affairs seems to be unusual about Canadian literature. Atwood states the consequences of the traditional, strictly complementary, role distribution for character constellations in literature on the North: "I can't offer you any female Franklins—no one would have funded an expedition headed by such a person—or any female prospectors, ... or any female Mounties" (91). She points out that, as early as 1892, Canadian writer E. Pauline Johnson, partly of Mohawk ancestry, published a piece in a Toronto newspaper in which she criticized "white authors for dishing up, again and again, the same kind of Indian maiden in their books—a poor, doomed creature, who passionately loves the white hero ... and usually ends her life by suicide, because of the perfidy of her white lover" (93). Atwood also diagnoses other differences in the plots of early literature on the North written by women such as Anna Jameson, Susanna Moodie, and Catharine Parr Traill: female characters are usually presented at home with their families, not out on the land; nor, in their relation to nature, do they "utilize verbs of the staking and penetrating variety" (97).

Later women writers dealing with the North (Atwood discusses texts by Margaret Laurence, Joyce Marshall, Ethel Wilson, Marian Engel, Aritha van Herk, and Ann Tracy) deal with literary conventions even more creatively. Thus, "the old woman"—the power plant luring Molly's husband into madness in Marshall's eponymous short story—is not only a substitute for mother or wife but also the "incarnation of that cold, savage, alluring, female power of the North" (101). In literature from the middle of the twentieth century onward, female protagonists often "go off into the woods" by themselves, sometimes with the very purpose to distance themselves from a man, such as the protagonist Lou in Engel's novel *Bear*, who even falls in love with that animal: "She does not conquer the natural world, or penetrate it—she befriends it" (106). From the 1970s onward, there has been a notable increase in women who write about the North, and women have claimed the territory, finally, for their own purposes:

> When second-wave women write about the wilderness, they render it female in relation to male characters. ... But when the protagonist is a woman, the wilderness is apt to be sexually neuter. It's also apt to be refreshing or renewing in some way, and in the 1970s at any rate this renewal has something to do with the absence of men from the scene. (108)

The North, in other words, formerly the territory for men to test their masculine strength and power, has become an area of retreat and intensified identity formation for female characters. Yet, in a typical Atwoodian manner, Atwood ends her lectures/book on an even more fundamental note, channelling questions of gender into questions of humanity. She warns of the pressing ecological problems endangering the North, former incarnation of pristine nature: "The North will be neither female nor male, neither fearful nor health-giving, because it will be dead. The earth, like trees, dies from top down. The things that are killing the North will kill, if left unchecked, everything else" (116).

Negotiating with the Dead: A Writer on Writing, though not focusing explicitly on gender either, states in the introduction what we are reminded of in places throughout the volume: the book is "about the position the writer finds himself in; or herself, which is always a little different" (xvii). Somewhat tongue-in-cheek, Atwood goes on: "If I had suspected anything about the role I would be expected to fulfil, not just as a writer, but as a *female* writer—how irrevocably doomed!— I would have ... plastered myself over with an impenetrable *nom de plume*, ... never have done any interviews, nor allowed my photo to appear on book jackets" (15). The persistent gender contrasting also in the context of writing, most frequently disadvantageous to women, refers to principles Atwood has pointed out before in her critical writing: the irrational professional role distribution between women and men (on her early idea of becoming a journalist, she notes, "I changed my mind, because he [a journalist] told me that as a girl I would be put to work writing the obituaries and the ladies' pages, and nothing else" [17]); the ascription of "masculine" and "feminine" writing styles, so that Atwood in her early writing used initials instead of her first name (21); the different expectations/treatments of reviewers concerning male and female authors (21) and of society concerning the writing life ("You couldn't be a wife and mother and also an artist, because each one of these things required total dedication. ... Love and marriage pulled one way, Art another. ... Art would dance you to death. ... Or it would destroy you as an ordinary woman" [85]); the prejudices in language use, indicative of the collective mentality behind it ("the word 'genius' and the word 'woman' just don't really fit together in our language, because the kind of eccentricity expected of male 'geniuses' would simply result in the label 'crazy,' should it be practiced by woman" [100]); "the F-word. If you're a woman and a writer, does the combination of gender and vocation automatically make you a feminist, and what does that mean, exactly?" (106). Although the intricacies of gender still make life hard for female writers, it is some consolation that nowadays things do not seem to be as bad as they used to be. As Atwood cautiously states at the end of chapter 3 of *Negotiating with the Dead*, "Now it is more possible for a woman writer to be seen as, well, just that: neither nun nor orgiastic priestess, neither more nor less than human. Nevertheless, the mythology still has power, because such mythologies about women still have power" (90).

Atwood's latest essay collection, *Payback: Debt and the Shadow Side of Wealth*, based on her Massey Lectures, investigates (with what seems to be uncanny prescience of the current global economic crisis) how the cultural concept of debt has structured human thinking and behaviour from antiquity to the present day. Not surprisingly for Atwood, she repeatedly looks at this topic with an awareness of gender, though in this collection, too, gender is not one of her focal concerns. She points out gender imbalances by showing that Christianity has no goddesses, just female saints (33), that the first slaves were women because they could be controlled more easily (59), that women, just like slaves, were excluded from citizenship in ancient Athens (though the allegorical figure of Justice remained female [39]), and that ruin for a man in the nineteenth century meant financial ruin, whereas for a woman it meant sexual ruin (by having extramarital sex, 106–07). With an autobiographical touch, Atwood repeatedly draws on her family's experience during the Great Depression and her own childhood in the still credit-card-free Canada of the 1940s. She points out that in her family her mother was the keeper of finances and that she therefore was instrumental in forming Atwood's sense of balance (43). That mothers have not been as appreciated in their role as they should be is suggested by this sarcastic comparison in her remodelling of Dickens's *A Christmas Carol* for the twenty-first century in chapter 5: "It's like Mother's Day—dump a card and some flowers on the old hen once a year, then exploit her the rest of the time" (179). Yet, as Atwood reveals, it was her mother who showed wise premonition in keeping a newspaper clipping from 1972 that featured an MIT study predicting that "the world economy is headed for collapse within 70 years—bringing widespread pestilence, poverty and starvation—unless economic growth is halted soon" (196). In chapter 3, "Debt as Plot," Atwood deals with debt as a literary motif. She points out that much of the money-lending business has been in male hands, and she treats a broad range of novels demonstrating debt as it impacts women (105–19). She concludes from her reading of Victorian novels that, "When I was young and simple, I thought the nineteenth-century novel was driven by love; but now, in my more complicated riper years, I see that it's also driven by money, which indeed holds a more central place in it than love does, no matter how much the virtues of love may be waved idealistically aloft" (100).

CONCLUSION

Atwood's status as a literary and cultural critic has repeatedly been evaluated, in spite of all the critical turmoil over *Survival*, in a predominantly positive manner (see the works mentioned at the beginning of this chapter). In trying to assess her critical writing, we can first of all distinguish broadly between two different traditions of essay writing: the first going back to Michel de Montaigne, characterized by meandering, subjective, detail-oriented progress of thought; the second going back to Sir Francis Bacon and the English tradition of essay writing, in which there is a more logical, didactic, rational progress of thought. Clearly Atwood's sharply analytical essays are more indebted to the latter tradition.

Her special contribution to Canadian criticism is her blend of partly self-ironic, humorous, always highly readable, and engaging presentation—appealing to a large readership—and serious, demanding, often problematic topics, on which Atwood presents her illuminating arguments in "didactic," convincing diction and rhetoric. As with her fiction, she is a rare case of a critic reaching both scholars and the general reading public. Her sometimes playful attitude and flippant style should not distract, however, from the fact that there is an analytical, highly perceptive, and intellectual mind at work on complex, sometimes notoriously difficult because emotion-laden gender issues, which are embedded in traditional power structures and supported by time-honoured social systems. Atwood's kind of criticism has been characterized as "literary journalism" and "practical-mediational criticism" (Woodcock 1981, 224, 236), as "practical, text-centered, and value-oriented craft," "mediator between art and the audience, between an increasingly elusive and elitist literary theory on the one hand and a non-committal *anything goes* on the other," and "criticism as creative art" (Pache 2000/02, 132, 133). In her pragmatic effort to reach mainly the public with her criticism and to provide helpful guiding—rather than to write merely for scholars (whom she repeatedly and facetiously calls "the footnote crowd")—Atwood has been an important counterbalance against a long trend of criticism in Canada (and elsewhere, e.g., the United States) between the 1950s and the 1990s that Robert Lecker diagnosed and deplored in 1994: "Canadian criticism has become a private affair, removed from public access. ... [S]cholars write for each other, rather than for the public. ... Atwood, an exacademic, sees the academic walls closing in on Canadian literature. She wants to break the trend towards privacy. She wants a public" (88, 93, 94).

At the same time, with her turning to issues of gender right from her early through to her later criticism, particularly in the context of writing, Atwood tackled a crucial problem that had long been ignored or, as the case may be, silently taken for granted, until Virginia Woolf put the question on the map with her "writerly" *A Room of One's Own* (first published in 1929):[12] the difference it makes to be a woman writer. With a wealth of first-hand experience in the literary world and her breadth of knowledge of world literature, Atwood gives us her view on women and literature, countering the male master discourse. Her essays "On Being a 'Woman Writer,'" "The Curse of Eve," "Writing the Male Character" (from *Second Words*), "Spotty-Handed Villainesses," and "Mortification" (from *Moving Targets*) may be regarded as classic statements on the issue. As with her creative writing, gender forms just one, albeit an important, strand of thought of this politically minded writer. Focusing on the status, situation, and discrimination of the woman writer and the handling of literary characters, Atwood rightly claims that this attention is part of her general humanistic involvement, her engagement with human rights. As she retorts to the offensive male interviewer in "Mortification," "'Women are human beings, don't you agree?'" (408). Similarly revealing what should be obvious is the following statement, from which it actually follows that every thinking human being, according to the logic of the sentence, would have to be called a "feminist": "'If feminism is dealing with women as independent entities, ... then I'm a feminist'" (cited in Rosenberg 1984, 147–48). Atwood thereby also questions the legitimacy of the breadth of meaning of this asymmetrically handled and often derogatorily used term "feminism." At the same time, she explicitly refused to be claimed by the Women's Liberation Movement, which may partly also be put down to her down-to-earth, straightforward style of essay writing (in the English tradition), which clearly distinguishes itself from the more inflammatory rhetorics of avowed feminists such as Hélène Cixous, whose "The Laugh of the Medusa" (1976) became a founding text of *écriture féminine*.

Atwood's critical essays also throw light on her own creative writing—compare *Survival* with *Surfacing*, "Great Aunts" with "Significant Moments in the Life of My Mother," "Spotty-Handed Villainesses" with *The Robber Bride* as well as *Cat's Eye*, "Mortification" with *The Edible Woman* as well as *Lady Oracle*, and so on. Yet Atwood's literary and cultural criticism, deriving as it does from a sharp intellect, effects important statements in its own right, often with a clearly political impact. Her critical writing is another instance of her firm view of the writer having moral and political responsibility toward the public, and it aims at what Margaret Atwood generally proposes in "What's So Funny? Notes on Canadian Humour" (1974, collected in *Second Words*) as the writer's task, where necessary, namely "to arouse moral indignation with a view to reform ... to expose, rebuke and correct" (183).

NOTES

1. "Witches" also falls into this category but is shorter and truly an "occasional piece"; Atwood alleges in the text that she wrote it in a restaurant on the very day of the speech.
2. E.g., "Sie kann's nicht" ("She is incapable of doing this"), as Chancellor Schroeder said about his later successor Angela Merkel, who then proved to be a very capable and powerful chancellor under adverse governing conditions; or the misogynist remarks about presidential candidate Hillary Clinton (often called a "bitch" on Internet sites).
3. Regarding the sadly revelatory phenomena characterizing the presidential primaries in the United States in 2008, for instance, see Metzler and Nischik 2010.
4. On the continued topicality of this argument, note that none less than a female Harvard professor in an interview in March 2008 called Hillary Clinton a "monster" (and had to resign from her post in the Obama campaign).
5. Those by male writers are more frequent (eight to six).
6. "Good" instead of "nice" earlier (78).
7. The ending may be fully appreciated in all its repercussions only with a closer knowledge of the essay as a whole, of course.
8. A surgical operation during which a permanent opening from the colon is made to allow feces to leave the patient's body via this opening.
9. On the restrictions on her text selection for the book and some of the partly harsh criticism launched against *Survival*, see Rosenberg 1984, 139–43.
10. From her stance of a roughly thirty-year-old at the time, she considers "over fifty" to be "old" (199).
11. See, e.g., "Canadians never developed the concept of women as merely brainless decoration. Canadian oral folklore is still full of tales of our grandmothers' generation, when women ran farms, chased off bears,

delivered their own babies in remote locations and bit off the umbilical cords" (90).

12. In what is widely considered one of the founding texts of feminist critique, Woolf, like Atwood, engages with questions concerning gender from a socioliterary perspective yet frames them within a markedly more experimental style than that of Atwood's sharp analytical prose. Woolf stretches the essay genre toward the fictional "liberties and licenses of the novel" (1929, 4)—and a modernist novel at that: blurring fiction and criticism, *A Room of One's Own* splits the first-person narrator into multiple personae and voices, argues for the (higher) truth of fiction, and embraces its own contradictions as inevitable and resonant.

7

"Survivalwoman, Survivalcreature, Womanwoman"
Atwood as Cartoonist

This chapter represents the first extended publication on Margaret Atwood's comics.[1] I want to introduce her comics oeuvre here, paying specific attention to the question of how far gender is also an important aspect of her comics with respect to content, theme, and, to some extent, even form. My analysis will be contextualized by a brief history of cartoon art in the United States and Canada as well as a short treatment of cartoon art as a motif in Atwood's literary works.

CARTOON ART IN THE UNITED STATES AND CANADA

The cartoon and the comic strip, the comic book, and the graphic novel[2] are popular forms of storytelling that usually combine images and words, which are equally important for the transportation of meaning.[3] These expressive formats of (short or long) "pictorial fiction" are usually geared to a broader consumer market, constituting a prime example of mass entertainment. After important European generic forerunners in the works of William Hogarth (1697–1764) and Wilhelm Busch (1832–1908), the cartoon and the comic strip in their modern-day conceptions were introduced in the United States at the end of the nineteenth century (1895),[4] when Richard Felton Outcault published a cartoon (i.e., a single image) called "The Yellow Kid," which was to develop into a successful series of comic strips.[5] Several internationally successful American comic strips have brought this hybrid art—which has been called one of the few indigenous American art forms[6]—into global popular culture and have repeatedly entered the world of Hollywood: *The Yellow Kid* (1896), *The Katzenjammer Kids* (1897), *Krazy Kat* (1913), *Tarzan* (1929), *Popeye* (1929), *Blondie* (1930), *Mickey Mouse* (1930), *Flash Gordon* (1934), *Superman* (1938), *Batman* (1939), *Wonder Woman* (1941), *Peanuts* (1950), *Spider Man* (1962).[7] For his graphic novel *Maus*, Spiegelman even won the American Pulitzer Prize.

As with every other art form, subgenres, transformations, and developments have emerged and still do. Whereas the main purpose of the earlier "comics" in the first three decades of their existence honoured their designation by being mainly funny (an alternative name for such comics, especially in colloquial North American English, is "the funnies"), this staple characteristic has been complemented over the course of time by, for example, traits of adventure, pornography, or horror. Comics have also been invested with conspicuous seriousness, such as a political,[8] sociocritical, or psychological agenda (see Charles Schulz's enormously popular *Peanuts* comics, which debuted in seven newspapers on 2 October 1950 and ran *daily* until 13 February 2000, one day after Schulz's death, in an uninterrupted sequence of 27,500 instalments).

The usual publication forums for cartoons and comic strips have been the newspapers and weekly magazines—such as *The New Yorker*[9]—which have ensured for comics both a regular and a large readership. It was estimated in 1963 that, "conservatively, six to seven hundred million readers weekly" read comics in the weekly magazines, "three times as many Americans as read the important daily news" (White and Abel 1963, 3, 7).[10] And in a recent study (2008) by the Newspaper Association of America, figures were still high: "39 per cent of readers polled said they read the comics each day. That's more than said they read movie reviews, food and fashion coverage and daily TV listings."[11] The comics have thus often been seen as an extra appeal that enlarges the readership of a newspaper (see O'Sullivan 1990, 10–12). At a time of shrinking newspaper markets, cartoons go increasingly online to more than make up for loss of readerships.[12] Judith O'Sullivan, surveying 100 years of cartoon art, has pointed out that "comics have achieved a high level of artistic and literary excellence within an intensely commercial environment and despite a sometimes hostile reception by critics, courts, and lawmakers" (1990, 10).

Another link between newspapers and comic art is the latter's frequent topicality, its reference to contemporary political or social issues. "The comics serve as revealing reflectors of popular attitudes, tastes and mores" (Inge 1990, xi). Perhaps it is not too surprising, then, that "cartooning remained for decades the exclusive territory of white males" (O'Sullivan 1990, 115). Most of the few well-known female comics heroines were created by male cartoonists (*Sheena, Queen of the Jungle*, 1942–52; *Wonder Woman*, 1941). After forerunners such as Nell Brinkley in the 1910s and Dale Messick (*Brenda Starr, Reporter,* 1940), it is mainly since the 1960s that there has been a significant increase in female cartoonists who, additionally, portray women not only as weak victims—insecure and dependent on their looks (e.g., Cathy Guisewite's *Cathy,* 1976)—but also, as is the case in Nicole Hollander's *Sylvia* (1979), create unconventional female characters who even serve a feminist agenda (see Montresor 1994). Pamela A. Boker points out yet a further step in gender representation in American comics:

> In the mainstream comic books of the last decade [the 1980s], the question of female inferiority is rarely verbalized within the text, and would be considered a cliché issue. The women superheroes are super-female in their appearance, and the men are super-male, but the concepts of femininity and masculinity, as cultural categories embodying the attributes of passivity and aggressiveness, are all but eliminated. A remarkable achievement in Western culture, even in fantasy. (1993, 109)

Canada's cartoon and comics industry was for a long time—and to some extent still is—heavily dominated by US productions. A case in point is the career of one of the creators of *Superman,* Joe Shuster, born in Toronto in 1914 and today honoured on Toronto's "Walk of Fame." There are architectural traces of Toronto, rather than any particular American city, in the anonymous "Metropolis" of the early instalments of *Superman.* Ultimately, however, Shuster must be regarded as an example of the continental exodus of talented Canadian cartoonists at the time, who usually went to the United States for better pay (Shuster went there even earlier, at the age of nine; on claiming Superman to be "Canadian," see, critically, Ferguson 1997). Especially up to the 1970s, the market for Canadian comic books in Canada had to struggle for survival due to a less developed publishing industry, higher production costs, and a much smaller readership than in the United States. An earlier flourishing period of Canadian comics was, again, linked to the powerful southern neighbour: with the adoption of the War Exchange Conservation Act in Canada in 1940 to alter the trade imbalance with the United States, the border was closed for "non-essentials," including comic books, which resulted in a brief thriving of Canadian comic art during the Second World War.[13]

In the past few decades, especially since the 1990s, Canada has joined the realm of first-rate, internationally acclaimed cartoon art[14] with artists such as Seth (pseudonym for Gregory Gallant) and Aislin (pseudonym for Terry Mosher).[15] Mosher/Aislin, the regular cartoonist for the editorial page of the Montreal *Gazette*, is Canada's most outstanding (and harshest) political cartoonist,[16] whereas Seth, with his use of "comics as a natural outlet for his own inner life" (2006, 4), has been influenced by Charles M. Schulz. Other important political cartoonists, of an earlier generation, were the late Len Norris (cartoonist for the *Vancouver Sun* from 1950 to 1988) and Ian Duncan Macpherson (cartoonist for the *Toronto Star* from 1958 to 1993; see Sabin 1977). Concerning the contemporary context, Bart Beaty summarizes the situation of comics art in North America as follows: "While Americans dominate the mass-market superhero comic industry, ... in the 1990s Canada emerged as a critical leader in the production of comic books that aspired to incorporate fewer generic elements and higher artistic aspirations" (2002, 223).

Earlier Canadian comics such as *Johnny Canuck* (1942)—"Canuck" being the Canadian slang term for a Canadian—and the later successful *Captain Canuck* (1975) flaunted stereotypical Canadian symbols and characteristics: "Captain Canuck, clad in a red and white suit and maple leaf emblems, used his strength—derived from a healthy diet and fitness—to fight for Canadian 'peace, order, and good government.' He avoided violence when possible, prayed before missions, and dedicated himself to protecting Canada and the world from evildoers"

(Edwardson 2003, 184). Something similar applies to Canada's first distinctly Canadian superhero in *Nelvana of the Northern Lights*, which came out in 1940: that is, in the four-year period sometimes called Canada's "Golden Age of Comics" (Ferguson 1997, 169). Nelvana of the North happens to be a female ("Canada's answer to Wonder Woman," Ferguson notes [1997, 169]), a fantastic Inuit goddess who, for instance, alights gracefully upon a snow altar to protect Canada's Inuit from the evil intentions of the "white man." Nelvana is also one of altogether five Canadian comic-book heroes who in 1995 appeared in a Canada Post booklet of ten stamps, featuring, next to Nelvana, Johnny and Captain Canuck, Fleur de Lys ("a modern Québécois Wonder Woman" [Ferguson 1997, 175]), and, interestingly, the "almost-Canadian" (see above) Superman, thereby "institutionalizing them as important cultural icons" (Edwardson 2003, 197).[17]

ATWOOD AND CARTOONS/COMIC STRIPS

It was against this background that Atwood took up the challenge to contribute to an expressive format dominated for a long time, particularly in Canada, by American productions. Atwood herself seems to have grown up with (American) comics. In the interview conducted for this book (see chapter 8), she answers the question "How did you develop into a cartoonist?" with "I *began* as a cartoonist!" Probably she is implying that her first steps toward writing were taken via this hybrid genre, which trains one toward pointed, minimalist, and often humorous language use. Atwood points out that she grew up at a time when TV had not yet been invented and that she thus belonged to "the comic-book generation":

> We didn't have TV and the comic books were very, very popular. Children collected them, and traded them, and had big stocks of them, and you might spend a Saturday morning with your friends reading comics. You know, a group activity was reading comics. And then trading, "I've read this," you would read them several times and keep them, put them under your bed. And of course it was something that parents disapproved of. (see chapter 8)[18]

Atwood also speaks of "amusing" and "narrative cartoon strips, featuring their protagonists just like novels." She thus draws attention to the *narrative* aspects of comics and thereby to an important similarity between fiction and comics.[19]

With her cultural background in the "comic-book generation," it is not surprising that a multitalented artist such as Atwood (see her long practical experience with several kinds of visual art, as she explains in the interview) should turn to the occasional production and publication of comic strips. This self-taught artistic activity ("I just did it ... children just do it," she notes in the interview) underwent a long gestation before Atwood started to publish comics in the 1970s, since she had already drawn comics on a larger scale as a child: "It was just a total culture that was very appealing to children, and therefore it was the normal form for children to practice. ... [T]his was just a natural thing to do, and we had comic strips that we drew."

Interestingly, in the interview, Atwood refers only to American comic strips—*Superman*, *Batman*, *X-Men* (apart from the very successful graphic novel *Persepolis* [2000–03] by Iranian artist Marjane Satrapi, who lives in France).[20] She does not mention any Canadian comics. Atwood may have been a little too young when, during the Second World War, comics sold in Canada were exclusively Canadian (see above), and after the reopening of the US-Canadian border for American comics the latter regained dominance in Canada. In an earlier interview, however, Atwood outs herself as a fan of Canadian cartoonist Aislin (Terry Mosher), who is, significantly, a *political* cartoonist: "Terry Mosher is one of my idols. I think he's really good" (in LaMarsh 1975, 03:06–03:09 min.).

It is not surprising, then, that Atwood has also repeatedly referred to comics in her literary writing. Although the visual medium that she most frequently makes thematic use of is photography (see Nischik and Breitbach 2006), her integration of comics into her literary works covers a wide range: from brief passing remarks[21] via indirect medial references (e.g., "Above the head of the [clothed] maid / is an invisible voice balloon: *slut*"[22]) toward an extended thematic treatment, as in Atwood's poems "Comic Books vs. History (1949, 1969)" and particularly "They Eat Out," collected in *Eating Fire* (1998, 94–95, 106).

In the former poem (from *Procedures for Underground*, 1970), the United States and Canada are contrasted in a classroom situation, with the United States being reduced by schoolchildren to its representations in comics: stylized "steel cities" and supernatural heroes ("they all wore capes, bullets / bounced off them" [95]). Canada, in contrast, anticlimactically and also reductively, is associated with "only / real-sized explorers, confined / to animal skin coats" who "in the winters / ... died of scurvy" (95). In a later, more realistic view, the American comics heroes "had collapsed inside / their rubber suits" (95). The final stanza sees the lyrical I distancing herself from high-blown representational distortions and turning instead to small-scale but "actual" historical endeavours in a "natural" context:

> I turn back, search
> for the actual, collect lost
> bones, burnt logs
> of campfires, pieces of fur. (95)

Gender is not made an issue in this poem, which emphasizes instead Atwood's involvement with problems of representation, particularly with questions of national (self-)conceptions regarding the contrast between the United States and Canada. "They Eat Out" (from *Power Politics*, 1971), in contrast, blends generic (here comics) and gender issues. In this somewhat surreal, tragicomic poem, a relatively harmless situation ("In restaurants we argue") quickly develops into a fantasized "murder" of the male partner by the female partner and his "funny pop art resurrection" (Hönnighausen 2000/02, 106) as Superman, in the manner of, say, Andy Warhol:

> the ceiling opens
> a voice sings Love Is A Many
>
> Splendoured Thing
> you hang suspended above the city
>
> in blue tights and a red cape,
> your eyes flashing in unison. (106)

As with "Comic Books vs. History," deflation follows inflation. The lyrical I not only denies any responsibility for her partner's transformation, but she[23] is also not at all impressed by his self-aggrandizement and his weird attempts to dominate and to attract (her) attention: "As for me, I continue eating; / I liked you better the way you were, / but you were always ambitious" (106). In this poem, it is not a "superman" who is in charge but the lyrical-I-cum-writer, who decides the male's longer-term significance:

> though the real question is
> whether or not I will make you immortal.
> At the moment only I
> can do it. (106)

It is the lyrical I who, through her self-confident detachment, over-rules any pretense on the part of the male figure at supernatural physical powers and who, through her writing, even has the power to immortalize. Atwood mocks the conventional "engendered" rules of hero worship, in which an adoring female "creates" a superman who then requires said adoring female to maintain the illusion of male dominance.

THE *KANADIAN KULTCHUR KOMIX* / SURVIVALWOMAN SERIES

Illuminating as such intermedial texts that interweave the motif of comics are, Atwood's most striking contribution to the genre of comics is, of course, her own production of comic strips. Her earliest published comics probably go back to the late 1950s: "I did comix stuff for Musical & Operetta programmes in the 1959–61 period."[24] It was in the 1970s that she published comic strips in greater numbers (twenty-five in this decade), and she has done so occasionally to this day. Her high productivity in the 1970s was due mainly to the editors of *This Magazine*. As Atwood explains, "I knew the people running it.[25] But I did a couple of big-page comics for a weekend supplement to newspapers called *Weekend*.[26] I did the hair comic and the "My Life" comic ["Portrait of the Artist as a Young Cipher"] for them" (see chapter 8). These early comics are classic examples of her ironic self-fashioning as a writer—an important tendency of her comics right from the beginning, which was to develop, particularly, into her *Book Tour Comics* of the 1990s.

It is the series of *Kanadian Kultchur Komix*, however (including the Survivalwoman comic strips), for which Atwood is best known as a cartoonist.[27] As she comments on the gestation of the Survivalwoman comics, "So then *This Magazine:* we got the idea of doing a comic in it. So I got the idea of having a superhero like the superheroes in real comics, except it was a Canadian superhero, so she didn't actually have any powers (laughs), and that was where that came from. ... I had already published *Survival* by that time" (see chapter 8). Atwood points out in her interview with Peter Gzowski that she would not have ventured into the *Kanadian Kultchur Komix* if *This Magazine* had not asked her to, for it was "not something that would have occurred to me by myself" (see Gzowski 1978, 14:14–14:30 min.). The first of these strips, which appeared in *This Magazine's* January–February issue 8.5–6 in 1975, began a series of altogether twenty-four instalments (seventeen of them featuring Survivalwoman), running over several years until the January–February issue 14.1 (1980).[28] Since the 1970s marked a decade of nationalist and identity debate in Canada, and since *This Magazine* (founded in 1966) is a Canadian leftist journal, concentrating on Canadian politics and culture, it is not surprising that Atwood's *Kanadian Kultchur Komix* of the 1970s should deal with topical Canadian issues of the political and especially cultural kinds. The official series title—spelled four different ways throughout the series—stresses Atwood's satirical involvement with Canadian culture:

Kanadian Kultchur Komix
Kanadian Kultchur Komics
Kanadian Kuultchr Komix
Canadian Kultchur Komix

Her facetious misspellings (the title is not once spelled correctly, "just one of those stupid jokes with which the strip abounds" [in Gzowski 1978, 03:08–03:12 min.]) can be seen in terms of the playful conventions of comics and, in particular, their tendency to play fast and loose with orthography. Perhaps they are also a hint of the hybrid nature of Canadian culture, with many Canadians having been born outside the country.[29] They might even be a mocking swipe at a lack of culture (if not even the correct spelling of the word *culture* can be counted on) or an eye-twinkling nod to Canada's continuous search for identity, particularly in the 1970s.

Another general noteworthy aspect of the *Kanadian Kultchur Komix* (Atwood, in another comic twist, also referred to them simply as "Kan Kutch"[30]) is the fact that Atwood published them under a pseudonym throughout, choosing the alias of a nineteenth-century Canadian political satirist/cartoonist, who simply signed with "B. G."[31] In the interview in chapter 8, she stresses that the male sex of the pseudonym was not an issue but the different "functionality" that a pseudonym lends: "it's a way of having another hat." In other words, Atwood slipped into the different persona of a male cartoonist (and by far most of the cartoonists of the time had, after all, been male, especially in Canada[32]) by choosing a pseudonym for this particular creative activity.[33] As she humorously commented in her interview with Gzowski, "It's a medium in which I can do all those rude things that I don't usually do, you see" (Gzowski 1978, 3:17–3:22 min.).

As Atwood points out in the passage quoted above, she deliberately created a *Canadian* superhero: that is, one without "actually ... any powers." But she does not stress the other specialty of her comics protagonist, that she invented a *female* superhero, thereby in a way suggesting a double powerlessness—as a Canadian and as a woman. Survivalwoman is the only figure of these twenty-four comics (all of which were published in *This Magazine*) that reappears many times in the series (in seventeen instalments).

Only seven *Kanadian Kultchur Komix* do not feature Survivalwoman. In "The Writers' Onion of Kanada" (1976), Atwood satirizes the Writers' Union of Canada (which she ridicules as "The Only Kollectiv Komic Superheroes in the World" in another comic from 1975). She tackles the precarious state of Canadian culture in the face of the domineering United States ("The Cultural Infiltration Agency," 1975; "Lightbulb Comic," 1975) and in connection with Canadian film ("The Kanadian Film Directors' Guild," 1975) and Canadian television ("The Ceebeecee Television Drama Dept," 1976). Last but not least, in "Recruiting for the Canadian National Revolution" (1977), Atwood comments on the "union-makes-us-two" relationship between the English and French Canadian parts of Canada. These seven comics thus treat pressing problems and challenges of a postcolonial country in the 1970s (or, regarding American cultural hegemony, a neocolonial one), preoccupied with questions of national and particularly cultural dependence and independence. Practically all identifiable figures—such as writers, film directors, television people, politicians, CIA agents—are male,[34] rather strikingly so for Atwood, but not striking for the 1970s, considering the professions represented.

Yet it is mainly with her seventeen Survivalwoman comics that Atwood notably "engenders" comics art, making gender a striking issue and combining it with other political and cultural agendas at the time. In the Survivalwoman comics, female figures are as frequent as male ones (next to the heroine, we are introduced to "Amphibianwoman," "Womanwoman," "lady," and the "Canadian Dream," the first two of which appear three times each in the series). This as well as the fact that the protagonist of this series is indeed female has to be considered unusual for the time.

And what a "heroine" she is: her name, Survivalwoman, goes back, of course, to Atwood's earlier "thematic guide to Canadian literature," *Survival* (1972), where Atwood claims that the most central theme/motif in CanLit is "survival" and where she develops her victim theory, with four different stages of victimization:

> *Position One: To deny the fact that you are a victim. ...*
> *Position Two: To acknowledge the fact that you are a victim, but to explain this as an act of Fate ... or any other large general powerful idea. ...*
> *Position Three: To acknowledge the fact that you are a victim but to refuse to accept the assumption that the role is inevitable. ...*
> *Position Four: To be a creative non-victim.* (36, 37, 38)

In connection with this theory, Survivalwoman is presented as a Canadian cliché. When she appears for the first time ("Survivalwoman and the Magic Word WHAMMIEQ," 1975), she is introduced with her typical paraphernalia, which she keeps throughout the rest of the series (see comic V, reprinted in Wilson 1993, 164). As Atwood says in the interview with Gzowski, "All superheroes are supposed to have a costume, and a magic word, and magic powers. ... Survivalwoman basically is supposed to have magic powers but doesn't have any"

(Gzowski 1978, 4:27–4:44 min.). She does have a "magic" word, though (which falls flat, however), and a costume: Survivalwoman's T-shirt bears the letter *S* for "Survivalwoman," in ironic similarity to the American Superman's *S*. She wears—also suggestive of her polar opposite, Superman—a long cape, in her case flaunting the Canadian flag with the maple leaf; and, again in ironic contrast to America's superhero and his black leather boots, she sports snowshoes (also in summer, as is pointed out) to indicate the more northern country from which she originates. Then, too, she is small—like Atwood herself—hardly taller than the garbage can next to which she is presented in the first panel of this first Survivalwoman comic. To further suggest similarities to Atwood herself, Survivalwoman features Atwood's characteristically curly hair.

Survivalwoman may thus be regarded as an ironic pictorial self-stylization of her creator, and, through the correlation between *Survival* and Survivalwoman, the latter comes to epitomize (the state of) Canada in Atwood's typical, and typically Canadian, self-ironic, sarcastic, even self-deprecatory view.[35] The superhero's gender is stressed by her alternative name "THE FLYING KOTEX® (Canada Limited)" in panel 1, reducing her, mischievously, to an article of female hygiene and, symbolically, to her biological sex. With a stereotypical Canadian inferiority complex, she asks herself why she is so down to earth, why she "can't fly like all the other superheroines [sic]" (panel 1),[36] and puts the blame partly down to her restricting snowshoes, that is, to an object clearly associated with Canada.

That Survivalwoman is truly Canadian and acts in a recognizably Canadian context is stressed in panels 2 and 3 when, even in her swearing, she resorts to one of Canada's "national animals": "BLITHERING BEAVERS ... it's a cry for help!" (V,1); this cry is—in politically correct fashion—put in Canada's two official languages, English and French: "**Help!** Au secours ... " (V,1). After several topical allusions to the political situation in Canada at the time (references to the "suffering Seebeecee" [CBC],[37] to "our fearless leader, Pierre ~~Burton~~ [Berton] Truedough" [Trudeau],[38] and to being "slighted by the Whitehouse" [USA]), Survivalwoman wants to come to Prime Minister Trudeau/Truedough's rescue by using a magic word supposed to lend her superpowers. This word, *WHAMMIEQ*, is an anagram of truly Canadian references to politicians, authors, regions, and ethnic groups, such as Quebec, Eskimo, Métis, or Hudson Bay. However, on conjuring up the word, Survivalwoman immediately deflates and withers to practically nothing: Survivalwoman, that Canadian female "fighting failure" (as she is called in comic strip VI), has lost her first battle and maybe even failed to *survive*.[39]

Yet Survivalwoman, honouring her name, is resurrected in one of the next issues of *This Magazine*, with the strip "Survivalwoman Renamed Survivalcreature (1975). The year 1975, when the comic was published, had been declared the International Women's Year by the United Nations, and around that time several commissions and agencies concerning the status of women were established in Canada, such as the Royal Commission on the Status of Women in 1967 by Prime Minister Lester B. Pearson or the minister for the status of women in 1971 (see Francis, Jones, and Smith 2000, 543).

In her comic strip "Survivalwoman Renamed Survivalcreature" (see figure 3), Atwood keeps a sarcastic eye on linguistic reforms concerning gender representation, which she suggests are insignificant as long as discriminatory mentalities and behaviour toward women remain constant. In this comic, the International Women's Year (of 1975) is directly addressed: "I wonder what I can do to help the Federal Government celebrate International Womens [sic] year with a truly Canadian slant ... " (VI,1). Panel 2 then refers to action directed against women that ranges from financial exploitation (e.g., unequal pay) through physical violence to denouncement of women on a symbolic level: "Exploit a female factory worker? Kick a waitress? Denounce Mothers Day?" Language regulations such as gender-neutral designations (e.g., "SURVIVALCREATURE," 3) are only a first step, this comic suggests, that has to be complemented by more significant actions. The government's attempts at the time to do something about discrimination against women are discussed in critical terms in this comic, suggesting that gender equality was no more than a political desideratum at the time.

In "Survivalwoman, Womanwoman, and the Canada Manpowerhole" (1978; see figure 4), Atwood blends questions of nationalism, regionalism, and feminism, highly topical issues in the 1970s. Both nationalism and feminism in Canada worked against supremacy and oppression by superior powers, mainly the United States on the

Figure 3.

one hand and masculinism on the other.[40] As Atwood states in an interview, "women as well as Canadians have been colonized or have been the victims of cultural imperialism" (in Ingersoll 1990, 94). In this context, regionalism, too, is a movement toward an idiosyncratic cultural self-image, liberating itself to some extent from larger defining frameworks.

Panel 1 shows Survivalwoman "entertaining her friend Womanwoman in the Survival-lair," hovering underground in a hole marked above ground by the sign "Beware Manhole" (XXI,1). Through her doubly typifying designation "Womanwoman," the latter is introduced as an extreme feminist, thinking only of the rights of women, in contrast to the conventional privileging of men. Atwood typifies the figure further by giving her a rather unfeminine look, with short hair and a full beer mug in front of her (the more feminine Survivalwoman, in contrast, has a cup of coffee or tea). Womanwoman questions nationalism and advocates regionalism instead ("Regionalism is the thing now"), defining nationalism, or probably both movements, in gendered terms of power politics: "any way it's a male Power Trip ... " (XXI,1). It is striking that Womanwoman is not given a mouth, because she represents the more radical part of the Women's Movement that made its voice heard in the 1970s. If this iconic specialty was effected by Atwood on purpose, then it may be meant to suggest that "mouthlessness" does not necessarily mean voicelessness, that oppressed, silenced groups can find ways to make themselves heard, after all. In addition, the lack of a mouth depersonalizes Womanwoman even further in the direction of an allegorical figure, representing an ideology rather than a character.

Panel 2 refers to a political situation of the 1970s that Atwood, critical observer as always, evaluated as follows in an interview: "Scratch the country and it's quite a fascist place. Look at the attitudes to the War Measures Act. ... Canada's not a goody-goody land of idealists" (in Ingersoll 1990, 122). The War Measures Act was a controversial, decisive reduction of civil rights that Trudeau put through in 1970 during the so-called October Crisis, in fear of an increase in Québécois terrorism. The War Measures Act had originally been put in force in 1914, yet its first and only application concerning a domestic crisis was in 1970, when Quebec nationalists fighting for Quebec's separation from the rest of Canada had kidnapped and murdered the provincial minister

Figure 4.

of immigration, manpower, and labour in Quebec and kidnapped the British trade commissioner in Montreal. In the wake of these terrorist events, the War Measures Act (replaced in 1988 by the more restricted Emergencies Act) granted police almost unlimited powers for a while.[41]

In panel 2, Atwood blends this political event with gender issues by having a determined-looking policeman, legitimized through a "Sexist Pig Whore Measures Act,"[42] "measure" the voluptuous breasts of a sexy-looking though irritated blonde (who, in view of her flaunting of her body, might indeed be a prostitute). The armed, intimidating policeman, calling the woman "lady" while in fact sexually harassing her (see chapter 4 on the "idealization" of women), sanctifies this outrageous degradation of the woman to her bust size/sexuality with political legislation: "hold still lady ... this is the P.M.'s orders." When the woman protests that she as a woman (and as a whore) has rights, too, the policeman bluntly denies this, with special reference to women: "Not in this country ya don't ... nobody does ... specially wimmin" (note that his speech—sentence structure and pronunciation—marks him as uneducated). As often with Atwood, power structures are seen in gendered terms, and oppression and the restriction of individual rights are presented as particularly pronounced in the case of women—Canadian women thus having to face a double challenge by being Canadian *and* female.

Panel 3, again very much up to date, picks up the contemporary debate on systematic discrimination of women through language (see chapter 4), particularly through grammar and word choice privileging the male gender (Womanwoman rightly calls this "Male Semantics," XXI,3). And the male gender, of course, still informs many designations of everyday usage and existence, such as the sign "Beware Manhole" used on construction sites—though in this case most of the workers on such sites are in fact men. Gender-conscious Womanwoman objects to this gender-exclusive designation and, being a feminist hardliner, is about to suggest a change to "Womanhole" (this is not spelled out explicitly, however, since Survivalwoman, irritated, interrupts her).[43] Probably also because of the sexual connotations that the female designation would have, Survivalwoman, though certainly not unaware of gender issues, proves to be more sober than Womanwoman as far as gender questions are concerned, protesting that Womanwoman, in her view, is going too far: "I draw the line!" (XXI,3; iconically, a concrete line is, in fact, drawn by the underlining of the utterance, cut short with an exclamation mark). As usual, Atwood is arguing against extreme positions and for sensible, balanced views instead, also on matters of gender.

In the final panel, Survivalwoman, representing Canadian nationalism, in fact reverts to a nationalistic approach, taking up the designation of the Canadian staffing firm Manpower[44] and suggesting the term "Canada Manpowerhole" as an alternative for "Manhole" on construction sites. Although this kind of negotiation over gendered terminology at first sight seems to ridicule the whole matter, it nevertheless points to the general significance—and, particularly at the time, virulence—of gender in language, raising consciousness about the grounds and legitimization of linguistic conventions in the represen-tation of men and women.

In the comic "Survivalwoman for Female P.M." (XXII, 1978), Survivalwoman and Womanwoman are talking about an upcoming spring election (see figure 5); the election referred to is the Canadian federal election of May 1979, which resulted in a defeat of the Liberal Party under Prime Minister Trudeau, to be succeeded by Joe Clark, candidate of the Progressive Conservative Party. Womanwoman—who in panel 3 is holding a beer mug again, whereas Survivalwoman is shown in a thinker's pose throughout all four panels—suggests that Survivalwoman run for prime minister, that is, that she enter the race for political power. In typical Canadian self-doubt, Survivalwoman replies, "But I'm not very together ... I'd run the country into debt ... everything would go to rat-shit ... " (3). Radical feminist Womanwoman does not seem to care: "So? At least you'd be female ... " (4).

Through this discrepancy between lack of confidence and/or com-petence on the one hand and, in the radical feminist's view, the capacity to lead the country merely on grounds of (female) gender on the other hand, Atwood once again positions herself against an absolute championing of women. As she has repeatedly stressed in interviews, she does not argue for "hardline, anti-male feminists [who] start castrating men" (in Ingersoll 1990, 183). Instead, she shrewdly defines her "feminism as human equality and freedom of choice" (142). Clearly radical feminism in the line of Womanwoman is not a solution to the problem of gender inequality: "I think that fanaticism—as apart from belief—is dangerous. Now belief in the rights of women is another thing" (183).

Figure 5.

The time for a female Canadian prime minister does not seem to be ripe yet, perhaps even today (consider, however, Kim Campbell's short stint as prime minister of Canada from June to December 1993). Atwood's comic strip "Survivalwoman and the Canadian Dream" (XXIII, 1978), however, sarcastically demonstrates (see figure 6) that women may at least figure as superheroines in comics, though in that case they will be of American origin (see again her implication in the interview in chapter 8 that a Canadian comics heroine by definition does not "actually have any powers"). The comic introduces a sexy, overpowering female figure, strongly resembling the American comics heroine Wonder Woman, clad in a tight, red-and-white-striped top and tight blue, star-studded shorts (see the American flag) as well as red leather boots. This "Über-woman" is suggested as a new identification figure for Canadians—named, with reference to the "American Dream," the "Canadian Dream." In panel 3, tiny Survivalwoman looks up at the huge figure of the "Canadian Dream" on a drawing board.[45]

This suggestion of a drastic "national symbol" (XXIII,2) in the context of a country known for its lack of grand master narratives (in contrast to the neighbouring United States) is put forward to Survivalwoman by a male representative of a so-called Task Force in National Unity (a small maple leaf, at the time still a rather new symbolic sign for Canada, is attached to this name).[46] Representing an officially bilingual country, the politician greets Survivalwoman in English and French with "Hi there! Bonjour!" (1). He suggests that Survival(woman) as a national symbol is "too DOOM & GLOOM!" (2) and, in true flamboyant marketing style, woos for a "more UPBEAT ... SEXIER ... IMAGE" (2), as embodied by the "Canadian Dream"/ Wonder Woman ("peppy, eh?" 3; note the typically Canadian question tag "eh?"). When Survivalwoman soberly questions having her country represented by an American iconic figure ("but what about those STARS and STRIPES?" 4), the representative of the task force, a "Liberal" Party member, dismisses her concern by calling this a "minor detail" and characterizing the stars and stripes as in fact "very UNIFYING" (4). The Canadian politician has apparently fully internalized the (neo) colonial subject mentality, not seeing the problem involved in importing American popular culture into Canada and allowing it to displace Canadian culture and national symbols. And, in fact, this politician is

Figure 6.

drawn by Atwood as a static, apparently rather brainless, figure through-out the comics: he holds on to his file of political documents, with a huge, broadly grinning mouth and motionless, almost closed eyes—blind to the neoimperialist implications of his suggestion and therefore stupidly happy about a sexually attractive American superheroine to symbolize Canada, his own country.

Apart from this neocolonial gesture, representing the problematic relationship between Canada and the United States, much could be made of the fact that the Wonder Woman comics were extraordinary in themselves (in creating the first mainstream, highly successful female/feminist superhero, next to the masculinist Superman and Batman) as well as controversial, which thus represents a further challenge to letting this figure represent Canada. The figure's inventor and first creator, William Moulton Marston,[47] was "a Harvard-educated psychologist who wanted a female warrior who could fight fascism while challenging the masculinist world of superhero adventures. ... Marston believed women were morally superior to men—and furthermore, that society was doomed unless strong women were to band together to overcome the masculinist social forces that restrict female life and possibility."[48] Since Canada has repeatedly been seen in a "female" subordinate position next to the domineering "male" United States, and as the morally "better" counterpart compared to a power-driven southern neighbour, the correlation between Wonder Woman and Canada would make sense to some extent at least. Yet other aspects of the original Wonder Woman suggest this correlation to be rather problematic from Canada's perspective. With her outfit in panel 3 exactly resembling that of the original heroine—strapless top, tight shorts, knee-high boots, headband, metal bracelets (which can deflect bullets in the original comics), and lasso (golden in the original, compelling anyone caught with it to tell the truth[49])—Wonder Woman/the Canadian Dream clearly conveys sadomasochistic associations, putting power relations in dubious terms. Marston's preoccupation with bondage and domination in the original Wonder Woman comics is notorious, as are statements of his such as "The only hope for peace is to teach people who are full of pep and unbound force to enjoy being bound. ... Only when the control of self by others is more pleasant than the unbound assertion of self in human relationships can we hope for a stable, peaceful human society."[50] Atwood provokes us in many ways with this comic: not only does a liberal Canadian politician, allegedly fighting for "national unity," advocate an *American female* icon of *popular culture* as Canada's national symbol, but also this figure stands in a rather dubious (sexual) relation to power structures, enjoying subordination and domination by her male lover (her weak spot), but at the same time, in Amazon style, trying to resist it and wield power herself.

In the earlier comic "Survivalwoman Meets Superham" (VII, 1976),[51] Atwood tackled a similar theme. This comic is her most explicit statement on the Canada-US relationship. In the squared-off introductory caption in panel 1, the problematic relationship is hyperbolically charac-terized as "the confrontation of the centuries" (true, perhaps, from a Canadian perspective because of the culturally existential relevance of this relationship for Canada). Superman, the megalomaniac popular culture icon of the United States, is renamed here, in a typically Atwoodian play on words, as "Superham," alluding to his pronounced muscles of a body builder and his rather "fleshy" body. And this Superman satirized as "Superham" is indeed past his prime: a bit too plump, unshaven, with a rather dumb look on his face and fleas jumping around his head, altogether giving a rather unkempt though still complacent impression. As Atwood described Superham in the Gzowski interview, this is "Superman sort of forty years later. He has bags under his eyes and whiskers and fleas. He's kind of sagging, he has a little potbelly" (Gzowski 1978, 7:46–7:58 min.). The figures' similar apparel notwith-standing (tops sporting a huge *S*; leather boots versus snowshoes), the choreography of panels 1 and 3 displays right away the major difference between the male superhero and the female superheroine, namely, their respective sizes. It indicates immediately who represents a big, powerful country and who a "smaller," relatively powerless country, making the neocolonial relationship between the two visible and palpable. As in the previously discussed comic, it is suggested, here by Superham, that there is really no difference between American and Canadian culture, in the sense that a hardly existent Canadian culture of its own is to be subsumed under American supremacy: "Aw come off it man—I mean, like, we're all the same culture—we see the same TV shows, we watch the same flicks, we read the same comics ... I mean, you aint [sic] got NO real culture, man" (VII,1). Superham thereby formulates any Canadian nationalist's nightmare, the imperialist incorporation of Canadian culture by the domineering United States or, even worse, the denial that there is an autonomous Canadian culture at all. Superham's slangy, blunt, "uncultured" language[52] even enhances the threat for Canadian culture—as does the fact that, with "TV shows," "flicks" (movies), and "comics," Superham seems to reduce North American culture to *American popular culture* only.

"Dwarfish" yet "intrepid" (1), Survivalwoman lives up to her name and, characterized as "the FIGHTING FAILURE exert[ing] her utmost powers" (2), takes up the challenge to help her culture "survive" against the odds of "our big, friendly neighbour to the south" (1). Using her knowledge and brain power rather than being able to rely on any physical strength like Superman, she counters by enumerating a long list of Canadian references. She cites names of writers (Al Purdy, Alan McPhee), politicians (Louis Riel, Thomas D'arcy [sic] McGee, Papineau), and other historical figures (Norman Bethune); political designations and events (Waffle, B[ritish]N[orth]A[merica]A[ct]); places (Klondike); cultural events/phenomena (the Grey Cup Playoffs, C[anadian]N[ational]E[xhibition], C[anadian]L[ibrary]M[onth], B[ed] & B[reakfast]); entertainment figures and programs/firms (Elwood Glover, The Happy Gang); historical dates (1837); products and firms (Moosehead Beer, Chinook, Resdan, Rawhide, Chesterfield); and Canadian English (Resdan). In a self-reflexive/-ironic manner, she even lists the magazine in which the *Kanadian Kultchur Komix*, including the very comic at hand, first appeared, namely, *This Magazine*. Survivalwoman's strategy, to foreground aspects of a truly Canadian culture, seems to be effective at first, since her huge speech bubble, in an iconic interplay between text and image, appears to be almost completely displacing Superham (only his feet/boots remain visible, indicating that he remains standing); in panel 3, it is even stated that "the BLIMPISH BEHEMOTH[53] admits ... defeat!!": "You're right, man ... I don't know what any of those mean ... " (3). Yet Survivalwoman's cheering triumph in victory pose (3) soon changes to thoughtful disillusionment when, in panel 4, Superham, taking off, adds self-righteously, "But neither do most Canadians ... same culture man. ..." He outsmarts Survivalwoman with her own weapons by pointing to Canadians' lack of knowledge of their own culture—which, in a way, was a significant reason why the prototext for Survivalwoman came into being in the first place: Atwood wrote *Survival* in part to show her compatriots that there was something like Canadian literature. And Superham likes to rub it in: referring to the "pipeline debate," he indirectly reminds Survivalwoman of Canada's economic dependence on the United States (see Bothwell 1985, 1419).

Although even a run-down Superham gets the better of Survivalwoman, he is further derided by Atwood. When flying away in typical Superman style—arms outstretched to the sky, fists clenched, billowing cape, taking off like a rocket or missile—panel 4 supplies a drawn sound effect, visually translated into several vertical lines snaking in parallel manner. These lines are complemented by the onomatopoeic word *poot*—Superham, apparently unashamedly, gives off a fart. The textual and, following from this, pictorial supremacy that the cultured and wordy Canadian figure briefly achieves in panel 2 is, in the final panel, obviously supplanted by a mainly visual hierarchy clearly in favour of America's Superham taking off to the sky. Apart from this pictorial choreography of the closing panel 4, the spoken text in this panel belongs solely to Superham. Diminutive Survivalwoman is reduced to silence by his deadly arguments, with her unspoken "sigh" marking the final printed word in this comic on US-Canadian relations.

Like all the other *Kanadian Kultchur Komix*, this comic, too, is closely tied to its historical context, the mid-1970s, when it was created and first published. While still involved with the finalizing of political independence (see the "Patriation of the Constitution," accomplished only in 1982 with the Canada Act by the British Parliament and the Constitution Act by the Canadian Parliament [see Sheppard 1985, 406–08]), Canada's preoccupation at the time was a *cultural* decolonization of its postcolonial status and mentality—no longer directed against Canada's former mother countries England and France but now against the American neocolonial influence. Although Survivalwoman is shown to lose this fight for cultural independence, she is nevertheless depicted as fighting, not giving up (victim position Number Three). And despite the obvious size difference between Superham and Survivalwoman, it should also be stressed that the American colonizer is depicted as run-down and past his prime; the Canadian fighter, in contrast, comes across as fresh, friendly, optimistic, witty, and intelligent/"cultured"—and very much aware of the postcolonial mentality (external and internal) that has to be resisted ("exerts her utmost powers" [2]). The time of an arrogant US imperialism toward Canada, though still existent, is slowly drawing to an end here, in the face of a small, young, yet determined and "intrepid" Survivalwoman. One important strategy of resistance is the insistence on cultural if not economic autonomy—soft (cultural) power for Canada versus America's hard (political, economic, military) power.[54] As often in the Survivalwoman series, such deliberations are paralleled by problems of gender, with Survivalwoman/Canada rendered as the supposedly smaller, weaker sex, aiming at "soft power" against a physically overpowering Superham/United States relying on traditional means of wielding power (e.g., physical/military supremacy).

As is suggested in this comic, the challenges to Canadian autonomy and strength derive as much from inner obstacles (see Canadians' ignorance of their own culture in comic VII) as from outer forces (mainly the United States). In "Survivalwoman Meets Amphibianwoman" (XII, 1977), Atwood turns to the conflictual relationship between English Canada and French Canada (see figure 7).[55] In this all-female comic,[56] Survivalwoman, representing English Canada, is joined by Amphibianwoman. The latter—as her name suggests—is a mixture of a woman and a frog,[57] drawn with a frog-like face (see her huge, protruding eyes and mouth and her animal-like nose) and frog feet. On the other hand, she appears on high heels, with a figure-hugging skirt, pronounced breasts, long eyelashes and styled hair, and a cigarette in an elegant cigarette holder. The hybrid nature attributed to the province's representative in this comic is probably due to Quebec's French heritage on a mainly English-speaking North American continent. In the first panel, Survivalwoman (i.e., Anglo-Canada) notes that she has not seen Amphibianwoman (i.e., Quebec) "for ages." Self-assured, vamp-like Amphibianwoman in her first statement makes clear that she has reached the "very high profile," with which Survivalwoman credits her admiringly, by way of cutting all ties with Anglo-Canada: "I got tired of the old Bondage routine—chains, rubber suits, Federal taxes, The Story of Q.[uebec]."[58] In panel 2, a thoughtful Survivalwoman compliments Amphibianwoman: "you were always more sophisticated than me ... ," perhaps referring to French culture in general and to Amphibianwoman's

Figure 7.

more pronounced sense of communal, here Québécois, identity. Amphibianwoman thereby also explains her decision for a (political) "separation" (from Anglo-Canada) and even for economic independence ("set up in business for myself. ..."). She mentions in panel 3 the help of her new lover, "a wonderful guy," whom in panel 4 she reveals as René (Lévesque): "René, René, you're so brainé[59] ... Heaven-sent ... make me SOLVENT. ..."

Survivalwoman's expression throughout the four panels changes from admiring friendliness (1) through thoughtfulness (2) and displeased surprise (3) to woeful despair (4). Survivalwoman does not focus on Amphibianwoman's story of growing up, greater self-awareness and independence, or her falling in love with René (i.e., Quebec regionalism/ nationalism). Instead, feeling threatened by Amphibianwoman's happy, self-confident, and apparently self-sufficient condition, she feels second rate in comparison and looks for largely superficial (and "feminine") reasons why "nobody loves" her: "how do you do it? Could I have the name of your HAIRDRESSER?" (3); "What can I do to improve my Image? Miss Dior? Pit cream? A new constitution?" (4). Instead of trying to develop her own personality/identity rather than worrying about her image and looks, Survivalwoman resorts to the guilty pleasure of reading "True Romance" trash fiction rather than living an authentic love story herself. "Sniffing"/crying, Survivalwoman belittles herself by literally squatting down next to a passionate, love-stricken Amphibianwoman, who stands (and looks) upright in the final panel.

This comic strip reflects on a political background that Atwood referred to in an interview as follows: "America is to English Canada as English Canada has been both to the Indians and the Quebecois. ... They [the French Canadians] are as ignorant of us [the English Canadians] as we are ignorant of them. When any question arises, the English-speaking sector, instead of knowing why, or responding with understanding, responds with bafflement and hurt feelings" (in Ingersoll 1990, 88, 87). Historically French Canadians, through a strong regional impetus, have had a deeper sense of their identity than self-questioning English Canada. The failure of the latter to give the French-speaking minority sufficient recognition ("Gee, Amphibianwoman—I hadn't seen you for ages," Survivalwoman says in panel 1) partly resulted in the Québécois separatist movement of the 1960s and 1970s: "English

Canada closed its eyes to the fact that a separate, older, and much more firmly rooted cultural nationalism had already evolved in Quebec" (Conlogue 1996, 16). In 1967, René Lévesque quit the Liberal Party and one year later founded the Parti Québécois, whose sovereignty-association policy aimed at political and cultural independence for Quebec, while also remaining in an economic union with Canada ("Heaven-sent ... make me SOLVENT" [4]). With his separatist policy, Lévesque was for many Québécois a "heaven-sent" spokesman who finally championed their heart-felt political desires. He also catapulted the Quebec question to the centre of national attention ("but suddenly you have a very high profile" [1]). On 15 November 1976, the Parti Québécois won the provincial election in Quebec, and Lévesque was able to establish a government under his leadership, aiming at Quebec's political separation from the rest of Canada. In the comic, Survivalwoman, fighting for the political and cultural survival of Canada at large, envies Amphibianwoman her firm and passionate sense of identity—"unlike Quebec nationalism, [English Canadian] nationalism lacked a clearly defined notion of a people or a national society" (McRoberts 1997, 116). Although Lévesque's policies did not lead to separation, the Quebec question repeatedly arises as an issue of concern.[60]

In this comic, charged with contemporary political and cultural problems, Atwood—inverting the traditional practice of letting "mankind" be (linguistically and mentally) represented by men only—chooses to represent Canada by two female figures and counterparts. As not infrequently in her comics, "romantic love" and sexuality are used as a popular metaphor for unpopular political/cultural statements, such as the sadomasochistic associations surrounding Amphibianwoman disentangling herself from "the old Bondage routine—chains, rubber suits" (1) and her love for René ("a good man is hard to find" [3]).[61] Just as men were often reproached for failing to understand women's desire for emancipation, particularly at this time of the second wave of feminism, so too Survivalwoman/English Canada fails—in fact does not even try—to understand Quebec's desire for political independence. Survivalwoman merely focuses on the external improvement of her self-image and is not interested in any deeper reasons for Amphibianwoman's infatuation with René/Quebec's nationalism or any constructive strategies to improve her own unstable condition. Again Atwood blends gender with political/ cultural questions, putting women at the centre of attention in this comic and having them perform the story of Quebec nationalism and Anglo-Canada's reaction to it.

In the last Survivalwoman comic to be discussed here (see figure 8), "Survivalwoman's Love Life" (X, 1976), Atwood sarcastically presents a panorama of three potential love relationships Survivalwoman may be involved in, all of which turn out to be unfulfilling, if not dangerous, for her. The first panel is made up of text only, demonstrating Atwood's knack for facetious wordplay: "Does SURVIVALWOMAN have a LOVE LIFE? ... is she whined and dinned by the TOP MAN in Noughtawa?" "Noughtawa," suggesting *naught* = "nill," refers to Ottawa, of course, which thus reduces Canada's capital, and by implication the whole country, to nothing. "Whined" correlates the sobbing/whining of the "TOP MAN," a beanstalk figure resembling then Prime Minister Pierre Elliott Trudeau, with the wine he consumes in panel 2. "Dinned" may be a reference to the dinner scene shown in panel 2 but also to the politician's laments over the budget (*din* = "a loud, continuous, and unpleasant noise"). This is a far cry from a romantic candlelight dinner in Ottawa; only the Trudeau figure has a glass of wine, whereas tiny Survivalwoman, looking greedily at Trudeau's wine, has nothing to eat or drink herself. A tight budget allegedly legitimizes the male politician's thinking only of himself—surely a sad view of romance or "love."

In panel 3, we meet a dismal-looking Superham again, who, very unromantically and without much ado, approaches Survivalwoman with barely camouflaged sexual innuendo: "Hey baby ... wanna play a little STRIP MINING?" "Strip mining" may have several meanings here, all of which have mainly sexual connotations: digging the ground, exploiting resources on a major scale, destructive explosion. The intimidated, submissive Survivalwoman, looking up to much larger Superham, spontaneously rejects his blunt sexual advance with the euphemism "Flake off!" Yet apparently not courageous enough to simply refute the much stronger Superham, she immediately relativizes her spontaneous statement undecidedly and open-endedly with "Well, uh ..." (3); she thus unfortunately panders to the clichéd view that women in sexual matters actually mean "yes" when they say "no."

Figure 8.

Panel 4 is a wonderful example of Atwood's turning around comics conventions for her own purposes. The speech balloons have to be read from right to left rather than the other way around as usual to make sense in sequence. This right-to-left direction is probably meant to suggest the deadlock our heroine finds herself in in this last instalment of her "love life." Out in the woods, she is pursued by several animals closing ranks around her: "Hey fellows ... it's a gang bang!"[62] The wild animals victimizing Survivalwoman are typically Canadian: a beaver, a squirrel/chipmunk, and what seems to be a (sexually precocious) bear cub, plus a mouse (the latter claiming that "Walt Disney [the creator of Mickey Mouse] was a Canadian!"[63]). The bear cub looks like a teddy bear but still feels threatening to tiny Survivalwoman—both on account of her female collective memory of sexual assault and because of the bear chasing her from right to left, so that in the choreography of this comic she seems to have no room left for escape. The personified animal seems to have a literary mind—"Just think of me as a metaphor!"—thereby suggesting that he is harmless, only fictional, trying to fool fleeing Survivalwoman with her own cultured weapons. The bear (and the sexual innuendo) are probably also a reference to Marian Engel's novel *Bear* (1976) and the controversies it stirred (the novel's protagonist falls in love and has sex with a bear). The year this Atwood cartoon appeared Engel's novel had just received the Governor General's Literary Award for fiction.

The overall impression of this comic is, of course, that Survivalwoman does not have a love life to speak of—she is at the mercy of egocentric male politicians, domineering Superham/the United States, and even Canadian wildlife. Her precarious state reminds us of what cultural and literary critic Northop Frye famously described as the "garrison mentality" of Canadians, that is, their feeling threatened and enclosed by an alien and hostile environment, particularly by a menacing and overwhelming nature. The desires of Survivalwoman remain unfulfilled. She seems to be lost, neglected, or pursued by stronger powers who want to use her for their selfish power games. Being presented only in hegemonic "relationships," she/Canada does not seem to have found her proper place and a sense of belonging and (self-)respect yet. All that is left for Survivalwoman/Canada to do in this situation is to defend at least her "low profile" (see comic XII): that is, to fight for her survival and repudiate "the Victim role," to use Atwood's phrase in *Survival* (1972, 38).[64]

THE AUTOBIOGRAPHICAL COMICS/*BOOK TOUR COMICS*

The *Kanadian Kultchur Komix* appeared in *This Magazine* in the middle of the 1970s. Around the same time, Atwood also published her first two autobiographical comics, "Portrait of the Artist as a Young Cipher" (1977) and "Hairdo" (1978). The strong autobiographical impetus of these two early comics[65] was taken up some two decades later when, in the early 1990s, Atwood started to publish her first *Book Tour Comics/Comix*.[66] At least six in number by now, they might indeed have started another longer comics series, but the more recent "LongPen" comic (2006) might also be an indication of Atwood's many book tours slowly drawing to an end. The early autobiographical comics self-ironically stylize a literary star in the making, whereas the *Book Tour Comics* have supplanted "Survivalwoman" with a female star author who has made it professionally but nevertheless still has to battle against an ignorant social context and various inclemencies of the writing profession.

In "Portrait of the Artist as a Young Cipher," first published in *The Graduate* in 1977 (reprinted in Nischik 2000/02, 316) under the name M. E.,[67] Atwood self-ironically substitutes in the title for the word *man* (see James Joyce's artist novel *Portrait of the Artist as a Young Man*) not the natural antonym *woman* but *cipher*—the implication being that woman equals cipher. The cartoon strip begins autobiographically with a small, curly-haired female student entering university (clearly the University of Toronto; see local references such as Bloor Street and the Park Plaza building[68]) and soon deciding to become a writer. The young student is sketched as an intimidated "Freshperson" (in contrast to the usual gendered designation "freshman") in English and philosophy at "Vic" (Victoria College), where—also true to life—Northrop Frye, Jay Macpherson (two of Atwood's teachers), and David Knight taught at the time. Atwood renders her 1960s university life by featuring herself as an outsider ("Why am I here?") in the grip of an existential zeitgeist: "My stockings darkened. My eyes bagged. Buttons fell from my clothes" (XVIII,14). She has her first short story accepted by *Acta Victoriana*, the student-run literary journal of Victoria College at the University of Toronto, consorts with her intellectual friends Dennis Lee[69] and Jack Robson (16), and has her first poetry readings at the Bohemian Embassy on St. Nicholas Street—all of these are autobiographical references. So are the young student's graduation from the University of Toronto in Honours English, her heightened awareness of her Canadian nationality at Harvard University, and finally her being a young mother in Alliston, Ontario (Atwood also calls this comic "The Story of My Life" in the interview in chapter 8). With the narrated events ending in 1977, it is significant—but not surprising for Atwood connoisseurs—that she does not make anything of her prominence and budding literary stardom at the time. Thus, the cartoon strip concludes with an anticlimax, yet an effective one, by merely suggesting that now freshmen find *her* intimidating and, adding sarcastically, that she has a lot of cats: "what else can you do with a B.A. these days?" (26). In this *reductio* style, Atwood ends "the story of her life" at the time, stressing her private life rather than her professional success, in typical Canadian/Atwoodian as well as female modesty.

"Hairdo," first published in the *Weekend Magazine* of the *Montreal Star* in February 1978 (a publication with a large circulation), is Atwood's longest comic strip so far. Usually her comics are made up of four panels (see her comments in chapter 8), like most of the *Kanadian Kultchur Komix*. "Portrait" is made up of twenty-six and "Hairdo" of as many as thirty panels. A lot can be said, and is being said, about the hairstyle of a female writer, Atwood seems to suggest. With "Hairdo" (and the later *Book Tour Comics*), we approach the realm of the following interview (chapter 8), dealing, among other things, with female celebrity.

"Hairdo," in its first, all-language panel, pretends to be a piece for a women's magazine, entitled "THE GLAMOUR & FASHION PAGE." Supposedly at stake here is how to become glamorous, largely through manipulative fashion. The subtitle of the magazine page is typically sensational, as such popular culture formats have to be to attract the masses and thereby be profitable: "How to achieve effects you would not have thought possible even in your wildest dreams!" That we have a stylized, Atwoodian autobiographical comic at hand becomes clear from the beginning, where Atwood outs herself as creator of this strip and is associated with the girl with the curly hair. A cute, modest, happy girl is admired as "fashionable" at the time because of her "natural curls! ... How cute! ... Just like Shirley Temple!" (2). Yet Atwood points out from the beginning of her pictorial representation of "stardom" that success/ celebrity and envy seem to go together, especially when the audience is not at ease with itself, as is the case with Canadians and their often problematic relation to stars from their own country (see chapter 8). In panel 3, the "glamorous" girl is persecuted by other girls as well as an older woman,[70] who with scissors, knife, and axe want to cut off her beautiful curly hair—that is, rob her of her (at the time) only sign of glamour. This panel in a way is a self-ironic depiction of Atwood's statement in *Second Words* that "'We [Canadians] cut tall poppies'" (1982, 305).

The following panels show young Margaret in conscious pursuit of "glamour." The representations work on two levels: first, by rendering direct speeches at the time of the events; second, by giving retrospective comments in captions and four text panels by the writer-"narrator," an older Atwood who has achieved fame and looks back on the strenuous path to it. This duet of two different time levels/aspects of the same person—presenting the innocent girl and the knowledgeable, famous writer—adds a humorous contrast. Panels 4–14 show young Margaret looking out for models in her pursuit of glamour and her desperate attempts to adapt to ruling/changing fashion dictates, such as feminine elegant clothes or straight hair. Her mother is not of much help since she is shown to be interested in having her own fun, for instance with speed-skating in practical, sporty dresses. Other mothers look either drab or ridiculously styled and uncomfortably artificial. Since young Margaret cannot find in real life the glamour propagated in the fashion magazines, she "turned to literature, where all things are possible" (7). In high school (panels 8–13), she again feels out of place: "I was 12. Everyone else was 18" (8).[71] Perhaps also as compensation, young Margaret starts to read voraciously (e.g., Walter Scott novels), "ruin[ing]" her "eyes" (9). Home economics classes, where she is taught "how to serve a formal tea," or all about germs, are sarcastically called "aids to the glamorous life" (10).

At university (panels 14–18), a more educated and self-assured Margaret "renounced the quest for glamour and became unkempt" (15). Again glamour is humorously reduced to the hairstyle. When she is granted the Governor General's Literary Award (panels 19–22), her

American roommates (supposedly at Harvard University) show their ignorance of Canada by being "impressed by the idea of a Governor-General" (19), perhaps even surmising him to be the Canadian boyfriend of the Atwood character. They burn her comfortable Hush Puppies shoes, again trying to force her into some preordained, more elegant, and more feminine fashion. It is in panels 23–30 that Margaret, a prize-winning writer by now, accepts her natural curly hair in "new utilitarian honesty" (23). This is made out to be the turning point of her life. Reading in a "how-to" book that "the main thing is to look like Who You Are!" Margaret asks the quintessential identity question, "Who am I?" (23). Nevertheless, she has learned her lesson. At readings, at parties, and at home, she seems to be herself now, doing and saying what she likes and thinks right, irrespective of any prescribed fashions, which are subject to change in any case.

As the last two panels indirectly claim, Margaret did not in fact start out by trying to be glamorous—which throws another ironic light on the preceding panels—nor did she consciously achieve glamour; rather, it was "thrust upon" her (29). In other words, simply by being herself and mainly by being successful in her profession, people make her out to be "glamorous." In the final panel, she is ironically shown to have unwittingly become a fashion model for enviable hair when a woman addresses another woman with "Hey ... when did ya get the Margaret Atwood hairdo?" (30). Margaret, the artist-outsider, compares her fate to that of other artists who have made it, if mainly in popular culture: Bette Davis (30), Emily Brontë (20), Debbie Reynolds (8), and Shirley Temple (2). What all these artists have in common is their (naturally?) curly hair.

In this autobiographical comic, Atwood presents a story about a developing artist who is depicted as an outsider in all periods of her development and is always out of tune with her social surroundings— people, fashions, and behavioural codes. Atwood writes about the constraints of fashion and selects as a symbol what has become her personal trademark, her curly hair, which in fact refuses to be restrained. She argues that she is not an essentially "glamorous" person and that people added this aspect to her image once she had become successful in her writing—a professional action that is, after all, largely conducted in privacy. As she stated self-ironically in an interview, "The truth is that I am not a very glamorous person. Writers aren't, really. All they do is sit around and write, which I suppose is as commendable as sitting around painting your toenails, but will never make it into the fashion magazines" (in Ingersoll 1990, 82). The subtitle of "THE GLAMOUR & FASHION PAGE" as announced in panel 1 is thus highly ironic: in a way, no glamorous effects are achieved while young Margaret tries hard to fit into changing fashion codes. It is only by being herself—unconsciously so as a young girl (2) and mainly after being very successful in her work—that she achieves "effects you would not have thought possible even in your wildest dreams!" (1)—in her case, that she is now regarded as a fashion model in terms of the curly hair that some time earlier she tried so hard to get rid of. As Sharon R. Wilson states, "Atwood here ridicules female fashions, conformity to changing definitions of glamour, and the role conditioning that makes female glamour seem more important than intelligence" (1993, 165). Thus, for the writer, "having curly hair" has not at all "blurred [her] image" (14)—that is, distracted from what is essential to her, her writing. For the less bright among her audience, however, her hair *has* "blurred her image;" during a reading, someone in the audience asks, "Is your hair really like that or do you get it done?" Atwood counters the irrelevance of this question and the invasion of her privacy in a public situation by ridiculing the question with an absurd question of her own: "do chickens have lips?" (24).

In some of the *Book Tour Comics*, too, Atwood shows the female body and its accoutrements such as hair(style)—traditionally a sign of femininity—getting an illogically large share of attention, even when writers are at work or reading or talking about their work. In contrast to their male colleagues, women in this profession are often subjected to a physical code, which in the final analysis functions as a signal as to who is in power—for the physical appearance of the writer, of course, has nothing to do with (the quality of) her writing. To focus on externals such as a writer's hairstyle thus disregards and thereby diminishes her art. As usual, Atwood in her comics also cleverly refutes, reverses, or at least disturbs such power codes. The second main issue of the *Book Tour Comics* is the audience's appalling ignorance about literature, particularly in connection with media people interviewing the writer about her works. A third issue of the *Book Tour Comics* is the strain of such tours, which exhaust the writer and keep her from doing her main job—that is, writing—instead investing her energies in helping the publisher to sell her books.

The *Book Tour Comics* were initiated at the time of Atwood's novel *The Robber Bride* (1993). As Atwood says in the interview in chapter 8, "I started the *Book Tour Comics* after one of these horrible book tours."[72] Perhaps this novel, with its intriguing *femme fatale* Zenia at its centre, triggered particularly personal, curious questions to the author on her book tours. In any case, her first *Book Tour Comic*, "The Robber Bride—A Roaring Success!" (XXVII, 1993), connects with the third topic of the *Book Tour Comics* mentioned above: the book tour as such is sarcastically thanked for helping to make the novel "a roaring success." The writer, surrounded by her travelling suitcases, picks up the same word—"Roar!"—so that for once the utter strain of such tours for her is "roared" out.[73] Atwood mentioned in an interview that she produced this cartoon (i.e., a single image, unique in her cartoon/comics oeuvre, which is otherwise made up exclusively of comic strips) as a Christmas present for her publisher (thus the added writing and signature) "to make them feel guilty" (see chapter 8).

The second *Book Tour Comic* devoted to *The Robber Bride*, "The Radio Interview" (XXVIII, 1994), features a tiny Atwood stylization with curly hair and elegant hat, physically so small that, sitting on a chair at a table, her feet do not even reach the ground (see figure 9). Mentally, however, she is fully in charge, defeating the physically much larger male interviewer with her intelligence and wit. The interviewer is shown to be utterly ignorant in matters of literature. He is not interested in the book as fiction, as artifact, but mainly, or even exclusively, as alleged autobiography. Whereas a writer such as Atwood dedicated to her art wants to be acknowledged for, and presumably mainly talk about, her work, the casual-looking interviewer in our "auto/biographical age" (Grace 2006, 123) seems to be interested only in the writer as person/woman, who allegedly writes about herself in her fiction—yet another way of diminishing a female writer's imaginative capabilities: "Now tell us, Ms. Atwood—which of the characters in The Robber Bride is really YOU?" (1).

The Atwood figure counters by taking up the interviewer's weapons, pretending that his question is legitimate. However, by laconically

Figure 9.

claiming "Zenia" (1) to be her alter ego, she gets the better of the interviewer, who by picturing Zenia as a sexually attractive *femme fatale* at least proves that he has read the novel. Obviously, the interviewer is stunned not only by her overpowering sexuality, as he imagines her, but also by the suggestion that Atwood herself—whose appearance is a far cry from the interviewer's fantasy of Zenia—is Zenia. With few words, the interviewee thus makes the tactless interviewer speechless.

Yet the answer "Zenia" is even more effective, at least for a perceptive reader of *The Robber Bride*, than simply disconcerting the ignorant interviewer. Zenia in *The Robber Bride* comes across as mysterious not least because she is hardly ever allowed to speak for herself. Her character is the montage product of other characters' projections. In this way, the figure of Atwood in the comic *does* have similarities to Zenia, after all: namely, concerning the public image that Atwood can control only to some extent; she is mostly at the mercy of a public largely ignorant of literature and projecting their simplistic views and prejudices onto her. That Atwood is not only used by the media but also cleverly makes use of them is also suggested by the fact that this self-referential three-panel comic first appeared on Atwood's website (www.owtoad.com).

"The Television Interview" (1993) features a similar-looking Atwood figure. This comic might also have been prompted by Atwood's *The Robber Bride*, though the title of the book that this television interview is about is—probably intentionally—not decipherable in the comic. Again a tiny, elegantly dressed Atwood figure is confronted with an ignorant interviewer, in this case drastically so since Atwood panders to the cliché of the dumb blonde here. A very "feminine"-looking, styled, and made-up blonde female interviewer charges the writer with writing "depressing" books, unlike romances or pulp fiction that the interviewer may be more familiar with: "now honestly—wouldn't you say your work is on the <u>depressing</u> side? I mean it's not exactly an <u>upper</u>! What exactly is the <u>message</u>?" (1). The interviewer's distance from the book is also visualized by her fingering and holding it up as if it were some detestable object. The writer's strategy to keep ignorant interviewers in their places is similar to the one in the previously discussed comic strip. Again the Atwood figure takes up the interviewer's suggestion—here implying the dubious assumption that a book can be reduced to *one* message—and mystifies it with disconcerting effect: "The message is: Eat more prunes" (2). The shocked reaction "<u>What?</u>" is answered by the writer with a concise repetition and short alleged clarification: "Eat more prunes. It's a cautionary tale" (3). The final panel sees the interviewer recovering her blandness in the face of a stoic, superior Atwood figure. The interviewer drops the book, which she seemed wary of right from the beginning. Probably she directly correlates the writer's answer with constipation and scatological matters, as a consequence trying to get rid of the book—and the writer, for she ends the interview as quickly as possible (4).

At second glance, the writer's answer, "Eat more prunes. It's a cautionary tale," might be less absurd than it seems in the context. It might refer indirectly to the apparent need of the interviewer to really "digest"—that is, understand—the book. A further alternative reading of this somewhat cryptic statement might be geared to the fact that the female interviewer appears utterly stiff and artificial and not at ease with herself. Whereas the writer sits comfortably with her legs slightly apart like men do, the interviewer, also due to her very tight, elegant dress, sits upright with her legs crossed, altogether making an uncomfortable impression. The writer's spontaneous response to the interviewer's provocative question might thus also be interpreted as the writer's perceptive taking-in of her constrained female counterpart, not only countering her verbal attack but also giving her indirectly a good piece of advice. This is lost, however, on the dumb interviewer, who looks as constrained in the final panel as in the first panel.

In "The Blind Assa" (XXX, 2001), published in connection with her book tours for her Booker Prize–winning novel *The Blind Assassin* (2000), Atwood again ridicules an interviewer asking ignorant questions, but she mainly jabs at reviewers in this *Book Tour Comic* (see figure 10).[74] Reviewers (especially those of the *National Post*, Canada's conservative national newspaper, which seems to be constantly sparring with Atwood) and publishers are portrayed as infantile here, in contrast to the self-assured, "stoic" (4) writer, who, for the first time, is not drawn smaller than the other figures in the comic.

Atwood uncovers the uncalled-for severity of some book reviewers ("a critic exposes himself in the N.Y. Times ... 'I pooh-pooh on this book'" [3]) and engenders this statement by having a male critic literally "exposing" himself physically (seen from behind) in panel 3.

Figure 10.

The reference to a *New York Times* critic is probably to Thomas Mellon's negative review of *The Blind Assassin* in this newspaper.[75] *The Handmaid's Tale* is also associated with sexuality by renaming it "the Handmaid's Tail," in connection with a negative review of the novel by fellow writer Mary McCarthy. This linguistic twist is all the more appropriate as one major motif of *The Handmaid's Tale* is the (in)capacity to produce children, especially concerning the book's male characters (consider the sexual innuendo of "tail"). The male "National Posties" reviewers, "all of whom are 12" (5), indeed behave like giggling, silly, gloating little boys, happy about bad reviews concerning Canada's leading writer. In the lower caption of panel 4, Atwood sarcastically draws attention to how Canada treats its own renowned writers: "World famous in Canada can be fun" (5). The last three panels again foreground the writer's sex. After having won the prestigious Booker Prize for *The Blind Assassin*, the (name of the) prize is mangled by two gossiping men to "the hooker prize," mentioned together with the exclamation "go figure" (6). The latter is a colloquial phrase used by itself as an interjection to mean "How can one explain that?" or "Who would have thought?" or to express puzzlement over some seeming contradiction; it can also be used sarcastically, implying that the speaker is in fact not at all surprised. Similarly the interviewer of panel 7, apparently quite ignorant of and uninterested in literature, mangles the novel's title—again pandering to sexist clichés—to "The Blonde Assertion" (7).

No wonder that a disgruntled writer in panel 7 is then seen thoughtfully back at her desk in the final panel, wishfully thinking to write herself into the male tradition of (*American*) writing by starting with "Call me Ishmael," the famous first words of Herman Melville's classic novel *Moby Dick* (1851). She thereby briefly slips into the male persona of a canonical *American* writer (potential implication: a world-famous writer is treated differently in the United States). Perhaps this final panel, where the writer briefly borrows from earlier writers rather than being imaginative and productive herself, also suggests how the sometimes destructive or at least hindering side-effects of being a female writer of world fame in Canada might temporarily have a negative influence on her creativity. Yet the comic strip ends with the Atwood figure (writing with her left hand, thus stressing her specialness) being aware that she has to keep on producing something new and outside a male tradition of writing, in spite of all potentially obstructive interventions of critics, reviewers, and interviewers (mostly male in these comics).

Atwood's comic strip "The LongPen" (XXXII, 2006) takes up her recent real "invention" of the "long pen," an autograph-signing machine, which might make book tours obsolete. Atwood came up with the idea of the LongPen during one of her book tours. She wondered how long she would still be able to meet the demands of her publishers and audiences to go on book tours. Inspired by the signing device that package delivery firms use, she invented the LongPen and handed the

Figure 11.

technical accomplishment and the marketing (and substantial sums of her money) over to Unochit (standing for U No Touch It), a company run by Matthew Gibson, the son of her partner, Graeme Gibson. With the help of the LongPen, Atwood can now sign books without being physically present at the book-signing event. "'You can't be in ten places at once, and because of the Amazon-thing we have now, English-speaking countries, and increasingly Germany, all want to publish at the same time. ... Then they all want you to be there and you can't.'"[76]

The book tour seems to be the incorporated devil in the "LongPen" comic. An avid, optimistic young writer ("Fine! Where do I sign? What are book tours?" [1]) is contrasted with a much older writer exhausted from book tours disarranging her in time, place, and inner balance ("Where am I? What time is it? Why am I doing this? I can't go on!" [2]). The rest of the comic then once more proves Atwood's knack for putting the media or, in this case, technology to work for her own purposes: her invention of the LongPen enables Atwood to be more stationary without giving up signing books for her numerous readers all over the world, thus underlining the connectedness of the writer and her readers and the necessity of communication, as well as the distance, between them. The LongPen may indeed put an end to book tours—even the devil capitulates in the final panel in the face of a recovered, younger-looking, and cheerful, even triumphant, writer. She is certainly not a victim any longer as the younger Survivalwoman was; she is a winner now and in control, even in the face of complicated challenges: "Just think of it as a very long pen, with you at one end of it and your writing at the other" (6).

CONCLUSION: ATWOOD AS A CARTOONIST

Although Atwood's more than thirty comics may be subdivided into two broad subcategories—the *Kanadian Kultchur Komix* and the autobiographical *Book Tour Comics*—her comics production has nevertheless a wide topical range. This is especially true of the *Kanadian Kultchur Comix* of the 1970s. In their many topical implications and references, they can be regarded as a critical national chronicle of the 1970s, challenging and demanding, particularly for readers thirty years after their production. Even when disregarding their topicality, these comics are more or less complex mini narratives that, as usual with Atwood, manage to tackle complicated issues in humorous terms. Although the *Kanadian Kultchur Komix* also feature a protagonist who, in many respects, reminds us of Atwood herself, the autobiographical impulse is much more pronounced in the later comics. The *Book Tour Comics*—in contrast to two early autobiographical comics, which also present some private aspects of the budding writer—focus exclusively on the Atwood figure in her professional function. These later comics show her grappling with the drawbacks of being a world-famous writer, in Canada in particular, and with the means and media of star formation and deconstruction (television, radio, newspaper reviewing, literary prizes, public readings, and book signings).

Atwood's self-fashioning as a writer, "from Survivalwoman to literary icon,"[77] has changed somewhat over the past thirty years. The apparel of Survivalwoman mirroring to some extent that of Superman, and therefore suggesting perhaps masculinity, changes to the more feminine look of the female literary star in the *Book Tour Comics*, clad in a black dress and sometimes with an elegant black hat. Her curly hair— Atwood's main visual trademark next to her small stature—also indicates the passing of time. Although the curls as such form a constant, the length of hair and, more importantly, its density change, just as they do in real life with the passing of time. In the Survivalwoman comics, the relatively young protagonist's hair is dense and nicely trimmed. In the two *Robber Bride* comics, produced almost twenty years later, and in the "Blind Assa" comic, produced at the turn of the millennium, the author's hair is still dense and rather voluminous because longer, yet also rather wild and "spacious," signifying a self-assured, but also stressed, author at the height of her success (having just received a very important literary prize in the English-speaking world). In Atwood's two more recent comics, "Negotiating with the De(a)d" (2002) and "The LongPen" (2006), the protagonist's voluminous hair has thinned out, thus signalling her growing older. Her mental capacities are more than intact, however, and the protagonist still gets the better of everyone else.

Yet the autobiographically inspired variations of the Atwood figure's hair are merely a natural side-effect of growing older. What this time indicator also shows is the extent to which both Survivalwoman and the author figure in the autobiographical comics are really humorous projections of Atwood the writer. There are other developments in Atwood's comics art production over thirty years that are more significant. The Atwood persona over the decades develops from a budding writer to an overtaxed, sometimes exhausted, star author of world renown. Along the way, her strategies for dealing with problems such as ignorance and/or gender discrimination change. One might argue that they change according to the very development of victim positions that Atwood presented in her influential book *Survival* (1972). The early comics start out by implying Position Three (in speaking out, they are not representative of Victim Positions One and Two): "*To acknowledge the fact that you are a victim but to refuse to accept the assumption that the role is inevitable*" (1972, 37). This position is valid for all the *Kanadian Kultchur Comix* featuring Survivalwoman. Victim Position Three is not a static but a dynamic state of affairs that offers a way out of the victim state since it makes it possible to "distinguish between the *role* of Victim ... and the *objective experience* that is making you a victim" (38). Being able to identify "the real source of oppression" and "how much of [this victim] position can be changed and how much can't," Survivalwoman's experiences in the *Kanadian Kultchur Comix* therefore are steps toward the constructive action of "repudiating the Victim role" (38).

As the analyses of the comics have shown, this impetus toward Canada's disentangling itself from postcolonial "external and/or ... internal causes of victimization" (38) on a national level is paralleled throughout in the *Kanadian Kultchur Comix* with similar negotiations concerning the status and self-image of women (and men). In this context, too, the "external and/or the internal causes of victimization" are at stake. With respect to gender issues as well, Atwood opts against extreme positions, as can be seen in the critical light she throws on Womanwoman—to substitute the domination of women by men by simply exchanging the sexes' positions is no solution on the path toward becoming "*a creative non-victim*" (38).

This desirable state of affairs is almost reached in the autobiographical comics, especially the *Book Tour Comics*. Although the "external causes of victimization" are still shown to be existent, the Atwood figure in these autobiographical comics is shown to free herself, or to have freed herself, from the "internal causes of victimization" and to fight in her own ways against external causes. The two early autobiographical comics, "Portrait of the Artist as a Young Cipher" (1977) and "Hairdo" (1978), cautiously show this emancipatory process toward self-determination.

It is in the *Book Tour Comics* that Atwood the cartoonist comes close to showing, or does show, the female writer as a creative non-victim and mostly as a superior, authoritative literary celebrity, nevertheless still grappling with inclemencies of the literary circus. These difficulties, due to a social context largely ignorant of the essentials of literary communication, are even more pronounced in the case of a female writer, who is often seen as a woman first and foremost and as a writer second (see also chapter 5). Whereas comics XXVII and XXX show the writer at the mercy of strenuous book tours with hardly any inspiring, helpful experiences (so that the writer roars out her exhaustion and frustration [XXVII] and temporarily even seems to lose her sense of originality and uniqueness, trying to write herself into a male American tradition [XXX]), she is mainly depicted as being in charge of the situation. She fights back and—quite in contrast to the Survivalwoman comics— outwits everyone else, thus providing a sensible model of a superior woman, superior certainly not because of any external "glamour" but because of the wit, intelligence, self-assurance, and creativity of a successful writer. In her later comic "The LongPen" (2006), the Atwood figure even manages to outwit the devil, successfully fighting off and finding an alternative solution for what she finds particularly oppressive at this stage in her successful life, namely, book tours. Her creative imagination as well as the autobiographical foundation of this second group of her comics are suggested by the fact that the LongPen is indeed an industrial invention inspired by Atwood, which could put an end to, or at least reduce the number of, her numerous book tours—thereby undermining the concept of a book tour, premised on physical presence.

At the end of this analysis of Atwood's comics, we can ask ourselves whether we have to regard this multifarious author as a remarkable cartoonist as well. I think the answer must be affirmative, though Atwood's comics, of course, rank behind her other literary achievements. Nevertheless, also in her own view of this hybrid genre and of her competence in it, there might have been a development. Whereas in the earlier Gzowski interview Atwood said, with a lot of wonderful self-irony, "Basically I can't draw" (in Gzowski 1978, 0:48–1:03 min.), in the latest interview on her comics (see chapter 8) she links her competence in this matter with the amount of time she chooses to set aside for it—not much so far. And she intimates in this interview that, if she applied herself, she might even feel fit to produce a graphic novel (which she does not intend to do, however).

Although Atwood never had any training in drawing apart from a few school lessons, being thus a self-made cartoonist (see chapter 8), and though her visual art cannot compete with, for instance, the Canadian masters of this genre, she obviously knows the tricks of the trade and has a talent for the visual arts. She picks up the generic conventions of comic strips and basically conforms to them: panels, gutters, captions, speech and thought balloons with pointed projections to indicate the source character, the verbalization of sound effects, special simplified language, such as the spelling of *comix* for *comics*, special signs to substitute for questionable terms such as the swear word *damn*, pointed language—all these comics conventions are heeded by Atwood as cartoonist.[78] By and large, she also keeps up the comics-specific interaction between images and words, generally avoiding the trap of the writer to let the language take precedence over the images.

Nevertheless, though, it would be surprising if Atwood's comics were not also somewhat extraordinary for the genre. After all, Atwood regards herself as an "amateur cartoonist": "I hesitate to call this a 'talent,' since I know I'm not very good; that is, I have to rub out a lot in order to get the heads the same size and I have difficulty drawing owls flying sideways" (in Ingersoll 1990, 80). The positioning of the feet in the Survivalwoman comics, for instance, is certainly not always professionally drawn. The order of the speech balloons is not always sensible or logical. Everything in her comics is hand drawn, including the panel lines, in contrast to the standard layouts of commercial comics.

Yet where her drawing sometimes does not quite come up to professional standards of comics art, Atwood can certainly hold her own, to say the least, with respect to the narrative material and the humour, irony, satire, and wit transmitted in her comics, particularly their thematic impact. The *Kanadian Kultchur Komix* in particular are complex, topical, satirical statements on contemporary Canadian culture, sometimes difficult to decipher even for knowledgeable readers nowadays. In this series, Atwood combines the comics genre with the political cartoon, making funny yet biting statements about Canadian culture and politics at the time. She sometimes also draws on caricature when she refers to historical figures such as Pierre Trudeau or Pierre Berton in her comics—a broad range of Canadian politics and culture is at the mercy of the caustic pen of Atwood the cartoonist.

"The history of cartooning is mostly the history of famous cartoon 'characters'—not powerful or meaningful stories," said Seth in 2006. Whereas the United States adopted Superman as its main comics representative, Atwood provided a memorable Canadian comics figure with Survivalwoman, who embodies typical Canadian self-deprecating irony and humour. As usual with Atwood, her protagonist is female, as in all her comic strips. Particularly in this genre, this is not a matter of course and thereby significant in itself. As Nicole Hollander, the American creator of the successful *Sylvia* comics (1979), stated, "'It didn't occur to me to be a cartoonist. [In cartoons by men,] women as characters make up a lesser proportion of images than men do. ... It's just one more instance where little girls don't get to see themselves. I think it's damaging. I think it reinforces being invisible, and it reinforces being powerless'" (cited in O'Sullivan 1990, 123). As usual, Atwood inverts conventions, and this can be seen particularly directly and graphically in her comics. They are indeed Atwoodian in their intellectual sharpness, their utter inventiveness, their wit, their verbal pointedness, their topicality, and, last but not least, their gender awareness. With this awareness, Atwood's comics formed part of their temporal context in North America, when Atwood started to publish comics in the 1970s. As Joyce D. Hammond explains about this time,

> During the 1960s and 1970s the women's movement in the United States engendered public debate on a wide range of issues centering around appropriate roles for women and men. Opinions about the feminist movement and its goals were expressed in many media forms, including the graphic cartoon. Cartoons combined words and pictures to make concise and humorous comments about a subject matter which was serious enough to be highly controversial. The cartoons' impact was quick and to the point. (1991, 145)

And as this chapter has demonstrated, gender has remained an issue also in Atwood's later autobiographical *Book Tour Comics*. Having long been an unjustly neglected part of her vast oeuvre, these comics are quintessential Atwood—making us laugh until we cry.

NOTES

1. The only (brief) publication on Atwood's comics I am aware of is Sharon Wilson's one-page, highly selective survey, a small part of a more than forty-page article on Atwood's visual arts (1993, 163–64).

2. The terms "comic book" and "graphic novel" are sometimes used interchangeably, yet more often a comic book is seen as a collection of comic strips (previously published in newspapers), whereas a graphic novel tends to be longer and needs an integrated story to warrant the term "novel." Usually a graphic novel is written in one piece, to be published in book form right away, and tends to be printed on higher-quality paper than the conventional comic books. Good examples of graphic novels are Art Spiegelman's *Maus: A Survivor's Tale* (1986) or David Cronenberg's *existenz* (1999), adapted from his eponymous film. Atwood's children's books (partly collaborations with other authors) may not, strictly speaking, be considered "graphic novels"— that is, as instances of long pictorial fiction—since in these texts the pictures are largely illustrations of the accompanying text and do not intertwine in the way that text and image work together in comic strips or graphic novels.

3. A broader definition would be that comics tell stories graphically because images without written text may still count as a cartoon or comic; see Atwood's "Lightbulb" comic (III in the comics list at the end of this book).

4. Generic forerunners of the cartoon or comics may be traced back as far as the murals of ancient Egypt and the Greek and Roman reliefs (see O'Sullivan 1990, 9); see also Inge 1990 as well as the interview with Atwood in chapter 8 of this volume.

5. "The comic strip may be defined as an open-ended dramatic narrative about a recurring set of characters, told in a series of drawings, often including dialogue in balloons and a narrative text, and published serially in newspapers" (Inge 1990, xi).

6. "Along with jazz, the comic strip as we know it perhaps represents America's major indigenous contribution to world culture" (Inge 1990, xi); see also White and Abel 1963, 1.

7. Here and in the following, the year refers to the first publication of a comic strip in serial production.

8. The forerunner of political cartoons in North America was created by Benjamin Franklin. It was entitled "Join, or Die" and was published on 9 May 1754 in the *Pennsylvania Gazette* at the beginning of the French and Indian War. It expressed Franklin's warning to the British colonies in America, exhorting them to unite against the French and the Natives. Showing a snake cut into eight segments, the cartoon depicts the colonies divided over the war. The caption and the editorial that accompanied the cartoon suggest that the divisions must be overcome and a union of the colonies be achieved, in order to ensure the survival of the British colonies. The first Canadian political cartoon, "The Mitret Minnet," was published only a few years later (1774); see Sabin 1977.

9. The first issue of *The New Yorker* (21 February 1925) featured a cartoon on its cover. "The editors receive today over 2,500 submissions a week from which approximately 20 are selected for publication, and most of these come from the 40 to 50 artists on whose works they have first option. *The New Yorker* remains for cartoonists the most prestigious place to publish" (Inge 1990, 115).

10. For a succinct survey of the ups and downs of comics reception, see Eklund 2006.

11. Kathy English, "Comic Strip's Fans Get Shirty," 14 March 2009, www.thestar.com/printArticle/602203 [consulted 25 March 2009].

12. See Brad Mackay, "Cartoons Go Online," 9 March 2005, www.cbc.ca/arts/media/cartoonsgoonline.html; and Leslie Berlin, "The Comics Are Feeling the Pain of Print," 28 December 2008, www.nytimes.com/2008/12/28/business/media/28proto.html [both consulted 25 March 2009].

13. For an excellent survey of the history of comics production in Canada, see Edwardson 2003.

14. "Canada has more good cartoonists per capita than any other country, save perhaps England, but even that exception is not unanimous" (Sabin 1977, 8).

15. See, e.g., Aislin 1999; and Seth 2006.

16. See "Often Called Canada's Nastiest Political Cartoonist," www.aislin.com/pages/aislindepth.html [consulted 25 October 2006]. On the strong tradition of political cartooning in Canada, see Sabin 1977.

17. A more recent example: one of the twenty questions put to the three candidates for mayor of Toronto in autumn 2006 was "Who's your favorite cartoon character?" See *Toronto Star*, 2 November 2006, R7.

18. See also Atwood in Atwood and Beaulieu: "When it rains and you're a child and you're in your little wood cabin in the forest, you have two choices: read or draw. I drew a lot when I was a child, I drew a lot of comic books, and I continued to draw them as an adult, because we were the comic book generation" (1998, 29). In a radio interview, Atwood even confesses "a real fascination with ... horror comics"; in LaMarsh 1975, 01:05–01:08 min.

19. On the characteristics and potentialities of comics as a narrative medium, see Abbott 1986.

20. As gleaned from several statements, Atwood's favourite comics/figures are Wonder Woman, Superman, Mickey Mouse, Plastic Man, Donald Duck, all of which, apart from the last mentioned, are referred to in her own comics occasionally; see below.

21. Thus in "Chicken Little Goes Too Far," in *The Tent:* "Chicken Little slammed Turkey Lurkey's office door, causing Turkey Lurkey's corkboard decorated with clever newspaper cartoons to fall onto the floor" (2006, 69). In Atwood's latest short-story collection, *Moral Disorder* (2006), for instance, there are four references to comic books (30, 77, 140) and cartoons (59).

22. From "Manet's Olympia," in *Eating Fire* (1998, 306). Here the short, sometimes abrupt, disjointed, and incomplete phrasing in cartoon language becomes an effective means of including an invective in the poem.

23. See chapter 1, 25.

24. Margaret Atwood, email to Reingard M. Nischik, 20 December 2006.

25. She refers mainly to Rick Salutin here (journalist and member of the board of *This Magazine* and a good friend of Atwood), who "thought that it would be good to have a comics section at the back since the middle was all so serious" (in Gzowski 1978, 14:21–14:30 min).

26. Atwood's "Hairdo" appeared in the *Weekend Magazine* of the *Montreal Star*, 4 February 1978.

27. In the interview (chapter 8), she states that she may publish her visual art, including her comics, in a collection someday.

28. Three of these twenty-three comics apparently do not explicitly bear the series title but clearly belong to the *Kanadian Kultchur Komix*.

29. "Multicultural chaos is the single most exhilarating aspect of being Canadian" (Ferguson 2003, 26).

30. Twice in an email to Reingard M. Nischik, 20 December 2006; maybe this is also an allusion to "catch-as-catch-can"—using or making do with whatever means are available.

31. As Atwood notes in her interview with Gzowski, "When I started doing this [the *Kanadian Kultchur Komix*], I took the initials B. G. from a nineteenth-century Canadian political satirist. And then we felt that this was a bit too skimpy, so we turned it into Bart Gerrard. ... This kind of social-political satire seems to be something that we [Canadians] do" (in Gzowski 1978, 1:33–2:12 min.). She also notes that "It's a reference to the first cartoonist in Canada, that was his name."

32. Even in 1977, it could still be stated that "Canadian cartoonists are ... all male, except Emily Carr who made two attempts at cartooning for WOMEN'S WEEKLY in 1905 and 1918" (Sabin 1977, 8).

33. "It's just a pseudonym but with a different functionality and a somewhat different personality," she says in the interview. Atwood also states that covering up her identity was not at stake for her, although in the earlier interview with Gzowski she intimated that she had received "hate mail" at the time on account of the *Kanadian Kultchur Komix* ("I got hate mail for being Bart as well, it wasn't just me" [Gzowski 1978, 2:20–2:39 min.), something she denies in the more recent interview.

34. Excluding the onions, lemons (see "lament"), frogs, and camouflaged representatives of "The Toronto Kultchural Mafia," who all appear sexless.

35. "Survivalwoman is the superhero that represents Canada in the same way that Superman represents the United States" (Atwood in Gzowski 1978, 4:14–4:22 min.).

36. In what follows, short references to the Atwood comics are based on the comics list at the end of this book, with I,1 meaning, for instance, panel 1 of comic I in the chronological listing.

37. Perhaps a reference to the Canadian Content Regulation (for television programming effective since 1961, for Canadian musical selections used on radio since 1972). See "Cancon Costs Canadian Taxpayers Billions and Curtails Freedom of Expression," www.fraserinstitute.ca/shared/readmore. asp?sNav=nr&id=353 [consulted 9 April 2007].

38. Atwood combines the two names of "Pierre Berton" and "Pierre Trudeau" into a single name. The reason might be that both men occupied outstanding positions in Canada's cultural and political life at the time— Berton as popular historian and Trudeau as prime minister. In addition, the spelling of Trudeau as "Truedough" suggests another connection, "true" and "dough," which might relate to "sourdough." The latter is the name for a "real" gold seeker during the Klondike Gold Rush and is generally defined as somebody who has wintered at least once in the Yukon during the gold rush. If one equates sourdough with a "real Klondiker," who in literature is

frequently seen as a prototype of the inhabitant of the "True North Strong and Free" and thus a "real Canadian," one can draw the conclusion that Atwood alludes to Berton and Trudeau as being "real Canadians."

39. Note that the blame for this is attributed to a man, finally, who allegedly provided her with the wrong kind of energy: "I should've asked for Regular ... damn that fast-talking ESSO® OIL man ... " (V,4).

40. Masculinism was much more powerful than feminism up to that time, though it was not generally designated that way.

41. On the October Crisis in Quebec, see Bothwell, Drummand, and English 1981, 388–406; see also Smith 1985a, 1311. On the War Measures Act, see Smith 1985b, 1917.

42. Note the phonetic similarity between the words *war* and *whore* as well as the ambiguity of the noun *measure*, which Atwood transfers here to its pragmatic verbal meaning, in a sexist context too.

43. With this language play, Atwood probably also ridicules the short-sighted gender-inversion cartoons that appeared at the time: "The inversion cartoon depicted women and men in a manner which inverted societal expectations associated with the status quo" (Hammond 1991, 145).

44. "Manpower, the world's leading staffing firm, provides ... workforce solutions and career management." See www.ca.manpower.com/cacom/index.html [consulted 6 March 2007].

45. See also Atwood's statement in the interview about the large size of comics when they are devised on the drawing board, to be reduced only later in print.

46. The red Canadian maple leaf flag was not officially adopted as Canada's national flag, replacing the Union Jack and the Canadian Red Ensign, until 1965.

47. There were several subsequent ones after Marston's death in 1947.

48. Joshua Glenn, "Wonder-Working Power," *Boston Globe*, 4 April 2004, www.boston.com/news/globe/ideas/articles/2004/04/04 [consulted 8 January 2007].

49. See Charles Lyons, "Suffering Sappho! A Look at the Creator and Creation of Wonder Woman," 1, www.comicbookresources.com [consulted 12 October 2006].

50. Cited in ibid., 3.

51. Reprinted in Nischik 2000/02, 315.

52. Note the padding words ("like," "I mean"), the double negative and the contraction "aint" ("you aint got NO real culture"), and the stereotypical address of "man," though Survivalwoman is clearly female ("Aw come off it man"), all suggesting a lack of education or wrong grammar of the speaker.

53. These are unflattering terms, "behemoth" signifying something of oppressive or monstrous size or power or appearance, "blimpish" referring to a diehard or ultraconservative nationalistic outlook and complacent stupidity (according to *Webster's Dictionary*).

54. See von Flotow 2007. Perhaps significantly so, European (and Asian) countries play a larger role in this context for Canadians right now than the United States.

55. Other comic strips that make a topic of the English and French Canadian duality are XIII, XIV, XV, and XVII.

56. As regards on-stage appearance; see also comics V, VI, XVII, XXII, and XXIV, in which only a female character or characters appear.

57. The French are stereotypically associated with frogs due to frogs' legs being a delicacy in traditional French cuisine.

58. A reference to *Histoire d'O* (1954; English edition *Story of O*, 1965), an erotic novel dealing with sadomasochism by Pauline Réage, the pen name of French author Anne Desclos.

59. A joual neologism: a mixture of an English noun and a French adjectival derivation.

60. Consider, e.g., the controversial resolution of the Quebec faction of the Liberal Party, advocated prominently by Michael Ignatieff when he was a candidate (eventually defeated by Stéphane Dion) for the Liberal Party leadership in autumn 2006.

61. "A Good Man Is Hard to Find" is the ironic title of a short story by Flannery O'Connor.

62. Copulation by several persons in succession with the same passive partner; gang rape (*Webster's Dictionary*).

63. Disney was a pioneer of animated cartoon films and a film producer, mainly well known for his series *Mickey Mouse*. Disney was born and died in the United States but had a Canadian father.

64. I am indebted to a former student, Mirjam Berle, whose attention I drew to Atwood's comics a couple of years ago and who then, thrilled about this topic, went to Toronto on an ICCS scholarship to write her MA thesis on Atwood's comics. She collected most of the comics I deal with in this chapter, apart from the later *Book Tour Comics*.

65. William New states that the beginnings of the autobiographical comic in Canada at large were in the 1960s (see Crosbie 1994, 29). "Contemporary cartoonists are also using the confessional model as a way of locating the personal subject—the artist/author—within diverse public spheres" (Crosbie 1994, 30).

66. Again the designation of the series title varies: "Comics" is used more often, though, so I have chosen this variant in what follows.

67. Atwood's second name is Eleanor.

68. The Park Plaza Hotel (Bloor Street and Avenue Road) used to be a meeting place for Toronto's literati in the 1970s to 1990s. Today the building is the Park Hyatt Toronto.

69. See Atwood's references to Lee in the interview in chapter 8.

70. Kindergarten supervisor, teacher?

71. This is probably an exaggerated reference to the biographical fact that Atwood skipped her seventh year of school, not unusual for bright children at the time (Sullivan 1998, 59).

72. John Shoesmith from the Thomas Fisher Rare Book Library at the University of Toronto writes that, "As for the Book Tour Comics, ... I think these were originally produced (in 1993) as a Christmas card to the people she worked with at Doubleday." Email to Reingard M. Nischik, 8 August 2008.

73. With her productivity (and thus the number of books to launch), no wonder Atwood has come to regard such tours, with long, packed days, as gruelling. She has gone through them anyway, also because such tours are said to increase sales by thirty to eighty percent (see Cooke 1998, 280).

74. And, particularly in the second panel, at her publishers, who send her to the "Priemière" [sic] of this "heavy book" (1) all the way to Whitehorse, the capital of Yukon, where she reads at night to a small number of listeners resembling animals rather than people; they make "the Blind Bit of Difference" in selling figures, as Atwood retitles *The Blind Assa(ssin)* here to satirize, perhaps, the book tour planning and advertisement strategies of her publishers, who overtax the writer.

75. Thomas Mellon, "Wheels within Wheels," *New York Times*, 3 September 2000; for a scholarly response to this ill-informed review, see Roy 2006.

76. Atwood in Julie Wheelwright, "A Sure Sign of Things to Come," 2006, www.living.scotsman.com/books.cfm?id=365352006 [consulted 10 April 2007].

77. See the title for my interview with Atwood in chapter 8.

78. Judith O'Sullivan summarizes the lexicon, syntax, and grammar of comics art as follows: "Richly various, comics have communicated over the years through different devices, including continuous narration, whereby a single set of characters appears repeatedly from frame to frame and the action progresses from left to right; calligraphic caricature, which renders the protagonists and their adversaries immediately recognizable; facial and gestural schemata, which express the characters' actions and reactions; action abstraction, a pictorial shorthand, universally understood, in which

exploding lines indicate sudden impact, stars unconsciousness, light bulb ideas, and balloon puffs thoughts; literary legend, conveyed in the balloon, which clarifies the comic's visual message; and specialized vocabularies, such as ... 'Pow!' which heighten the extreme emotion or action manifested by the characters" (1990, 9).

8

From Survivalwoman to Literary Icon
An Interview with Margaret Atwood

This interview (shortened for publication) took place in Toronto in a café on Bloor Street on 10 November 2006. Margaret was between numerous trips, as usual, while I, on sabbatical, was at the end of a three-week stay in Vancouver and Toronto before flying home to Zurich/Constance the following day. The interview was typically Atwoodian in that we had a lot of fun while discussing serious subjects.

RN: Margaret, thank you very much for being prepared to meet, and even in the morning...

MA: Yes...

RN: (laughs) You once said that breakfast time is the weakest time of your day...

MA: That's true, but I've had my breakfast!

RN: (laughs) That's what I thought. ... First of all, pre-outlining, I would like to touch upon three aspects of your creativity and some of its manifold results. First, your comics; second, what I would like to call "art work"; and third, photographs published of you, which are an important aspect of literary stardom. So first of all cartoons and comics then. As far as I know, you have published some thirty comics to date. How did you develop into a cartoonist? (laughs)

MA: I *began* as a cartoonist! (laughs) Because as a child I belonged to the comic-book generation. We didn't have TV, and the comic books were very, very popular. Children collected them, and traded them, and had big stocks of them, and you might spend a Saturday morning with your friends reading comics. You know, a group activity was reading comics. And then trading—"I've read this"—you would read them several times and keep them, put them under your bed. And of course it was something that parents disapproved of. But it was also an age in which there were much more extensive comics in newspapers than there are now. Some of them were amusing cartoon strips, and others were narrative cartoon strips, featuring their protagonists just like novels. And you could then get books of those, comic books featuring the same people. So it was an extensive culture. And if you went to the movies at all—which I didn't much because I wasn't near very many movie theatres—but when you did go to the movies there would be a cartoon before the main event, always these short cartoons that you now get reruns of on TV. Mickey Mouse cartoons and Donald Duck cartoons, many different kinds of cartoons. It was just a total culture that was very appealing to children, and therefore it was the normal form for children to practise. Now we see a new phenomenon: comics have come back or, say, drawn books, drawn novels. I don't know whether you saw *Persepolis*, by the Iranian woman who lives in France [Marjane Satrapi]. They are like old comic books except that the subject matter is serious. They frequently have hard covers on them, they are sold like books. The comics have now come full circle, from being a frivolous entertainment to being a serious art form. And some of these are now migrating into films: *Superman*, *Batman*, *X-Men* all were comic strips. They were comic strips, they were comic books. So on the weekends you got a colour supplement. They didn't used to be called comics, they used to be called "funnies."

RN: The funnies, right!

MA: The funnies would come in the weekend newspaper and would immediately be snatched up by children, who would read them all. But a lot of adults were fans of these comic strips, too. *Krazy Kat* is now regarded as an art form. So this was just a natural thing to do, and we had comic strips that we drew.

RN: At school?

MA: No, no, this is myself and my brother [who] drew comic strips.

RN: Well, you didn't go to school anyway... (laughs)

MA: Well, I did, in the winters. I didn't start school early, the way children do now, because there wasn't any. So I went from the age of six—in the winters, I would be in school, and then the other times of year I would not be in school. But that was not a school activity, of course, because adults didn't approve of it. (laughs) We did it outside of the school. We did it with coloured pencils. Ballpoint pens hadn't been invented. Coloured pencils had.

RN: All right, so you started out as a cartoonist with the cooperation of your brother?

MA: No, we had our separate strips, we were each other's audiences, he wasn't helping me, I wasn't helping him. We would draw away on our comics, and then we would trade them. (laughs)

RN: (laughs) Wonderful! So, in other words, you haven't had any training whatsoever, in painting or drawing, you just did it?

MA: I just did it. Well, children just do it. They will do it anyway. We had art in school in those days. There would be some portion of the day devoted to painting or drawing. And at Christmas and sometimes at other times... I remember particularly in grade five we were allowed to paint on the blackboard with poster paints, and we were supposed to paint Santa Claus and Christmas things. (laughs)

RN: But then came the 1970s, when I think *This Magazine* approached you to draw...

MA: Yes. I knew the people running it. But I did a couple of big-page comics for a weekend supplement to newspapers called *Weekend*. I did the hair comic and the "My Life" comic for them.

RN: Ah, the "Hairdo" comic...

MA: The "Hairdo" comic and "The Story of My Life" one ["Portrait of the Artist as a Young Cipher"] were done for *Weekend Magazine*.

RN: That was before the 1970s?

MA: No, it was during the 1970s. Let's go back in time. Although that may take you to "art work." But they're the same kind of activity. In college, I did covers for the literary magazine, illustrations within it, and I had this poster business whereby I did silk screen posters for events, such as plays and musicals. We did big posters which we stuck up on campus, advertising. This was before computers, and therefore these were actual cerographs.

RN: Cerographs...

MA: You have a frame, you have a piece of silk stretched within that frame, you block out part of the silk with either acetate film, or there is a kind of glue that you could paint on to get a wash effect. If you were doing lettering, you had to cut the letters out of the acetate film with a little knife and stick it onto the silk, and then you have to dissolve it in your finish and the acetate dissolver. You make one screen for every colour. And you therefore have to align the screens so that the second colour will come through in relation with the first one where you want it to go. If you have a third colour, then you have a third screen. So for each colour the posters would be run through once. You put the paper underneath the frame, which is on a hinge. You lift it up and put the paper on the centre, and you lock it down. And then you take a big thing like a window cleaner squeegee; it's rubber, and it has a pull handle, and you pull the colour over the poster. You have to pull it evenly, or you'll get blobs. (laughs) And then you very carefully lift the screen and take the poster out, and you dry it. So, for three colours, it would probably take three days to pull out an edition of posters, because you have to let them dry in between. I did this on the ping-pong table (laughter). And I had my little business, and I charged money and all the rest of it. So I did that, and to go with those posters I would do the cover designs on the fronts of the programs. So I did quite a lot of that kind of art work during those years. Why? Because there wasn't anybody else doing it. There was only one other person on campus who was doing silk screen posters. He went on to become a designer in New York.

RN: And then eventually came the *Kanadian Kultchur Komix*, spelt in so many different ways.

MA: Yeah. But let's just put something in between. Then I started publishing poetry books. And I was pretty involved with the covers of those. *The Circle Game* was done by me, using something called Letraset, which are those stick-on letters. You could get them at stationery shops, different typefaces. And the circles on *The Circle Game* cover are made from stick-on dots, the kinds that you put on legal documents. So I did that cover. Why did we all do those kinds of things? Because it was cheap. It was a very do-it-yourself, low-budget era of Canadian publishing. I did that cover, I didn't do the Oxford covers. I did the collages for *Susanna Moodie*. I did the cover for that, and they kind of messed it up, they put red on it. I didn't want them to do that, they didn't tell me they were going to. I guess they intervened in my cover, which annoyed me. So the recap: before the *Kanadian Kultchur Komix*, you have all of this other kind of visual work that was going on. So then *This Magazine*. We got the idea of doing a comic in it. So I got the idea of having a superhero like the superheroes in real comics, except it was a Canadian superhero, so she didn't actually have any powers (laughs), and that was where that came from.

RN: So this is how Survivalwoman came into being.

MA: Exactly. I had already published *Survival* by that time. I was doing that comic, I was living on the farm at that point in time. And at that time I also did *Up in the Tree*, you can see that it's related. They've just done a new edition, by the way, a facsimile edition, and they kept the original colours. The reason it was those colours was that it was the early years of Canadian children's publishing, and they could not afford three-coloured printing. Three-coloured printing is what gives you the full range of colours. So I chose this red and blue, and together they make this funny kind of purplely brown. But the only alternative would have been red and black or blue and black; so we got a much more colourful effect with the red and blue, given that there were only two colours that we could have.

RN: You decided to publish the *Kanadian Kultchur Komix* under a pseudonym—and under a male one at that.

MA: It's a reference to the first cartoonist in Canada, that was his name.

RN: Bart Gerrard. But why not Margaret Atwood?

MA: Why Margaret Atwood? I've used pseudonyms before. (laughs) You just don't know about it. (laughs)

RN: (laughs) Oh, I see! And you won't tell me... (laughter)

MA: Well, I can tell you about one of them. When we were in college, my friend Dennis Lee and myself... Dennis Lee who went on to become House of Anansi and then wrote all of these children's books—*Alligator Pie* and those books which have been so extremely popular. Anyway, when we were in college, we were involved in literary things of various kinds—no, he wasn't my boyfriend (laughs); it was possible to have friends who were boys, even then. Kids do it much more now, but it was possible then. We both had rather silly senses of humour, and we made up a person called Shakesbeat Latweed (laughter), Lee and Atwood = Latweed. We took the first thing we wrote together—we laughed our heads off, we had so much fun—it was Jack Sprat, the nursery rhyme: "Jack Sprat could eat no fat, his wife could eat no lean, and so betwixt them both they licked the platter clean." We took four lines of this poem, and we did interpretations according to, in the first instance, Shakespeare. Shakespeare wrote the first line, except that it was more than a line, it was a sort of blank verse on the subject of "Jack Sprat could eat no fat." (laughter) And then the second line, "his wife could eat no lean," I forget who wrote that, I think it was Alexander Pope. And somebody else wrote the third one, and the fourth one was written by a Beatnik poet: "they licked the platter clean" was sort of an Allen Ginsberg-Jack Kerouac run-on Beatnik sort of thing. So that was our first work of art, and then the pseudonym remained. Dennis went off—I think he spent a year in Germany—I continued to write Shakesbeat Latweed, and Shakesbeat Latweed wrote satire, basically. So Shakesbeat Latweed wrote an analysis of singing commercials in the mode of Northrop Frye's archetypes. (laughter) Shakesbeat Latweed wrote a piece on the difficulties of Anglo-Saxon. You know, that was the kind of thing that Shakesbeat Latweed wrote. And then after I left college, some people continued on writing Shakesbeat Latweed, which has confused scholars. Because they think it's all me, whereas in fact I left, and the name continued on. So you have to be very careful in looking at Shakesbeat Latweed, which year you're at (laughs), because for a couple of years after I wasn't there anymore. Shakesbeat Latweed—it's like the queen. You know, there's always the queen, it's just not always the same person.

RN: So was that published in *Acta Victoriana*?

MA: Yes, you can go back and find old Shakesbeat Latweed there. (laughter)

RN: Well, OK, so much about pseudonyms. So Bart Gerrard was not the first one you chose.

MA: No, by no means. (laughs)

RN: Was it known that you published these [comics by Bart Gerrard]... ?

MA: It became known.

RN: About roughly which time?

MA: I don't know.

RN: But after a while it became known?

MA: I think so, yes; I mean, it was pretty obvious anyway. If somebody is called Survivalwoman, who else is it going to be? But I think a pseudonym is a way of having another functionality, another function. So it's a way of having another hat. For instance, John Banville, who won the Booker last year, has just published a mystery novel under a different name. But it says right on the cover flap that this is John Banville. (laughter) And Ruth Rendell writes several different kinds of mysteries. But some books she writes under a different name, because she considers them to be a different kind of book. So she publishes sometimes under Ruth Rendell and sometimes under this other name—Barbara Vine. So a lot of people have done this.

RN: That would also work very well for you because every book you write is completely different from the one before. (laughs)

MA: Hm, yes. Well, not completely. (laughter) Anyway, the cartoons that I was doing for *This Magazine* were just another functionality, like Shakesbeat Latweed, a different area. And when you have a pseudonym like that you also get another personality. Mr. Pessoa [Fernando Pessoa], the Portuguese modernist, had fifty-four—he didn't call them pseudonyms, he called them heteronyms. A pseudonym is really you with another name, whereas he considers these to be separate individuals, although he was fully conscious all the time, it wasn't a case of multiple personalities. Among his poet personalities, he had three who were well known and even have their own websites to this day (laughter), and they wrote quite different kinds of poetry, and sometimes they wrote critical articles, tearing down the other ones. (laughter) And he wrote prose and poetry and critical articles, and some of his heteronyms were women. So this is an old story. If what you're saying is "Did you want to be a man?" or "Did you want to conceal the fact that you were a woman?" or any of that kind of thing, that didn't enter into it. It's just a pseudonym but with a different functionality and a somewhat different personality.

RN: I think you said in an earlier interview that you sometimes got hate mails—well, emails weren't around yet—hate *mail* for these comics at the time?

MA: Not for these. Not particularly, no. The audience was really too small, and it selected itself.

RN: OK, not for those. I think the series of comics for *This Magazine* was commissioned work, right?

MA: Do you mean did I get paid for it? Not that I recall. (laughter) If anybody got paid for any of this stuff, it sure wasn't much. These were all collective efforts at that time. There was a lot of volunteer work, as it were, that went into every one of those enterprises, *This Magazine* or the House of Anansi. I've run their poetry line for some years, and they've paid me this much, but it's not anything that you would call real money. And I did a lot of editing of other books as well, for instance *Eleven Canadian Novelists* that Graeme [Gibson] did. It was me who went through the transcripts. He had taped them, and then he had a typist type them out, but as it turned out she was a bit deaf (laughs), so I had to go through this. You know how it is when you're doing transcripts of conversations, there's miles of it that you just take out and turn into something that looks like English. So I was doing that with just mounds of paper that hadn't been accurately transcribed anyway, so I couldn't guess (laughter) what the person had said and made it up. And then we would send it to the writer and say, "Is this what you said?" She had transcribed the House of Anansi as "the House of Nazis."

RN: Oh dear! Oh no!

MA: She was really a little bit deaf... We all were doing this as a new cultural initiative that we were very involved in. And because it had been poetry throughout the 1960s, because it was so difficult to get novels published, we all were involved and knew each other and published each other's books and that kind of thing. It was just taken for granted that you would help other people. The further away from subsistence communities you get, the more that disappears.

RN: And when you created those comics at that time, you knew that they were going to end up in *This Magazine*?

MA: Oh yeah, I did it for them. I did it exclusively for them, and then they used some of those images as promotions. They made little note cards out of them and later on used them to sell subscriptions. But you have to remember that I wasn't as famous then as I am now, but I was somewhat famous. So it gave them something to help the magazine, people liked them [the comics].

RN: And by now you've produced something that might develop into a new series?

MA: Oh, the *Book Tour* series. (laughs) Well, I started the *Book Tour Comics* after one of these horrible book tours, and I did it as a Christmas present for my publishers to make them feel guilty. (laughter)

RN: Which is the purpose of a present... (laughs)

MA: It was "The Robber Bride." That was the first one, which I really did from that experience, more or less. They're saying, "Which character is the closest to you?" and I said, "Zenia." (long laughter)

RN: So you will keep on doing those...

MA: Who knows? I never make predictions about the future. It's not a lucky thing to do.

RN: OK, all right. Now here comes a very heavy question, you might cut my head off for this. Why don't you let the intrigued Atwoodians, or the interested readers at large, have a collection of your comics?

MA: It has been proposed. Number one, it was proposed by you, and before that it was proposed by the very same Anansi Press that I first started out with. And maybe I'll do it. But I think I would want to do not just the comics, I would want to do some of the other comic-like art work, such as the posters...

RN: Ah, that would be interesting!

MA: ... such as some of the cover designs that I've done. And I still like to mess with my cover designs, I still like to get involved. *Moral Disorder*, have you seen it?

RN: Yes.

MA: That picture was chosen by me, the colours were chosen by me, the layout was suggested by me. And then the designer made it more beautiful by colourizing the girls a bit and putting the red lines around. But that picture, it's a real picture from the real cookbook called *The Art of Cooking and Serving*, which was really put out by the Crisco Company about 1929–30. One of the first pictures is what the maid is supposed to wear during the day, the white stockings (laughs), and the other is what the maid is supposed to wear in the evenings. They do look like a couple of strange twins.

RN: I presume that you always take an interest like that?

MA: I always take an interest like that in my book covers, if I'm close enough to the publisher in time and space to be able to get my hands on it. Some of them, of course, have gone right by me. (laughs)

RN: Bantam Books, for instance...

MA: Well, those, ... and I think when the wall came down in Eastern Europe, all of a sudden they could publish anything they wanted. They had not been allowed to have pornography for so long, they just went wild. So *The Robber Bride*, I think it's from Estonia or Lithuania, has black satin... (laughter) It's incredible what they put on that book, and I thought, "Uh-oh, I'm going to get some really disappointed men readers." (long laughter)

RN: Oh dear... Well, when you start creating a comic, or a cartoon, do you have an overall idea first, or do you... ?

MA: I draw it out.

RN: So you start with the images?

MA: I sketch it out with a pencil. I'll show you exactly what I do. There's no secret, anybody does this who's doing a cartoon. You decide how many panels you're gonna have. Usually there's four in a strip like that. And then you make what they're going to say, where they're going to be. And then you can rub that out and change it around. And then you do it with quite a fine pencil, you draw it more perfectly. Here's Reingard (draws a cartoon), ... here's Reingard's hands, and she's saying, "Why don't you have a book of comics published?" (laughter) Then you have to see whether it's all gonna fit, and then you letter it. If you want to do serifs, ... (still drawing) it depends how fancy you want it to be. You could have any kind of lettering, really. So that's how it all goes forward, and then you ink it. When you read a comic book, it will say "drawn by such and such, inked by so and so."

RN: That's interesting! Let me see if I've got this correct. Now, after you've done the panelling, then you start with the language first?

MA: I start with the figures, who's gonna be in it, and then what they're gonna say, what they're gonna be doing... It's all part of the same process. So, for instance, Superman is jumping off a roof, (laughter) and there is magic, there's some Kryptonite here, so he's not gonna be able to fly, so he's saying... It's all one. But that would never happen, or else Superman would be dead, but just supposing. (laughter) Yeah, there was a lot of flying in our early comics, we had flying rabbits.

RN: Flying rabbits...

MA: Yeah, they had little capes. (laughs)

RN: One of my favourite animals because of the ears! Have you ever made use of my favourite Canadian animal, which is frequenting your street... ?

MA: Skunks? (laughter) Raccoons?

RN: (laughs) No, they are not in your street, are they?

MA: Beavers?

RN: Squirrels...

MA: (simultaneously) Oh, squirrels! I'm at war with them!

RN: Oh, because they climb into your window?

MA: No, they dig up my tulip bulbs. (laughter) I fox them, I know how to get round them—you get chicken wire and put it all over where you plant them. They watch you, they watch you planting things, and as soon as you've left they will come and dig around and see what you've planted. It's an ingrained habit, they watch other squirrels to see where they've hidden things, so they can come and steal them.

RN: Clever animals...

MA: Crocuses and tulips are particularly vulnerable. Daffodils they will dig out but not eat because they're poisonous.

RN: All right... You said in an earlier interview, referring to differences in genre, that a novel for you is also sheer hard, physical work, and we can all understand why. And you said that with poetry you sometimes might get away with that sheer hard, physical work, because it just doesn't take you so long in writing. It might take you as long in conceiving, but...

MA: Yes, that's just the physical work...

RN: Yes, just the physical work. But how about comics, are comics for you fun or work or both? Or is that the same thing anyway?

MA: Everything is fun and work. (laughter) I'd like to have enough time to do them properly. If you're too rushed with them, of course you don't get what you want, because you might make a blot. (laughter) The other trick about comics is that you always draw them bigger than they are going to appear. Because then, when they are condensed, you get a much more delicate effect than you'd be able to achieve if you drew them the same size that they are. So open up your newspaper and turn to the comic strips at the back and look at how big they are, they're tiny. The person has drawn them on a big drawing board. If you've ever seen a photograph of somebody like Charlie Schulz at his drawing board doing his comics, they're big. And then they photograph that, and they get condensed.

RN: OK. Now, this is not too serious a question; on the other hand, it might be, one never knows with you. Can we anticipate, sometime, a graphic novel from you?

MA: No.

RN: (laughs) That's what I thought.

MA: The people who do graphic novels are actually pretty talented. They are often talented artists. I could probably apply myself and take the time... But they usually have a lot of cross-hatching. They are intricate, they're considerably more finished than plain old cartoons. To do a graphic novel, you'd also need to decide if you are going to use a sort of greyish style or whether it is going to be a sort of stark, black-and-white, ... just exactly how much art you're gonna put in it. And it takes them a long time, you know, to design those things and draw them out. Some of them are quite a lot better than others. Photo *romanzi*, in Italy, have you seen that at all?

RN: Photo romances?

MA: Yeah, photo *romanzi*. They're not drawn, people have posed for the pictures. They were still current in the 1970s. They are probably regarded as somewhat old-fashioned these days. The people posing for them always had their mouths closed, it was very funny. (laughter) They would shoot them like movies, except that they were all stills.

RN: Very dramatic.

MA: Yeah. They were basically soap operas in comic-book form. The drawn narrative is an old idea—it goes back to Egypt, it goes back to those action panels that you get on Roman commemoration statues. It goes back to Greece, really, it goes back to Egypt, to the Bayeux tapestries. They sometimes say that's the first comic, because it practically has voice balloons coming out of their mouths, Harold said this, William said that...

RN: It's a time-honoured tradition, really.

MA: It's very old! They're graffiti on old tombs—if you go to Orkney, there's a place where the Vikings broke into a place called Maes Howe, which is one of the Stone Age constructions, and they made graffiti on the walls. Some of them are little drawings. One of them is a dog with his tongue hanging out, and it's a comment about a woman, (laughter) sort of a "Olga is a babe" kind of thing. So it's just part of the long history of human beings using pictures and words together to depict something. All those lives of the saints, remember the lives of the saints? Have you ever been to Assisi?

RN: No.

MA: Well, the life of Saint Francis is up on a fresco. And they usually show, you know, first saintly deed, second saintly deed, angel appears, does something or other, some more saintly deeds, death appears, the saint dies and goes to heaven. They're narratives about the saint's life in pictures. When you recall that literacy is pretty recent, everybody being able to read, that's pretty recent. The Church used these to tell stories. Any cathedral of those times is going to have a narrative sequence all the way around in stained glass windows. There are going to be stations of the cross, or it's going to be the creation of the world, all the way through, ending with the Last Judgment. There's a beautiful one in Palermo. People knew the story, so they could follow the narrative, and they knew the iconography. We all know what Mickey Mouse looks like, they all knew what Moses looked like, from certain things that Moses always had. They knew which saints were which because they had their symbols with them. St. Agatha, I think it was, always had her tits on a plate, (laughter) she is the patron saint of bell makers, maybe because they look... (laughter) So people just knew that and could follow the story. It may sound kind of silly to connect that with cartooning, but it's the same idea, pictures connected with stories.

RN: OK. Well, maybe we could close the file on this first part? You've been so generous with all kinds of information. Now, the second part is very short, and the third part is even shorter. First question in the context of "art work" is: could you describe to us if there is such a thing as a typical workday for you?

MA: There is no such thing. But if there were, I would get up in the morning and would have my breakfast, I would go to my study, I would open my email. I would check through my email, I would maybe answer some of them and not answer the rest, (laughter) leave the rest till later. I would sit down at my other computer, because I don't have my work on the same computer as the one that I have email on. The screen is bigger on the one that I work on, the other one's a laptop. Will I ever get a Blackberry? I don't think so. They have a use for businesspeople, but you can't write anything very long on them. So I actually lug my laptop around when I'm travelling so I can pick my email up on it, but I think I'm gonna change that... I'm frequently writing things while I'm out on the road. For instance, I was doing a piece for the *New York Review of Books*, and I had to do the galleys while out on the road, and the first galleys I did got emailed to me, and I also had a fax to the hotel. So I had that, and then the second set, on which there weren't very many changes, were sent in a pdf, so I could look and see what they had done and then email back and say, "Looks fine to me." So in that respect it's pretty handy. You don't have to go through too much: "I thought I was receiving a fax. Where is it? There was supposed to be a courier bringing me these galleys, it's not here." It's faster to do it this way [via email], and also it reduces the packaging quite a bit. So, for that kind of purpose, it's very useful. But other kinds of purposes... And people have gotten into a habit of mind, which is they'll dash out something, and then—I do it myself, so I know how it is—and then they'll remember that they forgot to put something in, and they'll send another email, because it's so easy to do. Once upon a time, you would have sat down, you would have composed the letter, you would have reviewed it, you would have revised it, (laughs) it would have had several more reviews before being sent. And also people would not have expected an instant reply the way they do now. If they send you something and you haven't answered in a day or so, they send you another one saying, "Did you get this?"—which is a good precaution because sometimes these things just go out into the air, and you don't know if they ever got it, they don't know that you've sent it. OK, how has it affected my actual writing pattern? Well, once upon a time, I had to write in handwriting, which I still do.

RN: The first draft?

MA: Yes, pretty much, in handwriting, pretty much.

RN: So the computer would distract you from...

MA: I can't touch-type, that's the secret. If you can touch-type, you can work perfectly on the computer. I have to look at the keyboard, I never learned to do this thing of not looking. So I made a wrong career choice. (laughter) And I have never been able to take the time since. Actually I'm not interested. At my age I don't care. I'm fine the way I am. So then I used to transcribe on a typewriter. First it was a manual typewriter, then it became an electric typewriter, which I liked a lot better, but it was still a typewriter. And when you had a typescript like that, you would then correct on the typescript, manually. And you would use a little brush of white-out right on top of it, or you would get those white things that you stuck on, but then I would always have to send it to a typist, because it would be so messy. The typist would type it again, and then and not until then would I submit it to an agent, publisher, whatever. So it would have to go through several stages. The fact that I couldn't touch-type meant that it was, however, easier for me to go from country to country, rent a typewriter, and adjust to a different keyboard. I did that in France, where the keyboard is different, and I also did it in Germany, where the keyboard is again different. So it was easier for me to learn where those different things were than it would have been for somebody who could touch-type. So I wrote the first part of *The Handmaid's Tale* on a German keyboard in Berlin.

RN: Close to the wall, at the time...

MA: Yeah, but we're talking about the typewriter. (laughter) Even then, it was getting a bit hard to rent typewriters. Now it would probably be almost impossible because there isn't a business for it anymore. I did find one, and I remember carrying it home, this huge, enormous thing... But that's the picture [photo] that you will see, Isolde Ohlbaum took it in Berlin. That typewriter that I'm working on is one I rented in Germany, because, of course, you could not travel with such a typewriter. In the old days, you could have, because people had steamer trunks and a lot more luggage, but to get on an airplane with such a typewriter would have been out of the question. So I just rented them wherever I was. I had my first computer for *The Robber Bride*. And the screen was about this big, you couldn't see the whole page, you had to use floppy disks. But nonetheless it still allowed me to correct on screen, print out, and the people whose jobs then disappeared were the typists, a lot of typists' jobs. Michael Ondaatje, I think, still writes in handwriting, and a typist types it, but a lot of people now do what I do, and they revise on screen. So that's what I will do, I will type away at my things, fool around with them, revise them. Computers got better and better. Even now we have made a transition, you used to get something called a super disk, and you'd plug the super disk thing into your computer, and the super disk comes up, but now you just slip a CD in, and you can burn it. I think we're reaching the moment at which no more improvements are possible.

RN: If you take all of that together, writing by hand and also correcting on the computer screen, could you say for how long per day you can do that? Creative writing, I mean.

MA: That depends what part of the work I'm at.

RN: Does it take longer in the first stage of writing?

MA: No, I spend less time doing that in the first stage than in the later stages because I'm spending more time thinking. Whereas, when you've reached the other stages, you know where you're going, you know what you're doing, and you're just galloping towards the finish line. So I might spend six hours, six to eight hours doing it.

RN: Six to eight hours?

MA: Yeah.

RN: In the revisionary stage?

MA: No, no, just writing.

RN: Just writing.

MA: Writing, revising, I do them both at once. That's why it's physically hard.

RN: Yeah, exactly. From sitting so long.

MA: It's the arms, it's the back. The ice packs, the painkillers.

RN: (laughter) Yeah, I can imagine. Now, this is a hypothetical question. If you had not been successful in writing, would you have kept doing it anyway?

MA: Yes. Why not? Because, when I started, there was no possibility of poets being successful, it wasn't an option. When I started in Canada, who was a successful Canadian writer? There had been some. L. M. Montgomery with the *Anne* books, Mazo de la Roche with a series called *Jalna*, and there had been sort of single-novel people who had appeared here and there, but the idea of making a living on it, that didn't exist. I think Morley Callaghan did because he published a lot of magazine pieces in the States, but that option was closing for people like me because magazines were stopping publishing fiction even then. So you might have the idea that you could publish a book—and we did have that idea, and we did publish books, unless we published them ourselves—but the idea that you could make a living from it, that was far away. So of course I would have kept doing it, I did it for sixteen years before that moment arrived.

RN: Sixteen years?

MA: Sixteen years. I started when I was sixteen. When I was thirty-two, I was making a living from it.

RN: All right. Now, another hypothetical question. I think you touched upon it earlier already. Could you imagine a different type of profession for yourself?

MA: Oh, sure.

RN: Like gardening? (laughs)

MA: I'm a novelist, I can imagine anything. (laughter) Gardening? No. No, absolutely not. I've done gardening, but I wasn't doing it for a living, I was doing it to eat the veggies. What might I have been otherwise? I might have been a scientist. I might have been an academic. I might have been somebody in advertising, I was good at that. Market research, that field, I had a job in that. I could have stayed there and gone up the ladder, run the company.

RN: So lots of alternatives.

MA: I mean, Samuel Beckett announced why he was a writer: he said he was not good at anything else. (laughs)

RN: (laughs) You're not that kind of person, definitely not.

MA: No, I could have done other things, but this is what I wanted to do.

RN: What did you do about insecurity about writing, especially in the earlier stages of your career? Insecurity: am I good enough, is this publishable?

MA: I didn't worry much about that. You must realize that there wasn't a profession...

RN: Right, so you made up your own rules.

MA: It's harder for young people now, in that respect. There's many more opportunities open to them, there's also a lot more competition. There's a lot more young people doing it. It's tough. When we started—by "we" I mean our generation—there was hardly anybody doing it. It was an open field. So in some ways that was harder, because there weren't very many obvious, you know, doors to success. (laughs) There was an underground culture then, there really was a Bohemia. So your contacts were within the Bohemia, but the way from the Bohemia to being recognized in the outside world, that was pretty obscure. And you can read about that if you want to in a book called *Negotiating with the Dead*, first chapter. Some people had two lives: they had their life at work, whatever they did, and then they had their life as the poet that only the other poets knew about. It was like that. So the reason most of us started in poetry, or most of us became known as poets, although we were writing other things too, was that it was easier to publish poetry, it was shorter. It was cheaper, you could do it yourself, you could make a mimeographed book, staple it together, and that counted as a book. We read each other's mimeographed books.

(laughs) We were interested in not just writing, we were interested in bookmaking as well, making a book.

RN: And what you meant with competition now, we just saw that with the Giller Prize winner [Vincent Lam]—first-time book, right?

MA: Yes, but most of the people on that were first-time books. It was a young list. By young, I don't mean all the people were young, but there were no heavy hitters, there were no already established, well-known people. Gaetan Soucy is well known in Quebec but not so much in English Canada. So there were three first books, never before seen the light of day, and two books in translation. No matter who won, it was going to be a person previously unknown. It was an interesting list that way, because nobody could say, "Oh, it's obviously so-and-so..." You know the story of Vincent Lam's book?

RN: That he met you on a ship in the Arctic?

MA: He did.

RN: You were immediately convinced that he had some talent.

MA: No, I wasn't convinced of that until I had read his manuscript.

RN: Yeah, that's what I meant, of course.

MA: I could see how it could be a book. When I took it to one publisher, he didn't share my view. Then I took it to another one, who did.

RN: So you were right.

MA: I'm usually right (laughter) about that. I would not recommend something to a publisher that didn't have the talent. Obviously I wouldn't do it.

RN: No, of course not.

MA: Now that that story has gotten out, everybody's going to be sending me their books. I'll just have to send them back. I read his because I knew him.

RN: Mm, you knew him.

MA: I wouldn't read a manuscript for someone I didn't know. It's too risky. I'll tell you why it's risky. Somebody sends you their manuscript. You read it. You send them a letter saying blah, blah, blah. They now have a letter saying that you've read their manuscript. You publish your next book. They revise their typescript to make it like your book. They have a letter from you that says you've read it, and they can accuse you of plagiarism.

RN: Oh dear, that's awful!

MA: I know.

RN: And that has been done, obviously?

MA: Yeah, it's been done. And there's also people who are mistaken. In fact, I got a letter from somebody who said, "You went into the Sydney Public Library, and you read my unpublished manuscript, which is on deposit there, and you modelled *The Handmaid's Tale* on it." (laughs) I said, "No, I've never been in the Sydney Public Library, forget it." And another one who said, "You read my book"—and she had published a book—"You went onto my website, you took my ideas, you changed all of the words, and you changed the idea, and then you published it." (laughs) So you just have to be very careful about reading other people's things.

RN: Not to mention the time limitations one has.

MA: Yes, well, someone decided to have a poems-written-in-prison feature in their magazine, and they selected some poems by this woman and published them. They're actually my poems (laughs) out of one of my books. They hadn't recognized it.

RN: So that leads on to the third and last part, because that kind of thing is obviously a highly negative part of stardom.

MA: Yes, somebody's going to take a pop at you one way or another. Because you're visible. But I think it happens more to younger people.

RN: Well, one thing that would interest me, I spoke to a Toronto friend recently, and he saw you from somewhere in the Four Seasons Centre in the *Ring* cycle, during that performance, and he argues that it was something very Canadian, that you were left in peace there, that people don't approach you.

MA: Not much, no, they don't.

RN: And he argued that, if you were an American, in America, and as well known as you are here, in America this would be different.

MA: It would be somewhat different. But remember that pop stars, film stars, TV stars, and writers—it's a different thing. A writer is a different thing. Why is a writer a different thing? Because what people really identify with is the book. It's nice that you're a writer, and some people make the mistake of thinking you should be as wonderful as they hoped you would be, but really it's the book that has taken their imagination. So there's never going to be people wanting to rip off your shoelaces and take them home. (laughter) It's not like being Elizabeth Taylor or Robert Mitchum; oh, those are pretty old ones, but let's take somebody from this current culture. It's not like being a very, very well-known movie, TV pop star. It's not like that. You are not your work of art, they are. They and their work of art are pretty synonymous. So Britney Spears and the Britney Spears image, music, and everything, they're all in the one package. As I went to great lengths to point out in chapter 2 of *Negotiating with the Dead*, the writer and the book are separate as soon as that book is finished. Canadians would find it, not exactly bad taste, but uncool to make too much of a fuss. So I can work in my front garden, and people will stop, they won't necessarily say, "I loved your book," they'll say, "Nice garden." (laughter) But people were stopping me—this is very Canadian, too—people were stopping me *now* to tell *me* how much *they* loved Vincent Lam's book! (laughs) I said, "I didn't write it!" "Yes, but you helped him." (laughter) So they like the helping story, Canadians like the helping story. And they like if I say, "He's really a modest guy, he wasn't pushy," they like that part.

RN: Nevertheless, if you, as a Canadian celebrity writer, go to the United States, do you have the feeling that you're approached differently there than in Canada?

MA: Somewhat. People in the United States think I have a window into the future. (laughter) Because of *The Handmaid's Tale* and now increasingly because of *Oryx and Crake*. So they're going to be asking me more questions like "What's going to happen?" That happened as soon as *The Handmaid's Tale* was published. People in England said, "Jolly good yarn." (laughter) They had done their civil war centring on religion. They did it in the seventeenth century. They're not going to do it again. They may have some other kind of civil war, but it won't be that, unless it involves Muslims, but it's not going to be involving Christians. Canadians, being a nervous group of people, said, "Could it happen here?" (laughter) And Americans *immediately* said, "How long have we got?" And that has only become more so as we have moved through the '90s—the rise of the religious right as a factor in politics, the Bush administration—so they see me in a somewhat different light. They want to know about their political situation and what is going to happen. And at that point, I make my "you've got to save democracy within the United States now" speech. And I make the "you cannot have secret torture going on in something that calls itself a democracy," "you cannot have a situation where people are spirited away and it's illegal to say they're missing." And that gets you into the inquisition, the Bastille, the behaviour of the secret police in the Union of the Soviet Socialist Republics under people like Beria, I mean it's just not done in something that calls itself a democracy. It's the foot in the door, you know, if you allow that to happen, and think, well, that's other "bad" people that that's happening to—pretty soon it's going to be you!

(Two women enter our separate room in the café, look at us, and say, "Can we come in?" And then to Margaret, "You look familiar!"—as if to prove what Margaret and I were just talking about, Canadians' attitude toward the celebrity writer in Canada.)

RN: That's a rage! (laughs)

MA: See what I mean? "You look so familiar." Sometimes people taking my credit card in stores will say, "I thought it was you, but I didn't like to say." "Has anybody ever told you that you look quite a lot like Margaret Atwood?" (laughter) They'll say, "I've seen you before. I know I've seen you. Are you the, like, are you the writer?"

RN: Well, you said in an earlier interview, long ago, that when you went to the Toronto General Hospital to deliver your baby, the nurse said, "Oh, you're Margaret Atwood!"

MA: Yes, that's right.

RN: Perhaps just one more issue. Do you try to have any kind of control over the photographs that are taken of you?

MA: Of course.

RN: You do. But you can't in a newspaper, right?

MA: No, you can't in a newspaper. But you can for your jacket photo. And what I usually do, because it's less cumbersome, I buy the photo from the photographer. And then I don't have to get permission every time. Publishers want you to send them a photo. That's what they want, they ask everybody to do that, they don't want to do it themselves. So you send them the photo that you want on the jacket. They always want a new one. So you toodle off and get your picture taken by somebody. And then you send them the one you like. Everybody does that.

RN: Do you have a favourite photographer? Probably Graeme?

MA: I have several. No, Graeme has taken some of them, but if you look on *Moral Disorder*, the Canadian one, I like that picture quite a lot right now.

RN: OK. I think we should stop here because actually the tape tells me that we've been at this for two hours. From Survivalwoman to Literary Icon: Margaret Atwood, thank you very much for this interview.

List of Margaret Atwood's Comics

Assembled and mostly titled by Reingard M. Nischik

Apart from comics nos. 18, 20, and 28–32, these comics were first published with their series titles only—Kanadian Kultchur Komix *or* Book Tour Comics—*or with no title at all. The comics are listed in chronological order of appearance.*

   I *Kanadian Kultchur Komics:* "The Only Kollectiv Komic Superheroes in the World." *This Magazine* 8.5/6 (Jan.–Feb. 1975): 43.

  II *Kanadian Kultchur Komics:* "The Cultural Infiltration Agency." *This Magazine* 9.1 (Mar.–Apr. 1975): 35.

 III "Lightbulb Comic." *This Magazine* 9.1 (Mar.–Apr. 1975): 35; repr. in Nischik 2000/02, 313.

 IV *Kanadian Kultchur Komix:* "The Kanadian Film Directors' Guild." *This Magazine* 9.2 (May–June 1975): 35; repr. in Nischik 2000/02, 314.

  V *Kanadian Kultchur Komics:* "Survivalwoman and the Magic Word WHAMMIEQ." *This Magazine* 9.3 (July–Aug. 1975): 35; repr. in Wilson 1993, 164.

 VI *Kanadian Kultchur Komics:* "Survivalwoman Renamed Survivalcreature." *This Magazine* 9.5/6 (Nov.–Dec. 1975): 47.

VII   *Canadian Kultchur Komix:* "Survivalwoman Meets Superham." *This Magazine* 10.1 (Feb.–Mar. 1976): 35; repr. in Nischik 2000/02, 315; and in Wilson 2003, 4.

VIII   *Canadian Kultchur Komix:* "The Ceebeecee Television Drama Dept." *This Magazine* 10.2 (Apr.–May 1976): 35.

IX   *Canadian Kultchur Komics:* "The Writers' Onion of Kanada." *This Magazine* 10.3 (June–July 1976): 35.

X   *Kanadian Kulture Komix:* "Survivalwoman's Love Life." *This Magazine* 10.4 (Aug.–Sept. 1976): 35.

XI   *Canadian Kultchur Komix:* "Boughtman, Rodentman, & Other Kanadian Superheroes." *This Magazine* 10.5/6 (Nov.–Dec. 1976): 47.

XII   *Kanadian Kultchur Komix:* "Survivalwoman Meets Amphibianwoman." *This Magazine* 11.1 (Jan.–Feb. 1977): 35.

XIII   *Kanadian Kultchur Komix:* "The Fifth Column of English Canadian Businessmen Meet." *This Magazine* 11.2 (Mar.–Apr. 1977): 35.

XIV   *Kanadian Kultchur Komics:* "The Muffleman." *This Magazine* 11.3 (May–June 1977): 35.

XV   *Kanadian Kultchur Komix:* "Recruiting for the Canadian National Revolution" (1977?) (source unverified).

XVI   *Kanadian Kultchur Komics:* "Survivalwoman Meets the Symbol for the League of Canadian Poets." *This Magazine* 11.4 (July–Aug. 1977): 35.

XVII   *Kanadian Kultchur Komics:* "Survivalwoman Unemployed." *This Magazine* 11.5 (Oct. 1977): 35.

XVIII   "Portrait of the Artist as a Young Cipher." *The Graduate* 5.1 (Fall 1977): 8–9; repr. in Nischik 2000/02, 316; repr. in extracts also in Wilson 2003, 2.

XIX   *Kanadian Kultchur Komics:* "The Origin of Survivalwoman." *This Magazine* 11.6 (Dec. 1977): 35.

XX   "Hairdo." *Weekend Magazine in the Montreal Star* 28.5 (4 February 1978): 6–7.

XXI   *Kanadian Kultchur Komics:* "Survivalwoman, Womanwoman, and the Canada Manpowerhole." *This Magazine* 12.1 (March 1978): 35.

XXII   *Kanadian Kultchur Komics:* "Survivalwoman for Female P.M." *This Magazine* 12.2 (May–June 1978): 35.

XXIII *Kanadian Kuultchr Komics:* "Survivalwoman and the Canadian Dream." *This Magazine* 12.3 (July–Aug. 1978): 35.

XXIV   *Kanadian Kultchur Komics:* "Survivalwoman in Scotland." *This Magazine* 13.4 (Sept.–Oct. 1979): 47.

XXV   *Kanadian Kultchur Komics:* "Survivalwoman and a Boat Person at Canadian Immigration." *This Magazine* 13.5/6 (Nov.–Dec. 1979): 55.

XXVI   *Kanadian Kultchur Komics:* "Back in Glitter City." *This Magazine* 14.1 (Jan.–Feb. 1980): 47.

XXVII *Book Tour Comics:* "The Robber Bride—A Roaring Success!" (produced in 1993).

XXVIII *Book Tour Comics:* "…. vol. 1,963: The Radio Interview." *Publisher's Weekly* 241.4 (January 24, 1994); repr. in Wilson 2003, 4; also published on Atwood's website: www.owtoad. com [consulted 18 August 2008].

XXIX   *Book Tour Comix:* "# 911 …: The Television Interview" [produced in 1993]; published on Atwood's website: www.owtoad.com [consulted 18 August 2008].

XXX   *Book Tour Comix:* "# 4,397: The Blind Assa.". "More Booktour Comix." *Brick: A Literary Journal* (Fall 2001), 101–02; also on Atwood's website: www.owtoad.com [consulted 18 August 2008].

XXXI   *Book Tour Comix:* "# H2^5: Negotiating with the D(e)ad" [produced in 2002]; published on Atwood's website: www.owtoad.com [consulted 18 August 2008].

XXXII *Book Tour Comix:* "Number 8,963: The Long Pen" (produced in 2006).

Bibliography

1. CITED BOOKS BY MARGARET ATWOOD (CHRONOLOGICAL)

POETRY

Double Persephone. 1961. Toronto: Hawkshead Press.

The Circle Game. 1966. Toronto: Anansi.

The Journals of Susanna Moodie. 1970. Toronto: Oxford University Press.

Power Politics. 1971. Toronto: Anansi.

Two-Headed Poems. 1978. Toronto: Oxford University Press.

True Stories. 1981. Toronto: Oxford University Press.

Wahre Geschichten. 1984. Düsseldorf: Claassen.

Interlunar. 1984. Toronto: Oxford University Press.

Selected Poems 2: Poems Selected and New 1976–1986. 1986. Toronto: Oxford University Press.

Morning in the Burned House. 1995. Toronto: McClelland and Stewart.

Ein Morgen im verbrannten Haus: Gedichte. 1996. Translated by Beatrice Howeg. Berlin: Berlin Verlag [German translation of *Morning in the Burned House*].

Eating Fire: Selected Poetry, 1965–1995. 1998. London: Virago.

The Door. 2007. London: Virago.

NOVELS

The Edible Woman. 1969. Toronto: McClelland and Stewart; edition used: New York: Fawcett Public Library, 1976.

Surfacing. 1972. Toronto: McClelland and Stewart; edition used: New York: Fawcett Public Library, 1972.

Lady Oracle. 1976. Toronto: McClelland and Stewart; edition used: New York: Fawcett Crest, 1987.

Life Before Man. 1979. Toronto: McClelland and Stewart.

Bodily Harm. 1981. Toronto: McClelland and Stewart.

The Handmaid's Tale. 1985. Toronto: McClelland and Stewart.

Cat's Eye. 1988. Toronto: McClelland and Stewart; edition used: New York: Bantam, 1989.

The Robber Bride. 1993. Toronto: McClelland and Stewart; edition used: London: Virago, 1994.

Alias Grace. 1996. Toronto: McClelland and Stewart.

The Blind Assassin. 2000. Toronto: McClelland and Stewart.

Oryx and Crake. 2003. Toronto: McClelland and Stewart.

The Penelopiad. 2005. Toronto: Knopf; edition used: Toronto: Vintage Canada, 2006.

The Year of the Flood. 2009. Toronto: McClelland and Stewart.

SHORT STORIES

Dancing Girls and Other Stories. 1977. Toronto: McClelland and Stewart/ Bantam-Seal.

Bluebeard's Egg. 1983. Toronto: McClelland and Stewart.

Wilderness Tips. 1991. Toronto: McClelland and Stewart.

Moral Disorder and Other Stories. 2006. Toronto: McClelland and Stewart.

SHORT FICTIONS/PROSE POETRY

Murder in the Dark: Short Fictions and Prose Poems. 1983. Toronto: Coach House Press.

Good Bones. 1992. Toronto: Coach House Press.

Gute Knochen. 1995. Translated by Brigitte Walitzek. Berlin: Berlin Verlag [German translation of *Good Bones*].

The Tent. 2006. Toronto: McClelland and Stewart.

CRITICISM AND THEORY

Survival: A Thematic Guide to Canadian Literature. 1972. Toronto: Anansi.

"Introduction" to *The Edible Woman.* 1979. Reprinted in *The Edible Woman.* London: Virago, 1989. 7–8.

Second Words: Selected Critical Prose. 1982. Toronto: Anansi.

"Writing Utopia." 1989. Reprinted in *Moving Targets*, 102–11.

"If You Can't Say Something Nice, Don't Say Anything at All." 1990. In *Language in Her Eye: Views on Writing and Gender by Canadian Women Writing in English*, ed. Libby Scheier, Sarah Sheard, and Eleanor Wachtel, 15–25. Toronto: Coach House Press.

Strange Things: The Malevolent North in Canadian Literature. 1995. Oxford: Oxford University Press.

In Search of Alias Grace: On Writing Historical Fiction. 1997. Ottawa: University of Ottawa Press. Reprinted in *Moving Targets*, 196–217.

Negotiating with the Dead: A Writer on Writing. 2002. Cambridge: Cambridge University Press.

Moving Targets: Writing with Intent 1982–2004. 2005 [2004]. Toronto: Anansi.

Payback: Debt and the Shadow Side of Wealth. 2008. Toronto: Anansi.

DRAMA

The Penelopiad: The Play. 2007. London: Faber and Faber.

FURTHER WORKS

The CanLit Foodbook: From Pen to Palate—A Collection of Tasty Literary Fare. 1987. Toronto: Totem Books.

Barbed Lyres: Canadian Venomous Verse. 1990. Toronto: Key Porter Books.

The Poetry of Gwendolyn MacEwen. 1993. Vols. 1 and 2, ed. Margaret Atwood and Barry Callaghan. Toronto: Exile.

(with Victor-Lévy Beaulieu). *Two Solicitudes: Conversations.* 1998. Toronto: McClelland and Stewart.

"The Myths Series and Me: Rewriting a Classic Is Its Own Epic Journey." 2005. *Publishers Weekly*, 28 November.

2. CITED WORKS ON MARGARET ATWOOD (ALPHABETICAL)

Becker, Susanne. 2000/02. "Celebrity, or a Disneyland of the Soul: Margaret Atwood and the Media." In Nischik, ed. 2000/02, 28–40.

Blakely, Barbara. 1983. "The Pronunciation of Flesh: A Feminist Reading of Margaret Atwood's Poetry." In *Margaret Atwood: Language, Text, and System*, ed. Sherrill E. Grace and Lorraine Weir, 33–51. Vancouver: UBC Press.

Bowering, George. 1981. "Margaret Atwood's Hands." *Studies in Canadian Literature* 6.1: 39–52.

Broege, Valerie. 1981. "Margaret Atwood's Americans and Canadians." *Essays on Canadian Writing* 20: 111–35.

Cooke, Nathalie. 2000/02. "Lions, Tigers, and Pussycats: Margaret Atwood (Auto-) Biographically." In Nischik, ed. 2000/02, 15–27.

————. 1998. *Margaret Atwood: A Biography.* Toronto: ECW Press.

————. 2004. *Margaret Atwood: A Critical Companion.* Westport, CT: Greenwood.

Cooley, Dennis. 1994. "Nearer by Far: The Upset 'I' in Margaret Atwood's Poetry." In *Margaret Atwood: Writing and Subjectivity*, ed. Colin Nicholson, 68–93. London: Macmillan.

Davey, Frank. 1986. "Alternate Stories: The Short Fiction of Audrey Thomas and Margaret Atwood." *Canadian Literature* 109: 5–14.

Davidson, Arnold E., and Cathy N. Davidson, eds. 1981. *The Art of Margaret Atwood: Essays in Criticism.* Toronto: Anansi.

Deer, Glenn. 1994. "*The Handmaid's Tale:* Dystopia and the Paradoxes of Power." In Deer, *Postmodern Canadian Fiction and the Rhetoric of Authority*, 110–29. Montreal: McGill-Queen's University Press.

Delville, Michel. 1997. "Murdering the Text: Genre and Gender Issues in Margaret Atwood's Short Short Fiction." In *The Contact and the Culmination*, ed. Marc Delrez and Bénédicte Ledent, 57–67. Liège, Belgium: University of Liège.

Epstein, Grace. 1993. "Nothing to Fight For: Repression of the Romance Plot in Harold Pinter's Screenplay of *The Handmaid's Tale*." *Pinter Review* 6: 54–60.

Ferguson, Stefan. 2007. "Margaret Atwood in German/y: A Case Study." In von Flotow and Nischik, eds. 2007, 93–110.

French, William. 1983. "Atwood's Snappy Snippets Pack a Wallop." Review of *Murder in the Dark. The Globe and Mail*, 15 March.

Gale, Steven H. 2003. "*The Handmaid's Tale*." In Gale, *Harold Pinter's Screenplays and the Artistic Process*, 315–21, 449–50. Lexington: University Press of Kentucky.

Goetsch, Paul. 2000/02. "Margaret Atwood: A Canadian Nationalist." In Nischik, ed. 2000/02, 166–79.

Grace, Sherrill E. 2006. "Atwood and the 'Autobiographical Pact'—*For Reingard Nischik*." In Moss and Kozakewich, eds. 2006, 121–34.

————. 1981. "Margaret Atwood and the Poetics of Duplicity." In Davidson and Davidson, eds. 1981, 55–68.

_____. 1980. *Violent Duality: A Study of Margaret Atwood.* Montreal: Véhicule Press.

Grace, Sherrill E., and Lorraine Weir, eds. 1983. *Margaret Atwood: Language, Text, and System.* Vancouver: UBC Press.

Gzowski, Peter, interviewer. 1978. "Closet Cartoonist." *The CBC Digital Archives Website* http://archives.cbc.ca/ [consulted 20 March 2007], 12 January, 14:32 min. Also on www.owtoad.com [consulted 20 March 2007].

Hammond, Karla, interviewer. 1979. "A Margaret Atwood Interview with Karla Hammond." *Concerning Poetry* 12: 73–81.

Hewitt, Pamela. 1996. "Understanding Contemporary American Culture through *The Handmaid's Tale:* A Sociology Class." In Wilson, Friedman, and Hengen, eds. 1996, 109–13.

Hönnighausen, Lothar. 2000/02. "Margaret Atwood's Poetry 1966–1995." In Nischik, ed. 2000/02, 97–119.

Howells, Coral Ann. 2006a. "Margaret Atwood's Dystopian Visions: *The Handmaid's Tale* and *Oryx and Crake.*" In Howells, ed. 2006b, 161–75.

_____, ed. 2006b. *The Cambridge Companion to Margaret Atwood.* Cambridge: Cambridge University Press.

_____. 2000/02. "Transgressing Genre: A Generic Approach to Margaret Atwood's Novels." In Nischik, ed. 2000/02, 139–56.

Ingersoll, Earl G., ed. 1990. *Margaret Atwood: Conversations.* Willowdale, ON: Firefly/Ontario Review Press.

_____, ed. 2006. *Waltzing Again: New and Selected Conversations With Margaret Atwood.* Princeton, NJ: Ontario Review Press.

Irvine, Lorna. 1988. "Murder and Mayhem: Margaret Atwood Deconstructs." *Contemporary Literature* 29.2: 265–76.

_____. 1979. "The Red and Silver Heroes Have Collapsed." *Concerning Poetry* 12.2: 59–68.

Keith, W. J. 1983. "Atwood as (Infuriating) Critic." *Canadian Forum* 62: 26–28.

Kirtz, Mary K. 1996. "Teaching Literature through Film: An Interdisciplinary Approach to *Surfacing* and *The Handmaid's Tale.*" In Wilson, Friedman, and Hengen, eds. 1996, 140–45.

Kuester, Martin. 1992. "Atwood: Parodies from a Feminist Point of View." In Kuester, *Framing Truths: Parodic Structures in Contemporary English-Canadian Historical Novels,* 124–47, 173–76. Toronto: University of Toronto Press.

LaMarsh, Judy, interviewer. 1975. "A Precocious and Creative Child." *The CBC Digital Archives Website* http://archives.cbc.ca/ [consulted 20 March 2007], 4 November. 17:21 min.

Ljungberg, Christina. 1999. *To Join, to Fit, and to Make: The Creative Craft of Margaret Atwood's Fiction*. Bern: Lang.

Lorinc, John. 2000. "'If You Like to Be in Control, You'd Better Stick to Novels.'" *The Globe and Mail*, 23 March.

MacDonald, John W. 1982. "Last, First, and Second Words." Review of *Second Words*. *Reviewing Librarian* 7: 38.

Mallinson, Jean. 1985. "Margaret Atwood." In *Canadian Writers and Their Works*, Poetry Series, vol. 9, ed. Robert Lecker, Jack David, and Ellen Quigley, 16–81. Toronto: ECW Press.

―――――. 1984. *Margaret Atwood and Her Works*. Toronto: ECW Press.

McCombs, Judith, ed. 1988a. *Critical Essays on Margaret Atwood*. Boston: Hall.

―――――. 1988b. "Politics, Structure, and Poetic Development in Atwood's Canadian-American Sequences." In VanSpanckeren and Castro, eds. 1988, 142–62.

―――――. 1973. "*Power Politics:* The Book and Its Cover." *Moving Out* 3.2: 54–69.

Merivale, Patricia. 1995. "From 'Bad News' to 'Good Bones': Margaret Atwood's Gendering of Art and Elegy." In York, ed. 1919, 253–70. Toronto: Anansi.

―――――. 1996. "'Hypocrite Lecteuse! Ma Semblable! Ma Soeur!': On Teaching *Murder in the Dark*." In Wilson, Friedman, and Hengen, eds. 1996, 99–106.

Moss, John, and Tobi Kozakewich, eds. 2006. *Margaret Atwood: The Open Eye*. Reappraisals: Canadian Writers 30. Ottawa: University of Ottawa Press.

Mycak, Sonia. 1996. *In Search of the Split Subject: Psychoanalysis, Phenomenology, and the Novels of Margaret Atwood*. Toronto: ECW Press.

Nicholson, Colin, ed. 1994. *Margaret Atwood: Writing and Subjectivity: New Critical Essays*. London: Macmillan.

Nischik, Reingard M. 1987. "Back to the Future: Margaret Atwood's Anti-Utopian Vision in *The Handmaid's Tale*." *Englisch Amerikanische Studien* 1: 139–48.

―――――. 1991b. *Mentalstilistik: Ein Beitrag zu Stiltheorie und Narrativik. Dargestellt am Erzählwerk Margaret Atwoods*. Tübingen: Narr.

―――――. 1993c. "Speech Act Theory, Speech Acts, and the Analysis of Fiction." *Modern Language Review* 88.2: 297–306.

―――――. 1994. "Sukzessive und simultane Aufspaltung der Erzählinstanz im Erzählwerk Margaret Atwoods." *Orbis Litterarum* 49: 233–51.

―――――. 2007. "'The Translation of the World into Words' and the Female Tradition: Margaret Atwood, 'Significant Moments in the Life of My

Mother' (1983)." In *The Canadian Short Story: Interpretations*, ed. Reingard M. Nischik, 331–40. Rochester, NY: Camden House.

_____, ed. 1994a. *Margaret Atwood: Polarities: Selected Stories*. Stuttgart: Reclam.

_____, ed. 2000/02. *Margaret Atwood: Works and Impact*. ESALC. Rochester, NY: Camden House/Toronto: Anansi.

Nischik, Reingard M., and Julia Breitbach. 2006. "Eye-Openers: Photography in Margaret Atwood's Poetry." In Moss and Kozakewich, eds. 2006, 331–46.

Oeding, Brita, and Luise von Flotow. 2007. "The 'Other Women': Canadian Women Writers Blazing a Trail into Germany." In von Flotow and Nischik, eds. 2007, 79–92.

Onley, Gloria. 1974. "Power Politics in Bluebeard's Castle." *Canadian Literature* 60: 21–42.

Pache, Walter. 2000/02. "'A Certain Frivolity': Margaret Atwood's Literary Criticism." In Nischik, ed. 2000/02, 120–35.

Rao, Eleonora. 1993. *Strategies for Identity: The Fiction of Margaret Atwood*. New York: Peter Lang.

Rigney, Barbara Hill. 1987. *Margaret Atwood*. London: Macmillan.

Rosenberg, Jerome H. 1984. *Margaret Atwood*. Boston: Twayne.

Roth, Verena Bühler. 1998. *Wilderness and the Natural Environment: Margaret Atwood's Recycling of a Canadian Theme*. Tübingen: Francke.

Roy, Wendy. 2006. "The Body of/as Evidence: Margaret Atwood, *The Blind Assassin*, and the Feminist Literary Mystery." In Moss and Kozakewich, eds. 2006, 361–71.

Somacarrera, Pilar. 2000. "'Barometer Couple': Balance and Parallelism in Margaret Atwood's *Power Politics*." *Language and Literature* 9.2: 135–49.

_____. 2006. "Power Politics: Power and Identity." In Howells, ed. 2006b, 43–57.

Spriet, Pierre. 1989. "Margaret Atwood's Post-Modernism in *Murder in the Dark*." *Commonwealth Essays and Studies* 11.2: 24–30.

Staels, Hilde. 1995. *Margaret Atwood's Novels: A Study of Narrative Discourse*. Tübingen: Francke.

Stein, Karen F. 1999. *Margaret Atwood Revisited*. Boston: Twayne.

Sturgess, Charlotte. 2000/02. "Margaret Atwood's Short Fiction." In Nischik, ed. 2000/02, 87–96.

Sullivan, Rosemary. 1998. *The Red Shoes: Margaret Atwood Starting Out*. Toronto: Harper Flamingo.

Teitelbaum, Sheldon. 1990. "*The Handmaid's Tale*." *Cinefantastique* 20.4: 16–25, 57–58, 61.

Thompson, Lee Briscoe. 1981. "Minuets and Madness: Margaret Atwood's *Dancing Girls*." In Davidson and Davidson, eds. 1981, 107–22.

VanSpanckeren, Kathryn, and Jan Garden Castro, eds. 1988. *Margaret Atwood: Vision and Forms*. Carbondale: Southern Illinois University Press.

Verduyn, Christl. 1986. "*Murder in the Dark*: Fiction/Theory by Margaret Atwood." *Canadian Fiction Magazine* 57: 124–31.

Walker, Susan. 2001. "Atwood at Work Again." *Toronto Star*, 9 September.

Willmott, Glenn. 1995. "O Say, Can You See: *The Handmaid's Tale* in Novel and Film." In York, ed. 1995, 167–90.

Wilson, Sharon R. 2003a. "Fiction Flashes: Genre and Intertexts in *Good Bones*." In Wilson, ed. 2003b, 18–41.

———, ed. 2003b. *Margaret Atwood's Textual Assassinations: Recent Poetry and Fiction*. Columbus: Ohio State University Press.

———. 1993. "Margaret Atwood's Visual Art." *Essays on Canadian Writing* 50: 129–73.

Wilson, Sharon R., Thomas B. Friedman, and Shannon Hengen, eds. 1996. *Approaches to Teaching Atwood's* The Handmaid's Tale *and Other Works*. New York: MLA.

Woodcock, George. 1981. "Bashful but Bold: Notes on Margaret Atwood as Critic." In Davidson and Davidson, eds. 1981, 223–41.

———. 1975. "Margaret Atwood: Poet as Novelist." In *The Canadian Novel in the 20th Century*, ed. George Woodcock, 312–27. Toronto: McClelland and Stewart; reprinted in McCombs, ed. 1988a, 90–104.

York, Lorraine M. 2007. *Literary Celebrity in Canada*. Toronto: University of Toronto Press; esp. chapter 3 on "Margaret Atwood's 'Uneasy Eminence': Negotiating with the Famous," 99–122.

———, ed. 1995. *Various Atwoods: Essays on the Later Poems, Short Fiction, and Novels*. Toronto: Anansi.

3. OTHER CITED WORKS

Abbott, Lawrence L. 1986. "Comic Art: Characteristics and Potentialities of a Narrative Medium." *Journal of Popular Culture* 19: 155–76.

Aislin (Mosher, Terry). 1999. *The Big Wind-Up! The Final Book of Nasty 90s Cartoons by Aislin*. Introduction by Pamela Wallen. Toronto: McArthur & Co.

Anthony, Carolyn, ed. 1989. *Family Portraits: Remembrances by Twenty Distinguished Writers*. New York: Doubleday.

Arendt, Hannah. 1969. *On Violence.* New York: Harcourt.

Baldick, Chris. 2001. *The Concise Oxford Dictionary of Literary Terms.* Oxford: Oxford University Press.

Barbour, Douglas, and Stephen Scobie, eds. 1981. *The Maple Laugh Forever: An Anthology of Comic Canadian Poetry.* Edmonton: Hurtig.

Baudelaire, Charles. 1973. *Die Blumen des Bösen, Der Spleen von Paris.* Leipzig: Insel [French and German versions of *Les Fleurs du mal* and *Le Spleen de Paris*].

_____. 1963. *The Flowers of Evil.* 2nd ed. Selected and ed. Marthiel Mathews and Jackson Mathews. New York: New Directions.

_____. 1989. *The Parisian Prowler: Le Spleen de Paris.* Translated by Edward K. Kaplan. Athens: University of Georgia Press [English translation of *Le Spleen de Paris*].

Beaty, Bart. 2002. "Comic Books and Graphic Novels." In *Encyclopedia of Literature in Canada*, ed. W. H. New, 221–23. Toronto: University of Toronto Press.

Beck, Ulrich, and Elisabeth Beck-Gernsheim. 1990. *Das ganz normale Chaos der Liebe.* Frankfurt: Suhrkamp.

Benjamin, Jessica. 1988. *The Bonds of Love: Psychoanalysis, Feminism, and the Problem of Domination.* New York: Pantheon.

Boker, Pamela A. 1993. "America's Women Superheroes: Power, Gender, and the Comics." *Mid-Atlantic Almanack* 2: 107–18.

Bonheim, Helmut. 1980–81. "Topoi of the Canadian Short Story." *Dalhousie Review* 60: 659–69.

Bothwell, Robert. 1985. "Pipeline Debate." In Marsh, ed. 1985, 1419.

Bothwell, Robert, Ian Drummand, and John English. 1981. *Canada since 1945: Power, Politics, and Provincialism.* Toronto: University of Toronto Press.

Braun, Friederike, Armin Kohz, and Klaus Schubert. 1986. *Anredeforschung: Kommentierte Bibliographie zur Soziolinguistik der Anrede.* Tübingen: Narr.

Burkart, Günter. 1997. *Lebensphasen—Liebesphasen: Vom Paar zur Ehe, zum Single und zurück?* Opladen: Leske & Budrich.

Butler, Judith. 1990. *Gender Trouble: Feminism and the Subversion of Identity.* London: Routledge.

Cameron, Deborah. 1985. *Feminism and Linguistic Theory.* London: Macmillan.

Cancian, Francesca M. 1987. *Love in America: Gender and Self-Development.* Cambridge: Cambridge University Press.

Cannon, Garland, and Susan Roberson. 1985. "Sexism in Present-Day English: Is It Diminishing?" *Word* 36.1: 23–35.

Chodorow, Nancy Julia. 1980. "Gender, Relation, and Difference in Psychoanalytic Perspective." In Eisenstein and Jardine, eds. 1980, 3–19.

Cixoux, Hélène. 1976. "The Laugh of the Medusa." *Signs* 1.4: 875–93.

Clack, Beverley, ed. 1999. *Misogyny in the Western Philosophical Tradition: A Reader.* Houndmills: Macmillan.

Conlogue, Ray. 1996. *Impossible Nation: The Longing for Homeland in Canada and Quebec.* Stratford, ON: Mercury.

Crosbie, Lynn. 1994. "The Compulsion to Confess: Autobiography and the Canadian Underground Comic." *Open Letter* 8th ser. 8: 29–40.

Daemmrich, Horst S., and Ingrid G. Daemmrich. 1987. *Themes and Motifs in Western Literature: A Handbook.* Tübingen: Francke.

de Bruyn, Frans. 2000. "Genre Criticism." In *Encyclopedia of Contemporary Literary Theory: Approaches, Scholars, Terms,* ed. Irena R. Makaryk, 79–85. Toronto: University of Toronto Press.

Denicolo, David. 1990. "Director's Chair." Interview with Volker Schlöndorff. *Interview* 20.3.

Dickinson, Peter. 2007. *Screening Gender, Framing Genre: Canadian Literature into Film.* Toronto: University of Toronto Press.

Dux, Günter. 1992. *Die Spur der Macht im Verhältnis der Geschlechter: Über den Ursprung der Ungleichheit zwischen Frau und Mann.* Frankfurt: Suhrkamp.

Edwardson, Ryan. 2003. "The Many Lives of Captain Canuck: Nationalism, Culture, and the Creation of a Canadian Comic Book Superhero." *Journal of Popular Culture* 37.2: 184–201.

Eisenstein, Hester, and Alice Jardine, eds. 1980. *The Future of Difference.* New Brunswick, NJ: Rutgers University Press.

Eklund, Christopher. 2006. "Comics Studies." In *Modern North American Criticism and Theory: A Critical Guide,* ed. Julian Wolfreys, 207–13. Edinburgh: Edinburgh University Press.

Evans, Margery A. 1993. *Baudelaire and Intertextuality: Poetry at the Crossroads.* Cambridge: Cambridge University Press.

Ferguson, Will. 2003. *How to Be a Canadian.* Vancouver: Douglas and McIntyre.

————. 1997. "Superman vs. Captain Canuck." In Ferguson, *Why I Hate Canadians,* 167–75. Vancouver: Douglas and McIntyre.

Fetherling, Douglas. 1994. *Travels by Night: A Memoir of the Sixties.* Toronto: Lester.

Fiedler, Leslie. 1966. *Love and Death in the American Novel.* Rev. ed. New York: Stein and Day.

Forster, Leonard. 1969. *The Icy Fire: Five Studies in European Petrarchism.* Cambridge: Cambridge University Press.

Fowler, Roger. 1991. *Language in the News: Discourse and Ideology in the Press.* London: Routledge.

_____. 1986. *Linguistic Criticism.* Oxford: Oxford University Press.

_____. 1977. *Linguistics and the Novel.* London: Methuen.

Francis, R. Douglas, Richard Jones, and Donald B. Smith. 2000. *Destinies: Canadian History since Confederation.* 4th ed. Toronto: Harcourt Canada.

Frenzel, Elisabeth. 1992. *Motive der Weltliteratur.* 4th rev. ed. Stuttgart: Kröner.

Friedan, Betty. 1963. *The Feminine Mystique.* New York: Norton.

Hahn, Kornelia, and Günter Burkart, eds. 1998. *Liebe am Ende des 20. Jahrhunderts: Studien zur Soziologie intimer Beziehungen.* Opladen: Leske & Budrich.

Hall, Catherine. 2004. "Of Gender and Empire: Reflections on the Nineteenth Century." In *Gender and Empire,* ed. Philipa Levine, 46–76. Oxford: Oxford University Press.

Hammond, Joyce D. 1991. "Gender Inversion Cartoons and Feminism." *Journal of Popular Culture* 24.4: 145–60.

Heffernan, James A. W. 1996. "Entering the Museum of Words: Browning's 'My Last Duchess' and Twentieth-Century Ekphrasis." In *Icons—Texts—Iconotexts: Essays on Ekphrasis and Intermediality,* ed. Peter Wagner, 262–80. Berlin: de Gruyter.

Henley, Nancy M. 1987. "This New Species That Seeks a New Language: On Sexism in Language and Language Change." In *Women and Language in Transition,* ed. Joyce Penfield, 3–27. New York: SUNY Press.

Hoffmeister, Gerhart. 1973. *Petrarkistische Lyrik.* Stuttgart: Metzler.

Hook, Donald D. 1974. "Sexism in English Pronouns and Forms of Address." *General Linguistics* 14.2: 86–96.

Hutcheon, Linda. 1991. *Splitting Images: Canadian Ironies.* Toronto: Oxford University Press.

_____. 2006. *A Theory of Adaptation.* New York: Routledge.

Inge, M. Thomas. 1990. *Comics as Culture.* Jackson: University Press of Mississippi.

Ingram, Forrest L. 1971. *Representative Short Story Cycles of the Twentieth Century: Studies in a Literary Genre.* The Hague: Mouton.

Key, Mary Ritchie. 1975. *Male/Female Language: With a Comprehensive Bibliography.* Metuchen, NJ: Scarecrow.

Kolodny, Annette. 1975. "Some Notes on Defining a 'Feminist Literary Criticism.'" *Critical Inquiry* 2: 75–92.

Kramer, Cheris. 1975. "Sex-Related Differences in Address Systems." *Anthropological Linguistics* 17.5: 198–210.

Kroetsch, Robert. 1989. "No Name Is My Name." In Kroetsch, *The Lovely Treachery of Words: Essays Selected and New,* 41–52. Toronto: Oxford University Press.

Laing, Ronald D. 1965 [1960]. *The Divided Self: An Existential Study in Sanity and Madness.* Harmondsworth: Penguin.

Lakoff, George, and Mark Johnson. 1980. *Metaphors We Live By.* Chicago: University of Chicago Press.

Lakoff, Robin. 1975. *Language and Woman's Place.* New York: Harper Octagon.

Lecker, Robert. 1994. "Professionalism and the Rhetoric of English-Canadian Criticism." *Zeitschrift für Kanada-Studien* 14.1: 87–103.

Lenz, Karl. 1998. "Romantische Liebe—Ende eines Beziehungsideals?" In Hahn and Burkart, eds. 1998, 65–85.

Marsh, James, ed. 1985. *The Canadian Encyclopedia.* Edmonton: Hurtig. 3 vols.

Mathews, Robin. 1969. *The Struggle for Canadian Universities.* Toronto: New Press.

McConnell-Ginet, Sally. 1978. "Address Forms in Sexual Politics." In *Women's Language and Style*, ed. Douglas Butturff and Edmund L. Epstein, 23–35. Akron: L & S Books.

McConnell-Ginet, Sally, et al., eds. 1980. *Women and Language in Literature and Society.* New York: Praeger.

McRoberts, Kenneth. 1997. *Misconceiving Canada: The Struggle for National Unity.* Toronto: Oxford University Press.

Miller, Michael G. 1989. "Browning's 'My Last Duchess.'" *Explicator* 47.4: 32–34.

Millett, Kate. 1970. *Sexual Politics.* New York: Doubleday.

Mitchell, Juliet. 1984. *Women: The Longest Revolution: Essays in Feminism, Literature, and Psychoanalysis.* London: Virago.

Moeller, Hans-Bernard, and George Lellis. 2002. *Volker Schlöndorff's Cinema: Adaptation, Politics, and the "Movie-Appropriate."* Carbondale: Southern Illinois University Press.

Montefiore, Jan. 1994 [1987]. *Feminism and Poetry: Language, Experience, Identity in Women's Writing.* 2nd ed. Hammersmith: Pandora.

Montresor, Jaye Berman. 1994. "Comic Strip-Tease: A Revealing Look at Women Cartoon Artists." In *Look Who's Laughing: Gender and Comedy*, ed. Gail Finney, 335–47. Amsterdam: Gordon and Breach.

Morgan, Robin, ed. 1970. *Sisterhood Is Powerful: An Anthology of Writings from the Women's Liberation Movement.* New York: Random House.

Nilsen, Alleen Pace. 1990. "Sexism in English: A 1990s Update." In *Language Awareness*, 5th ed., ed. Paul Eschholz et al., 277–88. New York: St. Martin's Press.

Nilsen, Alleen Pace, Haig Bosmajian, H. Lee Gershuny, and Julia P. Stanley. 1977. *Sexism and Language.* Urbana: National Council of Teachers of English.

Nischik, Reingard M. 1993a. "Mind Style Analysis and the Narrative Modes for the Presentation of Consciousness." In *Tales and "Their Telling Difference":* *Festschrift für Franz K. Stanzel,* ed. Herbert Foltinek, Wolfgang Riehle, and Waldemar Zacharasiewicz, 93–107. Heidelberg: Winter.

_____. 1993b. "Montage intermedial: Strukturelle Bezüge und Funktionen von Montage in Harold Pinters Arbeiten für Film, Fernsehen, und Theater." In *Montage in Theater und Film,* ed. Horst Fritz, 275–311. Tübingen: Francke.

_____. 1991a. "'Où maintenant? Quand maintenant? Qui maintenant?' Die namenlose Ich-Erzählfigur im Roman." *Poetica* 23.1–2: 257–75.

Nischik, Reingard M., and Gabriele Metzler. 2010. "Die Präsidentschaftswahl in den USA im November 2008: Politologische und kulturwissenschaftliche Überlegungen." In *Nationale und internationale Aspekte von Politikwissenschaft und politischer Bildung,* ed. Markus Gloe and Volker Reinhardt. Wiesbaden: VS Verlag.

Olsen, Christina. 1995. *The Art of Tarot.* New York: Abbeville Press.

Ostriker, Alicia. 1982. "The Thieves of Language: Women Poets and Revisionist Mythmaking." *Signs* 8: 68–90.

_____. 1984. "'What Are Patterns For?' Anger and Polarization in Women's Poetry." *Feminist Studies* 10.3: 485–503.

O'Sullivan, Judith. 1990. *The Great American Comic Strip: One Hundred Years of Cartoon Art.* Boston: Little, Brown.

Rubin, Gayle. 1975. "The Traffic in Women: Notes on the 'Political Economy' of Sex." In *Toward an Anthropology of Women,* ed. Rayna R. Reiter, 157–210. New York: Monthly Review Press.

Russel, Bertrand. 1925. *What I Believe.* London: Routledge, 2004.

Sabin, Roger. 1977. "Canadian Political Cartoons." In *Canadian Political Cartoons* [exhibition catalogue], Patricia E. Bovey (curator), 5–22. Winnipeg: Winnipeg Art Gallery.

Seth (Gallant, Gregory). 2006. "On Cartooning," interview, www.pbs.org/pov/pov2006/tintinandi/sfartists_seth.html [consulted 25 June 2008].

Shaw, George Bernard. 1964. *The Standard Edition of the Works.* 6th ed. Vol. 2. London: Constable and Company.

Sheppard, Robert. 1985. "Constitution, Patriation Of." In Marsh, ed. 1985, 1: 406–08.

Sloterdijk, Peter. 2000. "Entgöttlichte Passion: Interview zur modernen Liebe." *Focus* 52: 146–48.

Smith, Denis. 1985a. "October Crisis." In Marsh, ed. 1985, 2: 1311.

_____. 1985b. "War Measures Act." In Marsh, ed. 1985, 3: 1917.

Spender, Dale. 1980. *Man Made Language.* London: Routledge and Kegan Paul.

Stanzel, Franz K. 1984. *A Theory of Narrative*. Translated by Charlotte Goedsche. Cambridge: Cambridge University Press [German original 1979].

Thorne, Barrie, and Nancy Henley, eds. 1975. *Language and Sex: Difference and Dominance*. Rowley, MA: Newbury.

Trömel-Plötz, Senta. 1980. "Sexismus in der englischen Sprache." *Englisch Amerikanische Studien* 2: 189–204.

Tyrell, Hartmann. 1987. "Romantische Liebe: Überlegungen zu ihrer 'quantitativen Bestimmtheit.'" In *Theorie als Passion: Niklas Luhmann zum 60. Geburtstag*, ed. Dirk Baecker et al., 570–99. Frankfurt: Suhrkamp.

van Zoonen, Liesbet. 1994. *Feminist Media Studies*. London: Sage.

von Flotow, Luise. 2007. "Telling Canada's 'Story' in German: Using Cultural Diplomacy to Achieve Soft Power." In von Flotow and Nischik, eds. 2007, 9–26.

von Flotow, Luise, and Reingard M. Nischik, eds. 2007. *Translating Canada: Charting the Institutions and Influences of Cultural Transfer: Canadian Writing in German/y*. Ottawa: University of Ottawa Press.

Whitcut, Janet. 1980. "The Language of Address." In *The State of Language*, ed. Leonard Michaels and Christopher Ricks, 89–97. Berkeley: University of California Press.

White, David Manning, and Robert H. Abel, eds. 1963. *The Funnies: An American Idiom*. New York: Free Press; London: Collier-Macmillan.

Woolf, Virginia. 1993 [1929]. *A Room of One's Own* and *Three Guineas*. Ed. Michèle Barrett. London: Penguin.

Würzbach, Natascha. 1985. "Feministische Forschung in Literaturwissenschaft und Volkskunde: Neue Fragestellungen und Probleme der Theoriebildung." In *Die Frau im Märchen*, ed. Sigrid Früh und Rainer Wehse, 192–233. Kassel: Röth.

Wydra, Thilo. 1998. *Volker Schlöndorff und seine Filme*. Munich: Heyne.

Index

[underlined page numbers refer to illustrations]

Parti Québécois: 223 [see also Canadian dualism; October Crisis; Quebec
nationalism; Quebec dualism]

Peanuts (Charles M. Schulz; 1950): 196 [see also Schulz, Charles M.]

Pearson, Lester B.: 207

Performativity: [see Gender]

Pessoa, Fernando: 260

Petrarca, Francesco: 36

Piercy, Marge: 173

Pinter, Harold: 143–45, 146, 153, 164n26, 165n31

Plastic Man (Jack Cole; 1941): 247n20

Plath, Sylvia: 20, 36, 45–46n30, 173, 177
  – *Ariel* (1965): 20

Poetry: 1, 6, 6–7, 17–47 [see also Genre; Love poetry; Poetry cycle; Prose
  poetry]

Poetry cycle: 24, 134 [see also Genre; Love poetry; Poetry; Prose poetry]

Popeye (Elzie Crisler Segar; 1929): 196

Popular culture (in Atwood's works): 8, 63–66, 228–31

Postcolonialism: 13, 204–05, 241

Postmodernism: 51, 66–67

Power structures (esp. in connection with gender): 7, 13, 31, 32, 33, 34, 39,
  40, 42, 44n22, 44–45n23, 116–17, 143, 156, 190, 202, 206, 207–09,
  214–20, 224

Prizes: [see Giller Prize; Man Booker Prize; Nobel Prize for Literature;
  Pulitzer Prize]

Prose poetry: 1, 7–8, 49–70 (esp. 67, 68n6, 68n8, 69n13), 72 [see also
  Genre; Love poetry, Poetry, Poetry cycle]

Pseudonyms: [see Atwood, Margaret: Pseudonyms]

Pulitzer Prize: 196

Purdy, Al: 218

Q

Quebec nationalism: 12–13, 209–11, 220–24 [see also Canadian dualism;
  October Crisis; Parti Québécois; Quebec separatism]

Quebec separatism: 222–24 [see also Canadian dualism; October Crisis;
  Parti Québécois; Quebec nationalism]

Quigley, Paul
  – (dir.), *Reflections: Progressive Insanities of a Pioneer/Poem as Imagery*
  (1972/1974; short film): 134 [see also Adaptation; Atwood,
  Margaret: Adaptation; Atwood, Margaret: Works]

Composed in Adobe Garamond Pro 11 on 14

Printed and bound in Canada

4229